THE WEEKEND REFINISHER

The Weekend
REFINISHER

How to Make the Most of Your Furniture—
A Step-by-Step Guide

Bruce Johnson

Ballantine Books
New York

For my father,
who, while not a refinisher,
taught me more than
I could ever teach others.

Library of Congress Catalog Card Number: 88-92002

ISBN: 0-345-35866-X

Cover design by Sheryl Kagan
Cover photograph by George Kerrigan
Book design by Alex Jay/Studio J

Manufactured in the United States of America

First Edition: April 1989

20 19 18 17 16 15 14 13

Contents

Introduction

A few years ago, I made a statement that appeared in print in which I predicted the demise of the do-it-yourself refinisher. "The two-paycheck family signaled the end to amateur refinishing," I declared, "and opened the door for the professional refinishing shop."

At the time I had just expanded my own professional refinishing operation and no doubt was hoping that business would continue to improve; my banker was hoping so, too. While we certainly had our slow months those first few years, we never were without work.

But I had made one major mistake. I had underestimated the determination of the amateur refinisher.

Busy schedules are a fact of life, but they are not going to deter those who would rather do a refinishing project themselves than have it done by someone else. The desire to refinish the furniture you inherited from your parents, or picked up at a garage sale, or bought from the unfinished furniture store, has not diminished. But what many of you have been waiting for is someone to come forth with fresh, updated, useful information to help you fit those refinishing projects back into your busy schedule. Given a step-by-step, no-nonsense approach, you will realize that you won't need as much time, materials, or equipment as you thought you would.

I've now come full circle. After having spent nearly ten years as a full-time professional refinisher, I'm back where I started: stripping tables by hand in my driveway, rubbing on stains with a torn T-shirt, regluing chairs while they sit in my dining room, and brushing on varnishes with a disposable foam brush in my basement.

And I love it.

One reason that I enjoy refinishing so much more now than ever before is because my experience as a professional has taught me the shortcuts: knowing when to save rather than strip a finish; how to avoid sanding; how to remove stains from wood and marble; and how to pick the best finish for each project. I wouldn't go back to the professional shop, but I won't ever be without my own workbench and a couple of refinishing projects down in the basement. It's kept me out of trouble and off the psychiatrist's couch—and given me a house full of wonderful antiques and quality reproductions that look every bit as good and as old as the real ones.

A long time ago, I was a high school English teacher. Although people sometimes refer to me as a "former" teacher, I haven't really given it up. Once a teacher, always a teacher—I've discovered that it's the classroom, not the teacher, that changes. For me, I've gone from the classroom to the workshop to the word processor. I only hope that *The Weekend Refinisher* can do for you what ten years in the workshop has finally done for me.

CHAPTER 1
The Budget Workshop

Like most English teachers, I always dreamed of writing The Great American Novel, but at the age of twenty-seven I was still correcting papers and not writing, so I left the classroom. That first year I discovered that writing a novel didn't take as much time as teaching high school seniors, nor did it pay as well.

The novel waited while I went about setting up Knock On Wood Antique Repair & Restoration. Looking back, it was amazingly easy, but for good reason. If I had known back then what I know now, I probably would never have found the courage to open my own business. But fools rush in, and this fool was no different from all who had come before.

I must admit, as soon as I had picked out a location for my workshop, I was tempted to start buying all sorts of woodworking equipment: a table saw, a radial arm saw, a jointer, a lathe, a drill press, a shaper, a band saw, a stationary sander, even a planer. I wasn't convinced I needed all of them to refinish furniture, but I thought they would give me instant recognition as a professional.

Fortunately, I didn't have enough money to be a complete fool. I did buy a new table saw, and my brother-in-law gave me his old Sears lathe; I paid twenty dollars at a yard sale for a table-top drill press. The motor was extra. I also bought a band saw, but after the blade came off for the thirty-seventh time, I started using an electric saber saw and eventually gave my band saw away. My shop never looked as professional as the woodworker's, but, I had to remind myself, the woodworker was making furniture— I was simply refinishing it.

Granted, I ran into situations (still do, in fact) where I needed to have an edge straightened, a molding duplicated, or a new leaf planed, but I also found that most of the woodworkers I meet who have all of the precision equipment invariably fall into one of two categories: either they are so friendly that they enjoy doing those things for us, or they are so pinched for cash that they do it to help make their loan payments. Either way, paying a few dollars for their services was and is still a lot less expensive than owning and maintaining a shop full of expensive equipment.

Now that I have come full circle and am back to being a full-time writer and a weekend refinisher, I realize I was fortunate not to have been able to afford all of the machinery I thought I had to have. What was important then is still important today—and that is having a comfortable place to work and a few versatile tools.

Selecting ▶ a Work Space

You need a special place to work, a place where you can have some privacy, make your own mess, and listen to the music you like. It doesn't need to look like a woodworking shop and it doesn't have to be a large space, because you will only be working on one or two projects at a time. And you won't need a lot of expensive tools because you will want to save, not make, everything that is original to a piece of furniture—wood, finish, and hardware. The weekend refinisher would rather know how to reglue a broken chair rung than replace it with a new one, would rather learn to patch the nail holes in a desk than pay for a new top. Our approach will be just as fast, far more fun, and certainly less expensive than the woodworker's approach. Besides, most woodworkers are frustrated perfectionists; refinishers learn right away that no furniture—especially old furniture—can ever be perfect, so we don't have to be either.

Choosing a work space isn't difficult, but you do need to take into consideration a few practical requirements, such as space, lighting, ventilation, and electricity. You won't need the entire basement, half of the garage, or the guest bedroom, but you should have more than just the top of the picnic table. I have successfully reglued many chairs on the top of my picnic table, getting a tan, and listening to the radio at the same time, but only once did I make the mistake of varnishing outdoors. I naively assumed the sun would help my varnish dry, but instead it created hundreds of tiny moisture bubbles that dried like moon craters in the sticky finish. By that time, though, it really didn't matter; I had already picked off a dozen flying dandelion seeds, pulled out several drowning flies, and twice chased away Lucky, my neighbor's one-eyed cat.

Your choices will usually include part of the basement, a corner of the garage, or your kitchen floor, but if none of these are available, don't despair. One determined refinisher converted a metal storage shed in the corner of her yard into a small, but efficient, work space. An apartment-bound refinisher found it economical to lease a storage bay for his furniture projects, paying for it with money he earned regluing chairs for an Italian restaurant.

But the most creative refinishing shop I ever visited was inside a 1977 Ford van. The owner lived in a small second-floor Chicago apartment with no access to either a garage or a basement, so he adapted what little available space he had—the rear of his van. Weather permitting, he would pull out and assemble a pair of sawhorses to set his current project on and, when needed, drop an extension cord from his apartment for power. Rainy days restricted him to smaller projects inside the van, where he had built a narrow tool chest on one wall, a hinged workbench complete with a small vise on the other, clamp racks on the ceiling, and a special stain and varnish storage box, adapted from plans for kitchen quarters on a nineteenth-century sailing ship. When we last spoke he was thinking about leaving his construction job to start a unique traveling furniture repair and restoration business.

The best way for you to begin is by surveying the areas you have available and by finding out (1) what each has to offer and (2) what each would require to be converted to a refinishing work area. Your basic specifications will include:

Space—approximately one hundred square feet, enough to sit at a workbench and be able at the same time to work on a large piece of furniture sitting on the floor;

Lighting—as much natural light as possible, though you should be able to add a fluorescent light fixture overhead and one or two portable floodlights when needed;

Ventilation—an exterior window through which fumes can be safely exhausted;

Power—adequate outlets for moderate power demands, such as an electric drill or an extra light;

Storage—either stationary or portable shelving for tools, parts, and materials.

◀ The Basement Workshop

If you live in a modern house, what used to be called the basement may now be the family room. If you're lucky, the builder may have left an unfinished storage room that you can turn into a workshop. Given a window, some ceiling lights, and an outlet, you may only have to deal with ten years' accumulation of fondue pots, baby furniture, and broken bicycles. To start, gather the following at the door to your storage room: a dozen empty boxes, a dozen garbage bags, a felt-tipped pen, a roll of masking tape, some inexpensive shelving, and a current antiques and collectibles price guide. What you can't justify putting in a box, labeling, and storing should either be given away, thrown away, or, if you prefer, returned to its rightful owner.

Older houses generally have an abundance of unused basement space, but for two very good reasons: low ceilings and high humidity.

My parents still live in the house I grew up in, a sturdy 1912 two-story house with a huge attic upstairs, but only a six-foot-high ceiling in the basement. When I was fourteen years old and only five foot six, that didn't pose a problem, but if I were living there now and wanting to use the basement for a workshop, it would. If you are as tall as your basement ceiling, there really isn't much you can do about it, other than learn to work sitting down. All you'll need is an old office chair with smooth-rolling castors or an inexpensive bar stool with the legs cut down.

Much of the dampness associated with basements in older homes is simply due to a lack of circulating air. If your basement is ideal for raising mushrooms and mildew, try opening all of the doors and windows and setting up portable fans to circulate fresh air throughout the rooms. In the winter, open the basement furnace vents and use the fans to draw fresh air down from upstairs. You can monitor the humidity with a simple household humidistat; 45 to 55 percent is considered ideal, but not mandatory for anything except brushing on a finish.

Look for any signs of incoming moisture. A damp wall may indicate an outside leak—a rotting or clogged roof gutter or a missing downspout extension. If you can't find the cause yourself, you should call in a professional for a free inspection and repair estimate.

If high humidity is more of an inconvenience than a serious problem, there are other steps you can take by yourself to reduce and stabilize it. Paint and hardware stores stock special sealers designed to be brushed or rolled on basement floors and walls to prevent moisture in the bricks or concrete from constantly increasing the humidity level. A coat of paint will brighten up your work area and make sweeping the floor much easier.

Dehumidifiers can also be very effective, especially if your work area can be isolated from the rest of the basement. Installing an inexpensive prehung door in an open doorway should only take a few hours and, in addition to cutting down on the amount of air your dehumidifier has to wring out, will make the place a bit more private. A friend of mine even went to the extent of building a wall across one end of his basement to isolate a work area from the rest of the large, open space. Since he did all of the work himself, the cost was limited to two dozen two-by-fours, four sheets of drywall, and a door.

Basement lighting in older homes generally comes in one of two forms—inadequate or dangerous. A typical turn-of-the-century basement will have only one or two unshielded bulbs per room. You can buy wire guards to go over them or, if you want to increase your lighting, you can purchase prewired fluorescent light fixtures that you can attach to the ceiling joists and plug into the old light sockets. A pair of fluorescent lights can make a dramatic difference in how a dim room looks and can be safely installed between, rather than beneath, low ceiling joists. If you need flexible lighting, I would recommend a couple of portable floodlights, the type with six-foot cords, rotating socket joints, and rubber-coated spring clamps. You can temporarily attach them to ceiling joists, sawhorses, music stands, chair backs, camera tripods, or, for even more convenience, a simple plywood pedestal mounted on castors.

Good ventilation not only reduces the humidity in the basement, it also eliminates the flammable and oftentimes toxic fumes you and your family might be exposed to. You need only two portable household fans to establish a rapid ventilation system. The first should be positioned near the door to bring fresh air into the room. The other should be suspended from the ceiling in front of the window nearest where you will be working. It will pull the fumes away from you and push them out through the open window. By working between the two fans with your back or side always facing the fan in the doorway, the fumes and dust will be both blown and drawn away from your face and lungs and out the open window, making your work space a safer place to work.

Before deciding to work in your basement, be sure you take into consideration the location of the furnace, water heater, and any similar appliances, especially those with open pilot lights. I get nervous any time I see paint or varnish stored within ten feet of them, or when I see both stored in a small, enclosed room. More often than not, it will be the fumes that ignite before the liquid. You will also want to make sure that the cold air return on the furnace is not drawing air from your workshop area; otherwise the fumes and dust you may be creating will spread throughout the entire house—leaving you with more to clean up than just your work area.

The Garage ▶
Workshop

When we moved into our present home, a 1929 one-and-a-half-story bungalow, I had two options for my workshop. Downstairs we have a partial basement, meaning we have one room, fifteen by fifteen, that also holds the furnace and water heater. The ceiling is only a few inches taller than I am, but the basement does have two windows and several outlets.

In the backyard we had a typical Southern garage: two stalls for cars, a dirt floor, and no doors. Being from the Land of the Tall Corn and Deep Snows, I found that a little hard to comprehend until I went through my first winter without having to shovel snow. Basically, what we had bought were three walls and a roof—no doors, no windows, no lights, no power. It was obvious that the garage was going to take more time, more energy, and more money to convert into a workshop than the basement, but it also offered more room for expansion, more increased value for our property—and no flight of steps.

Within a few weeks I had sharpened my concrete-finishing skills, my carpentry, and my ability to understand simple electrical terms. When I was finished, we had four walls, both an overhead door and a standard door, a concrete floor, ceiling lights, and an outlet every six feet. In the Midwest, that's what they start with. For me, it represented two months' work.

If you have a garage, you probably don't have as many of the problems as I had. Most garages have windows, doors, and electricity, making it much easier to convert one corner or wall into a workshop. And most detached garages, unless you live further south, have at least concrete floors and doors. In either case, the garage is generally an excellent place for refinishing.

Electricity is essential, but it does not have to be permanent. If you can't afford to wire your garage, you can at least invest in a heavy-duty exterior extension cord, preferably the type with two recepticals. One can supply power to a clamp-on spotlight while the other can be available for an electric drill or saber saw. If you already have power in your garage, you may only need to decide if you have enough outlets in the right places. I'm scared to death of electricity, and that's probably kept me out of more trouble than I've been in, so I would recommend having an electrician check your wiring and approve the use of any multiple-plug extensions. If you are planning to use a table saw, jointer, or any other large equipment, it is vital that you first have your electrical system inspected before you run the risk of an overload.

Most garages have the advantage of offering a great deal of

natural light. You can open the overhead doors and pull your project into the light during warm days, but when you have to depend on artificial lighting, I suggest using fluorescent lights that come ready to hang and plug in. You can buy special adapters that will turn an ordinary light bulb socket into either an outlet or, if you prefer, a socket and an outlet. If your garage walls are unfinished, you can also use floodlights clamped onto the exposed studs. What I also find convenient, especially when I'm on the floor working on the underside of a dining room table, is an automotive trouble light. I bought a plastic model rather than the more expensive metal version simply because I can hook it over the rung of a chair or table without scratching the finish.

In the summer, ventilation is simple. You merely open the doors and windows and let the breezes blow your fumes away. Still, you need to plan for ventilation when you are varnishing, or working in the winter, since gusty winds also bring with them dust, dirt, and pesky insects, not to mention cold air. I use my workshop every day, so I mounted an exhaust fan over a hole I cut between two of the wall studs. The unit came completely assembled, with motor, fan blades, protective shield, and louvered shutters ready to screw to the wall. Less than two hours after it arrived, I had it installed and wired to a standard light switch. The total cost of the exhaust unit was less than one hundred dollars, and at the flick of a switch, it protects me from dangerous fumes. (See Sources, Chapter 12).

If a wall-mounted exhaust fan isn't practical for your situation, you can still use the two-fan method I prescribed for basement workshops. In the garage, one fan should be placed in front of a partially opened door, while the other will need to be set in or hung in front of an open window. They are a little more troublesome to arrange than a wall unit, but are far less expensive and more flexible in their uses.

While garages don't share the same problem basements have with high humidity and low ceilings, they often have one serious problem of their own: no heat. If you don't plan to do any refinishing when the temperature drops below sixty degrees, this isn't going to cause a problem for you. But if you want to refinish a pair of chairs for your daughter for Christmas, then it might. Unless you are really going to get serious about this, I wouldn't recommend installing a furnace in your garage, but you do have the option of using a portable heater on those days when you want to be refinishing. Kerosene heaters have become nearly as popular as electric heaters, but you *must* bear in mind that refinishing often involves highly flammable materials. I have safely used electric and kerosene heaters and even a wood stove in my various workshops, but to be totally honest, all three made me a little nervous. Use them if you must, but please be careful. Position them where it will be impossible for you to spill any stains or finishes next to them and where there is no material—be it wood, fabric, or liquid—being stored nearby. If you decide to put your refinishing projects in hibernation each winter, remember that all liquid refinishing supplies should be stored in a room that will remain above freezing even on the coldest of January nights.

What garages and basements do have in common is a tendency for them to become dumping grounds. Anything that is too good to throw away, but not good enough to use, inevitably ends up either in the basement or the garage. A friend who likes to buy old, damaged furniture at weekend auctions, fix it up, and sell it to antiques dealers started by cleaning out his entire garage. He held what really was a garage sale and with the profits purchased the tools and supplies he needed to turn one side of his clean garage into a well-equipped refinishing area. If your garage is anything like his, all it may really need is a good, ruthless cleaning. When I tackle my storage rooms, I try to stick to one rule: If I haven't used it in the last year, out it goes. If it is too good to throw away, I either sell it or give it to someone or some organization that can get some good out of it.

As in the basement, once your work space has been cleaned, additional lighting installed, and adequate ventilation assured, your only remaining problem may be in convincing everyone in your family that your refinishing work area is not where your son overhauls his motorbike, your daughter oils her softball glove, or your spouse repots the house-plants.

If your pleas, bargains, and threats don't work, be prepared to take some serious defensive measures. First, store and clearly label all disassembled parts in boxes, jars, and cans. Second, keep any furniture in your workshop covered with sheets of plastic and old blankets. Finally—though this is a bit drastic—lock your tool chests. You may not get any surprise parties from your family, but at least you'll always know where your hammer is when you need it.

For those of you who only repair or refinish one or two pieces a year and who don't have an available garage or basement, your kitchen floor, an extra bedroom, or even your balcony can become your weekend workshop. But as far as I am concerned, given the choice between working on carpeting and working on linoleum, there is no choice—not since my affair with Ginger.

◀ The Kitchen Floor Refinisher

While every professional refinisher would love to just work on fine, old antiques, the truth is that a good portion of their steady income comes from insurance work. One of my most memorable house calls was to a new home on a hill overlooking a large lake. The family had just moved in the week before, and the movers had left ample evidence of their skill: nicks, scratches, dented corners, chipped finishes. No piece escaped unharmed, but none was so serious as to need to be taken back to the shop.

The worst damage was in the bedroom, where I was met by the aroma of new carpeting—deep, plush, white shag carpeting. I kicked off my shoes at the doorway, carefully picked up my touch-up kit full of tubes and bottles of paints, stains, and finishes, and asked the woman if she would keep her two small children and pet poodle out of the bedroom while I was working.

"We're on our way to the store," she replied, "so I'll take Ginger with us."

With everyone out of the house, I sat down in front of the first dresser and began squeezing out puddles of stains and paints onto the middle of a two-foot square of thin plywood I had brought along with me. About an hour later I heard a car in the driveway, but didn't stop. I was in the midst of blending a deep cross-grain scratch and barely registered the door slamming down the hall. What I heard next I do recall very clearly—the panting of a small dog. Still seated, I slowly turned my head to see Ginger—standing in the middle of my pallet of paints, looking at me curiously.

Ginger kept lifting her paws and putting them back down again into the red, black, and brown puddles of paint, but so far she had stayed on the plywood. I laid my brush on top of the dresser and slowly edged toward her.

She stood quivering, like all poodles do when they don't know what to do, just a few inches from my outstretched hands. Just as I was about to scoop her up, the woman burst into the room.

"Ginger!" she shouted. "What are you doing in here?!"

Startled by the woman's voice, Ginger bolted. Across the pure white carpeting she ran for her life, which at that moment I wouldn't have given much for. Black, red, and brown footprints marked her route. As if to make sure she didn't leave any section of new carpeting unscarred, Ginger took another lap around the room, then dashed past the woman and disappeared down the hall, her footprints fading into the distance.

The woman stopped screaming. Before I could speak, she ran to the bathroom, came back with a wet towel, and frantically began scrubbing each fresh footprint. In a matter of seconds she managed to turn a half dozen one-inch paw prints into six large stains. She then realized that she was doing more harm than Ginger. The shag carpeting could have been trimmed and patched to minimize the damage, but in her panic, the woman turned a bad accident into a total disaster.

Since that day I have been unable to look at—let alone work on—a new carpet without thinking of Ginger. Actually, she was less to blame than anyone, and I had been taking a risk by not removing the furniture from the room.

But back to the kitchen floor. The advantage of working in the kitchen is that it, unlike the garage or the basement, is going to have all of the electricity, lights, heat, windows, and refreshments a refinisher could ever need. And since you are only going to be using it for a weekend, you don't have to build any walls, clean out any boxes, or move any old bicycles. For forty-eight hours you simply suspend all hot meals and dinner parties, as tools, cans, and brushes take the place of spatulas, pans, and dishes atop your Formica counters.

Before they do, however, you will want to protect nearby appliances and the floor itself. The most effective and least expensive method involves a fifty-foot roll of heavy plastic and some masking tape. Begin by draping and taping sections of plastic over the front of the refrigerator, counters, lower cabinets, and electric stove. If your stove is gas, turn off the main gas valve located behind it. The pilot lights not only can ignite the plastic, but could set off an explosion if the concentration of fumes ever reaches a significant level. You will find it easiest to work if you also move all other furniture out of the room. If you don't have a pair of sawhorses to support table leaves or dresser drawers, cover a pair of your kitchen chairs with a sheet of plastic and an old blanket.

Regardless of whether your kitchen floor is wooden, linoleum, or carpeted, you are going to want to protect it. The best method I have found also makes cleanup easy and painless. I start by stretching a thick sheet of plastic to all four corners of the room and fastening it to the floor with masking tape. I then cover it with five or six layers of newspaper; as the top layer becomes wet or dirty, rather than pick it up, I just add another layer. When the project is finished and moved out of the room, I simply roll or fold up the plastic sheet, newspapers, dirt, spills, rags, cans, and disposable brushes and deposit it all outside in a metal garbage container.

As in any workshop, you should place fans in front of open doors and kitchen windows for good ventilation. You can use your masking tape to hold down any newspapers or plastic that begins flapping in the breeze; tools and cans might seem like good paperweights, but they invariably end up scratching the furniture or getting knocked over. If your fans are going to be blowing dust and fumes through the rest of your apartment, consider taping a sheet of plastic over the doorway, letting it hang free when neither the dust nor the fumes are a problem, and taping it shut when they are. If you need additional lighting and have a number of widely scattered outlets, get a couple of clamp-on floodlights to be positioned wherever needed, using the edge of a counter or the top of a chair as a base.

Since your kitchen floor operation will be temporary and you must, for the sake of your sanity, proceed quickly, you will need to remain organized the entire time, and for that you will need three sturdy, medium-sized cardboard boxes. On the outside of one write "Tools"; the second should be marked "Supplies," for such things as steel wool, sandpaper, and stains; the third will store any and all "Parts" from your project, such as hardware, screws, and castors. I used this three-box system for several months while I lived in a third-floor apartment, storing them in my closet between projects. When my tools and supplies outgrew my boxes, I knew it was time to find a more permanent workshop—or a larger apartment.

I used to collect jars for storing screws, hinges, and other small items in my parts box, until another refinisher suggested self-sealing sandwich bags. They not only take up less room, they don't break either. Now I keep a box of bags in my workshop, along with a small pad of paper. Whenever I remove a set of screws, a knob, or even a splinter I want to reglue later, I simply drop it and a slip of paper identifying it in a bag and seal it shut.

Before jumping into your first project, you also need to be aware of what paint varnish remover and several other refinishing solvents can do to your telephone and plastic kitchen appliances. Although it's been there for less than a year, the phone next to my workbench bears a permanent reminder of nearly every phone call that came while I was in the middle of a project. I can point to the call that came while I was staining a walnut table, the one that came when I was stripping a footstool, and the one that came while I was hand-rubbing a coat of tung oil. I don't care what the phone in my garage looks like because it only cost $9.99, but you might feel differently about the one you have next to the refrigerator. If you do, then I would recommend two preventive measures. First, buy a box of surgical gloves. Then, when the phone rings, your stomach growls, or your poodle slips past the barricade, all you have to do is peal them off and toss them on the floor. *Voila!* Clean hands. Second, before you start, place a clean rag next to the light switch, one on the refrigerator door, and one over the telephone. If your gloves leak or you forget to put them on, you can still leave your phone looking as good as it did before your mother called.

Along that same line, I would advise you to wear a pair of old, loose-fitting sneakers or house slippers while in your kitchen refinishing shop. Then, when the doorbell does ring, the baby cries, or Nature calls, you can quickly kick them off—leaving your fresh varnish footprints on the newspapers and not following you down the hall.

Storage ▶ Regardless of whether you plan to work in your basement, out in the garage, on the kitchen floor, or in the back of a 1977 Ford van, one of the most important aspects of refinishing is storing your tools, parts, and refinishing materials. One of the easiest, least expensive, and most efficient systems that I have found is one that I mentioned earlier and simply call "the box system."

I begin by buying an inexpensive set of metal shelving, the type that stands on the floor, has three to five adjustable shelves, and comes unassembled. Before putting it together, I make the rounds at area copy centers, print shops, and office supply stores, picking up an assortment of empty cardboard boxes with lids. One of the best is the heavy white box used to ship reams of standard 8½-by-11-inch paper. They are strong enough to store power tools, extension cords, and bulky floodlights. Smaller boxes, such as the type used for manila envelopes, work well for hand tools, parts, and hardware. Extra lids, turned upside down, are perfect for preventing small cans of stain and varnish from sliding off the shelf.

Back at home, I begin transferring small tools to one box, larger tools to another, parts, stains, varnishes, and steel wool to their respective containers. I label the outside of each box clearly to save time rummaging through five or six boxes looking for a nail punch, a can of walnut stain, or box of screws. One box contains nothing but empty containers: baby food jars, peanut butter jars, sandwich bags, coffee cans, and almost anything else with a lid, plus a role of masking tape and a marking pen. Once I have all of my boxes organized, I then measure and space my shelves accordingly and assemble them.

The shelving itself can be placed wherever it is most practical, since you can easily carry each box wherever you need it. Even though you may be regluing a chair out on your deck, painting a bookcase on your kitchen floor, or touching up nicks on the grand piano in your living room, you can keep your storage shelves down in the basement, in the back of your pantry, or even inside the guest bedroom closet. It doesn't matter where you put them, just don't try to get along without them. Cardboard boxes are sturdy, but they quickly crumble when other boxes are stacked on top of them or if they are stored on a damp basement floor.

◄ The Weekend Refinisher Tool List

One of the most enjoyable and challenging aspects of being a weekend refinisher is utilizing a number of common tools for a variety of different purposes. A pair of old socks can turn an extra hammer into a padded mallet for tapping apart loose joints. A few strokes with a metal file can turn a screwdriver into a miniature scraper or a dull chisel into an upholstery tack remover. You can also use that same metal file to remove old glue from the end of a chair rung, or round a sharp edge on an unfinished reproduction corner cupboard.

Most refinishers buy tools only as they need them and then only as a last resort. Improvisation is as much a talent for us as it is for a young actor. If you can use a rubber band as a spindle clamp, a nail for a drill bit, or a coat hanger as an awl, then you can spare yourself a good deal of money and time from running back and forth to the hardware store.

One afternoon I was making an estimate for a couple who wanted to have their six dining room chairs completely refinished. The matching table was in excellent condition, but the veneer on the apron connecting the legs had come loose in several places. I didn't have time to go back to the shop for a dozen clamps, but

I could see that it was just a matter of time before someone snagged a skirt on the edge of the veneer, probably tearing both at the same time.

"Do you have any clamps?" I asked from under the table.

"Sorry—I'm a mechanic, not a woodworker."

I slid back out from underneath the table. "Then bring me all of your pliers and vise grips." He disappeared out the door while his wife stood there, looking at me as if I just stepped off a UFO. "How about some glue, a couple of heavy-duty rubber bands, and a lid from a cardboard box?" She sighed, but started rummaging through a kitchen cabinet. "And a toothpick."

In just a few minutes time I had all of the tools I needed to reglue the veneer that was coming off the apron. I started by using the toothpick to work the glue behind the veneer; I then started tearing the cardboard into strips, laid it on top of the veneer, and, starting at one end, began clamping the veneer and the table apron back together with the vise grips. When I ran out of vise grips I switched to his pliers: as soon as the glue began oozing out from between the veneer and the apron, I wrapped the rubber bands tightly around the handles to maintain the pressure. Together we wiped the excess glue off with wet paper towels and stood back to admire our work. It wasn't pretty, but it worked.

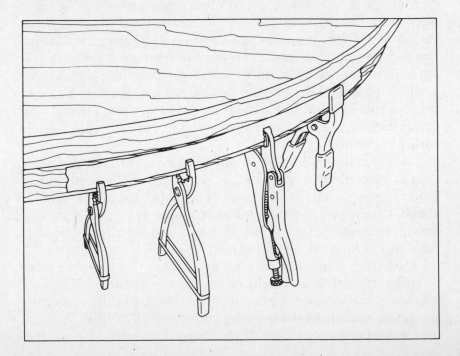

Many of the tools you may need, you already have, but can't very quickly put your hands on. One hammer is in the junk drawer in the kitchen, the other is in the basement; the vise grips are in the trunk of the car, the Phillips screwdriver is on the floor next to the bikes, and no one's seen the tape measure since Tommy went out for the track team. Take a few minutes to canvass your entire household, including the cars, the basement, and the garage, and assemble all of your household tools in one spot and put each in the appropriate storage box. Hopefully, when your search is completed you will have collected the majority of the tools you can expect to need on your refinishing projects:

The Weekend Refinisher Tool List

Regularly	*Occasionally*	*Rarely*
— Claw hammer	— Tack hammer	— Rubber mallet
— Screwdrivers	— Needle-nose	— Awl
— Standard pliers	pliers	— Block plane
— Diagonal pliers	— Crescent wrench	— Steel square
— Nail punch	— Vise grips	— Folding ruler
— Hobby knife	— Wood rasp	— Level
— Chisel	— Putty knife	
— Metal file	— Sharpening stone	
— Toothbrush	— Wire brush	
— Drill and bits	— Natural-bristle	
— Hacksaw	brush	
— Metal ruler	— Crosscut saw	
— Tape measure	— Fine-tooth saw	
— C-clamps	— Bench vise	
— Pipe clamps		
— Brushes		
— Jars and cans		
— Clock radio		

A friend of mine called not long ago to ask about a problem he was having getting his varnish to dry. He had brushed it on four days earlier, and while parts of it were starting to dry, large areas still remained tacky.

◀ **The Weekend Refinisher Materials List**

"I hope the finish didn't go bad on me," he moaned. "I've still got half a gallon left."

"Half a gallon? Brad, how much did you buy? And how long ago?"

"When Dutton's was going out of business."

"Brad—that was two years ago."

"Hey, it was cheap."

But his lesson wasn't. His finish had gone bad. He paid for a gallon of varnish, but only used half of it before it went bad. When we calculated what it had actually cost him—not to mention the extra time and materials needed to restrip his dresser—his bargain proved to be no bargain.

Refinishing supplies fall into two categories: liquid and solid. The liquids—stripper, glue, stains, and finishes—have a relatively short shelf life. Part of the problem with buying any of them is that you have no reliable way of knowing how old they are or whether they have been exposed to freezing temperatures, two factors that have a direct impact on their performance.

And with glues, stains, and finishes, a little does go a long way. In my refinishing career I can remember getting to the bottom of only a few cans of stain or finish; the rest I either had to throw away or managed to knock over before the can was empty.

Solids, on the other hand, such as steel wool and sandpaper, last indefinitely, so long as they remain dry. Mail-order firms and discount stores are apt to offer substantial discounts on quantity orders of both; sandpaper that costs as much as forty to sixty cents a sheet when bought individually can be purchased for as little as sixteen to twenty-six cents a sheet when bought in packs of one hundred.

What I would advise you to do, then, is to buy your sandpaper and steel wool in quantity, especially when it is on sale, and use the savings to compensate for the smaller, more expensive cans and bottles of glues, stains, and finishes.

Buying in small quantities is not necessarily a disadvantage, however, especially when you realize that ten dollars can buy either one gallon of Colonial Maple stain or a pint each of Golden Oak, Light Walnut, Mahogany, and Colonial Maple. Beside the fact that four small cans are easier to store than one large, bulky can, you can mix those four together in various combinations to create a limitless number of colors.

Not all of your supplies will have to be purchased at the hardware or paint store. Some you may already have, such as bleach, glass cleaner, and toothpicks. Those I have included on a separate list, to be purchased only if you can't find them in the medicine cabinet, the pantry, or under the kitchen sink.

From the Store

Regularly	*Occasionally*	*Rarely*
__ White glue	__ Denatured	__ Rubbing
__ Syringes	alcohol	compound
__ Sandpaper	__ Epoxy glue	__ Shellac sticks
__ Steel wool	__ Lacquer thinner	__ Paste filler
__ Turpentine		
(mineral spirits)		
__ Paint and		
varnish remover		
__ Paste wax		
__ Lemon oil		
__ Screws		
__ Nails and brads		
__ Wood dough		
__ Wood putty		

From the House

Regularly	*Occasionally*	*Rarely*
__ Wax paper	__ Toothpicks	__ Fingernail file
__ Masking tape	__ Clorox bleach	__ Crayons
__ Scissors	__ String	
__ Cotton swabs	__ Rubber bands	
__ Liquid detergent	__ Cotton balls	
__ Glass cleaner	__ Old cake pans	
__ All-purpose	__ Sponges	
cleaner		
__ Pencils and		
markers		
__ Worn towels		
__ Old blankets		
and sheets		
__ Canister		
vacuum cleaner		

**The Weekend ▶
Refinisher's
Workbench**

I have known cabinetmakers who have spent more time building a workbench than I would a simple piece of furniture, but for good reason. A workbench is as important to a cabinetmaker as a word processor is to a writer or a saddle is to a rider. Multiple vises, bench stops, tool trays, and parts drawers are vital to a professional woodworker, but then, so are shapers, planers, and jointers.

On the other hand, I have used picnic tables, sawhorses, kitchen chairs, a card table, the dining room table, my desk, and even a piece of plywood on top of a wheelbarrow for a workbench. They didn't all work as well, but when you have to make do, you make do. If you plan to make your living from your workbench, then your workbench should reflect that commitment. However, if you only want to reglue your office chair, stain your new computer table, or paint your granddaughter's rocker, then you shouldn't spend more time on your workbench than you will on your project.

**Designing ▶
Your
Workbench**

Several factors are going to determine what your workbench looks like. The first is purpose. If your workbench is only going to have to support a chair, a small end table, or a clock, then it won't need to be very large or extremely sturdy. But if you want to be able to nail boards on it, stand on it, or turn a dining room table upside down on it, then it had better be made of strong lumber.

The second factor is location. If you have an entire fifteen-foot wall available in your garage or basement, you may decide to build a workbench fifteen feet long that is permanently attached to the wall and floor. If, however, your workbench has to be able to move with you or dismantle when you are finished, fifteen feet may be a little awkward.

The third factor is you. If you prefer to work sitting down, then your workbench may be only twenty-seven inches high with no shelf or drawers underneath it. If, however, you are six foot four and like to work standing up, but not stooping over, the legs on your workbench may be over three feet long. Finding a comfortable height for you is simply a matter of experimentation. Start with your current dining room table, your desk, or even a card table, and using a set of encyclopedias or textbooks under the legs or across the top, begin changing the height. Each time you adjust the height, sit or stand next to it. If it helps, lay a blanket on the table and set a chair on it as if you were going to reglue it. Do whatever it takes to find the best height for you, then measure it and write it down. Don't worry about a "standard" height, because there isn't one. And don't hesitate to have two workbenches of different heights. I have one for small, intricate work, such as sanding knobs, polishing hardware, or regluing inlay. I have another that is several inches higher; I use it to set chairs on while I reglue them. Since I don't like working on my knees, and my back doesn't like stooping over, I designed it with legs longer than most people expect to find on a workbench. It looks funny, standing there like an awkward teenager, until I start working at it—then it suddenly appears to be the right height.

Finally, once you have determined how sturdy your bench needs to be and what dimensions it is going to be, you can start adding any extras you want. I like to have a splashboard across the back of my workbenches, not unlike that on the back of a kitchen counter. It keeps tools, cans, and furniture legs from sliding off the back when I'm moving things around on it. I have also had workbenches with shelves or drawers built underneath the top, a pegboard attached to the back, or a vise attached to one end. The number of options are endless, and you can keep adding them as the need arises, but only after you have determined the best height, width, and depth you feel comfortable working with.

◄ Styles of Workbenches

Once you determine the size of your workbench, you can then consider which style of bench would best suit your space and needs. In addition to the numerous impromptu workbenches—your kitchen table draped with an old blanket or your picnic table in the backyard—you have at least four basic styles to choose from: the portable workbench, the wall workbench, the stationary workbench, and the adapted workbench.

◄ The Portable Workbench

One of the oldest forms of workbenches consists of two sawhorses spanned by either a piece of plywood, a door, or several boards. It is ideal for the weekend refinisher who does not have a permanent work area, for the sawhorse workbench can easily be disassembled, moved, and stored when not in use.

Hardware stores and specialty woodworking companies stock sawhorse brackets, a metal device that enables you to turn a standard two-by-four into a sawhorse in minutes using only a saw to cut the four legs and crosspiece, and a hammer to nail it all together. This "five-board sawhorse" may feel a little wobbly, as most sawhorses do, but you can strengthen it simply by nailing cross braces between the legs. As with all workbenches, the height should be what feels the most comfortable to you. If you are still unsure what height is best for you, start by making the legs longer than what you would want. By cutting an inch off at a time, you can soon determine what is the most comfortable height for you.

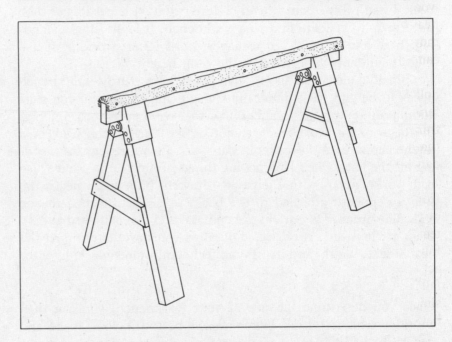

One problem with regular sawhorses is that they are too tall for most of us to get a large piece of furniture onto or to be able to see the top of it once we do. If you like to work on large pieces, such as dressers, library tables, or china cabinets, but don't enjoy lying or even sitting on the floor when you work on them, you may want to make a special pair of low sawhorses—anywhere from six to eighteen inches high—that will get your project off the ground without putting it through the ceiling.

You can use a pair of sawhorses with or without a piece of plywood or an old door spanning them. Then you'll want to protect your furniture from the tops of the sawhorses by covering each crosspiece with an old towel, blanket, or carpet scrap. You can hold them in place with masking tape or, if you prefer something more permanent, staples into the sides of the sawhorses. Do not use metal fasteners on the top of either sawhorse, however, for the staples or nails can work loose and eventually scratch any piece of furniture you place on them.

When you need a workbench, however, you will want to have a top to span your two sawhorses. Naturally, the heavier the pieces you want to work on, the stronger your top will need to be. A half-inch-thick piece of plywood is easy to move, but won't safely support much more than a single chair or rocker. Thicker plywood will take more weight, but not without becoming pretty heavy itself. If you are going to be working alone at any time, moving a large sheet of three-quarter-inch plywood by yourself can be both difficult and dangerous.

An inexpensive solution, though, comes in the form of a hollow-core door. You can buy these lightweight, yet sturdy, interior doors in several standard sizes ranging from eighteen to thirty-six inches wide and up to eighty inches long—and for less than twenty-six dollars. Many discount stores will sell slightly damaged doors at half of their regular price.

You can use hollow-core doors just as they come unfinished from the store, or you can take the time to brush on two coasts of polyurethane varnish. Then your new workbench will be protected from spills, stains, and minor scrapes. And if you nail a four-inch-wide strip of pine to the rear edge of the workbench to act as a splashboard, you won't have to worry about cans and tools falling off the back. I also used to have a problem with my door sliding off my sawhorses, until I nailed a strip of wood across the bottom side of either end to catch on the top of the sawhorse.

◄ The Folding Workbench

If the space where you'll be refinishing is going to be shared with the rest of the household, you may want to install a folding workbench. A stable, space-saving workbench can easily be made by first attaching three hinges—at either end and in the middle—to one edge of a door or sheet of three-quarter-inch plywood, and then screwing the hinges to the wall studs in your basement or garage. When not in use, you simply fold the workbench either up or down against the wall.

You can support the front corners of the folding workbench with a variety of devices. A pair of sawhorses, stacking metal milk crates, two-by-fours with one foot encased in concrete, or a pair of folding legs hinged to the underside of the workbench are just a few of the ways you can provide the necessary support when you want to work on the bench.

Each folding workbench has to be designed for the space into which it is going to fit. Before drilling the first hole, consider:

- Do I want it to swing up or down against the wall?
- Do my hinges line up with the wall studs?
- Will my workbench cover any electrical outlets?
- What height do I want the workbench?
- If I am going to use existing sawhorses as supports, what height are they?
- If I am going to attach legs under the front of my workbench, are they positioned to fold and fit between the wall studs when not in use?

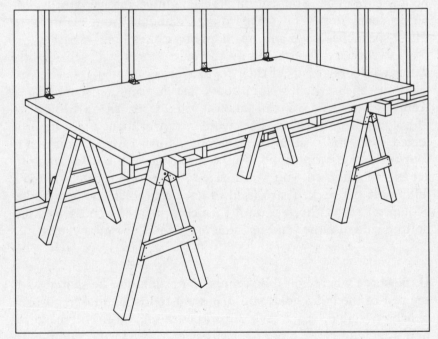

The Stationary ▶ Workbench

A standard workbench, reduced to its basic form, doesn't look much different from the traditional library table: an overhanging top supported by four vertical legs connected by four upper horizontal boards (also called the "skirt" or "apron") and either three or four lower horizontal boards (also called "stretchers" or "rungs"), depending on whether or not you wish to be able to sit with your feet and legs beneath the table.

The nice thing about workbenches is that anyone who can cut

a board and swing a hammer can make one. When I need another workbench I start by sitting down and sketching it out on a piece of paper, noting how long, wide, and tall I want it to be. Workbenches don't need to be very wide; I try to keep mine under thirty inches, so that I can carry (or drag) it through a standard doorway without having to turn it over on its side. If your doorway is only twenty-nine inches, I would suggest that you make your workbench an inch narrower. Its length will depend on the space you have and any turns you have to make moving it in or out of your workshop, and its height will be determined by yours.

After the sketch is completed, you next need to determine what materials you will require. Each of the four legs can either be two-by-fours nailed together or one four-by-four, whichever you prefer. The apron and stretchers can be standard construction-grade two-by-fours, nailed to either the inside or the outside of the legs. A typical six-foot-by-thirty-inch workbench will require six two-by-fours eight feet long for the apron and skirt and either four eight-foot two-by-fours or two eight-foot four-by-fours for the legs. Waste is unavoidable, but don't throw those scraps away; you can use them later to set furniture on or make sanding blocks, clamp pads, a furniture dolly, or a dozen other things.

The top can be made from any number of types of material: plywood, particle board, a hollow-core door, or even individual boards, such as one-by-fours or, for more strength, even two-by-fours. If you use relatively thin material, such as half-inch plywood or three-quarter-inch pine boards, you will need to provide extra support braces between the front and rear apron to prevent the top from sagging. In my experience, you can only have too little support under the top. I like a workbench I can jump up on if I have to and not worry about whether or not it is going to hold me. I like to nail two-by-four braces every twelve inches between the aprons; on a six-foot bench this only requires four more pieces cut from two more eight-foot two-by-fours. Total cost of extra bracing: three dollars.

Extra bracing can actually save you money. Instead of spending twenty dollars on a sheet of three-quarter-inch plywood for your top, you can spend three dollars in extra bracing and only have to buy half-inch plywood, which costs about six dollars less a sheet. If your top ever becomes too beat-up, cut up, and badly stained to use, simply nail or glue a piece of inexpensive quarter-inch plywood or particle board on top of it. If you nail your top

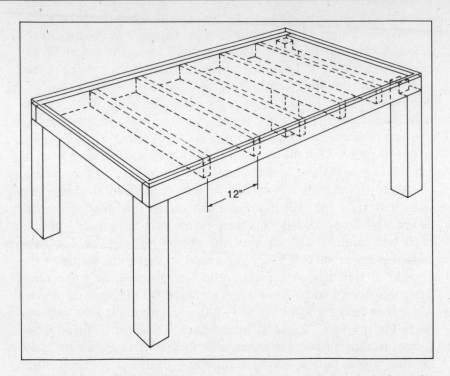

to your base, though, be sure to drive the nail heads below the surface of the wood to prevent them from scratching your furniture. Even then, you may want to have a protective pad for the top of your bench.

Shortly after moving to North Carolina I was driving down a busy street with my wife when, without a warning, I turned into a driveway.

"Do you know these people?" she asked as a couple of heads peered out the window at us.

"Of course not," I replied as I got out of the car. "I wouldn't dream of dropping in on friends unannounced."

She slumped down in her seat while I walked up to the front door. After a few minutes of conversation I returned.

"What was that all about?" she asked as I backed the car down the driveway.

"Carpeting."

"Carpeting?"

"This carpeting," I explained as I stopped beside a large piece of carpeting rolled up and sitting on the curb waiting for the garbage truck.

She slumped even deeper in her seat.

I jumped out and in less than forty-five seconds had checked out the carpeting, decided it was fine, and thrown it in the back of the van. She didn't act like she knew me until we were five miles farther down the road.

"What are you going to do with that?"

"Well, one strip is going to go on my workbench, another I'm going to use to stand on in front of my workbench, and whatever's left over I'm going to set out on the curb for someone else to pick up."

I like to have a piece of carpeting on top of my workbench. Not only does it protect the finish of my furniture from the workbench top, it soaks up spills, absorbs blows, and hides my plywood top. Don't make the mistake that one refinisher made, though, and glue or staple your carpeting to the top. You need to be able to roll it up, take it outside, and shake it like a rug every few days, and you can't do that very easily if it is attached to the top. Granted, it may slide a little, but if that becomes a real problem, use some double-sided carpet tape to hold it down temporarily.

If you end up with enough scraps of plywood or particle board, use them to make a shelf on top of the stretchers you nailed between the legs of your workbench. It doesn't have to be one continuous sheet of plywood because it is only going to hold a couple of boxes or perhaps your saber saw and electric drill. Like the top, it, too, may benefit by having a splashboard nailed across the back to keep tools and boxes from falling off.

◄ The Alternative Workbench

If you have the space for a workbench, but don't have the tools, skills, or interest required to construct one from two-by-fours and plywood, you still have plenty of options. In fact, some of the options are so inviting—and inexpensive—that you may decide to choose one of them even if you were thinking of making your own.

I was at an auction not long ago where rather ordinary round oak tables and five-drawer cherry dressers were selling for over five hundred dollars apiece. At the same auction, however, I spotted a older gentleman looking over a turn-of-the-century buffet that was in sad shape. Both lower doors were missing, the veneer on the sides was bubbling, and the top was badly water-stained. When it came up for sale an hour later, he was the first—and only—bidder. Always curious, I wandered over next to him.

"Say," I asked, "could you tell me why you bought that beat-up buffet?"

He looked me over carefully. "Tell me, son. When was the last time you bought an oak workbench for three dollars?"

I wished I had bid four.

When you consider how many old buffets, flat-topped desks, and library tables, too badly damaged or too common to justify restoration, are littering flea markets, secondhand furniture stores, yard sales, and community auction houses, you begin to wonder why anyone would even consider investing in the lumber and time required to make their own workbench. I built mine, and it doesn't have a splashboard, three drawers for tools, or a lower storage area, let alone a lifetime supply of oak veneer patches.

My favorite clock repairman spends most of his time sitting down, so his workbench is a forty-year-old flat-top desk that came from a university surplus store. The seven drawers hold everything from tiny springs to special pliers to invoices, and the five-foot-long top gives him enough room to dismantle and lay out an entire wall clock while remaining seated. He moved the desk to his basement, where he set it next to the washer and dryer. Above it he has both a fluorescent light and an adjustable study lamp, and there's a pegboard nailed to the wall for hanging tools and parts that won't fit in any of the drawers. The old schoolteacher's desk gives him work space, storage space, and organization—all for less than it would have cost him to build a plain plywood and two-by-four workbench.

Smaller flat-topped desks can work just as well as the large ones—and can be customized for expansion when needed. One weekend refinisher, borrowing an idea from her sewing machine cabinet, took a small desk, had a piece of three-quarter-inch plywood cut to the same dimensions as the top, and hinged the two together at one end. When she needs additional workbench space, she simply flips the plywood top over to rest on a sawhorse, instantly doubling her area. When floor space is more important, the plywood top remains folded over the desk to serve as a workbench top.

So before you take off for the hardware store and the lumberyard, stop by a couple of used furniture stores, a consignment shop, and the local auction house. Call Aunt Mildred, for that matter. You may find a library table this afternoon that is going to be a better—and cheaper—workbench than you could make in a week's time.

If you are anything like me, one of the reasons you like to refinish furniture is to be alone. No offense intended to close family members, it is just that all of us need time alone. When you first open your home workshop or start your first project, you may draw a small audience, but most people quickly grow tired of watching someone paint a bookcase or patch a sliver of veneer on an Art Deco radio. Most of the time you will be by yourself and, for that reason, must be extremely safety conscious.

◀ **Safety Precautions**

Safety precautions start with common sense. Consider the following:

Cigarettes pose a triple threat: exploding fumes, igniting flammable liquids, and burning wood—not to mention turning human lungs into a pair of charcoal briquettes. As soon as you have had to patch one cigarette burn, put out one fire, or attend one funeral, you'll no longer need to be reminded of the dangers cigarettes pose to all refinishers. If you must smoke, don't do it while you are refinishing.

Dull tools cause more accidents than sharp ones. I know; I am not particularly patient when it comes to sharpening tools—and I have the scars to prove it. The extra pressure that has to be exerted on a dull chisel or knife blade can send it flying across the wood—or the back of your hand. Either replace or hone your blades regularly. I use hobby knives often and with this rule: New project, new blade. They're cheaper than stitches.

Rags: If you want to meet your local fire department, call them—or start throwing used rags in a plastic trash bag. A rag soaked in linseed oil and tossed carelessly aside can burst into flame in less than two hours' time. Spread all rags, regardless of what they were used for, out to dry before discarding them in an outdoor, enclosed metal garbage can. There are some surprises you can live without, and spontaneous combustion is one of them.

Securing lids tightly on cans—immediately—can prevent the inevitable: grabbing a can from the shelf and instinctively shaking it, spewing stain all over your work and into your eyes. I did it to myself again yesterday. It missed my eyes, but I turned a perfectly good shirt into a work shirt with one quick shake of cherry stain.

Protect your eyes: Old iron nails often snap as they are being pried loose, flying up into your eyes at tremendous speeds. Safety glasses can keep nail heads, dangerous solvents, and shards of broken glass from ending your refinishing career prematurely. I have always had a pair around, but until I started hanging them directly over my workbench, I was still taking chances too often.

Now I don't have an excuse for not slipping them on when I'm using a power saw, prying out upholstery tacks, or grinding a new edge on a scraper. After you have used them for a while, take a close look at the lenses; any one of the things that made those scratches could have hit your eye instead.

Protect your lungs: Even though you may never have a heavy concentration of either dust or dangerous fumes in your workshop, your lungs act as constant vacuum sweepers while you work. They inhale fine dust particles and fumes rising up from the wood before even your exhaust fan system has a chance to pull them away. Many times I get so intent on my work that I don't realize that with each stroke of the brush or pass with the sanding block, my face comes closer and closer to the board. Sometimes it isn't until that evening when my eyes are burning or my sinuses swelling that I become conscious of how much dust and how many fumes I have inhaled working on a single piece of furniture.

The solution doesn't come in the form of a ten-foot-pole with a sanding block nailed to one end; rather, it comes in a small box of inexpensive particle masks designed to filter out dust before it reaches your lungs. These reusable, lightweight masks come with an elastic band and a thin metal strip that can be shaped to fit the contour of even the most unusual nose. If you use them, but have another refinisher in the family who doesn't, slip a box in his Christmas stocking—but don't wait until Christmas to give it to him.

What particle masks cannot stop are dangerous fumes. For that you need a respirator, a tough rubber mask that uses disposable charcoal filters to remove dangerous fumes from the air you inhale. Respirators were formerly available only through automotive supply shops, but now are stocked in many retail paint stores. A high-quality respirator and pair of extra filters will cost around fifty dollars, quite a bit more than a box of particle masks, but far less than a lung transplant.

Protection from chemicals: For many years it was presumed that commercially produced refinishing materials, including paint and varnish remover, lacquer thinner, and pigmented wiping stains, were perfectly safe to handle, especially when compared to some of the earlier homemade paint stripping formulas that called for lye. With the growing concern that is developing around the effects of all kinds of household materials, professional refinishers are taking additional precautions when using stains and stripper. Even though we nonprofessionals do not intend to be in constant contact with these same chemicals, it still is a good idea for you to invest in a pair of heavy rubber gloves to wear while stripping old finishes, and a box of thin surgical gloves for when you are staining and finishing. Each will prevent your skin from absorbing what may, months from now, be identified as a dangerous chemical—and will allow you to go to bed tonight and to work tomorrow without hiding your blackened hands in a pair of white cotton gloves.

Labeling and storage: It is absolutely imperative, though, that all of the materials you will be using, from paint and varnish remover to lemon oil, be clearly labeled and safely stored where small children and pets cannot conceivably come in contact with them. At the very least they should be kept out of their reach, but it would be even safer to store them in a cabinet or desk that can be locked. A padlock and latch, a bicycle lock, or even a chain and combination padlock will give you the assurance that when you are out of town on business, your children won't be able to get into your stains and finishes. I have a distinct memory of playing war games in a friend's basement when we were both seven years old that ended when a plastic grenade knocked a quart of red paint with a loose lid off a shelf and onto my head four feet below. I ran home crying, looking as if I had been hit by a real grenade.

Along this same line, make sure all sharp tools, such as chisels, scrapers, and hobby knives, are safely stored when you leave the workshop. If power tools become a part of your collection of tools, make sure that they are either locked up when not in use or have had trigger locks installed on each of them. Children have a way of sticking more than just power cords into electrical outlets. If there is any chance one of your children might be able to stick a screwdriver, a piece of wire, or a nail into one of those outlets placed so tantalizingly at their level, then perhaps you will want to install child-proof covers over the electrical outlets in your workshop.

Despite all of our precautions, accidents do happen, so regardless of how small or how seldom it is used, every workshop should contain:

- a certified fire extinguisher
- a standard first aid kit
- an eye-flush bottle

Don't wait until it is too late. Buy them now and hope that they will do nothing but collect dust.

P.S.—They make great gifts.

CHAPTER 2
First Aid for Furniture

When the phone rings or the letter comes announcing the forth-coming arrival of guests, family, or business associates, I suddenly start noticing little things, like the new scratch Spike, our cat, left on the dining room table, the scuff marks around the feet of the couch, the hazy spot where I forgot a hot coffee cup on the top of the end table, or the buildup of old wax on the backs of our dining room chairs. That's when I get out my little black bag and start making my rounds.

The Furniture ▶
First Aid Kit

My wife and I have a good deal of wooden furniture in our house. Some of it might be antique, but we both like dresser drawers that run smoothly and couches you feel comfortable on, so we have some new oak furniture as well.

Since we have more wooden furniture than upholstered furniture, plus a large dog and a grouchy cat, I find that I need a permanent first aid kit. I use a small oak toolbox I found at a flea market, but your first aid kit can range from a drawer in your kitchen cabinet to a cardboard box to a plastic dishpan. I would recommend a plastic dishpan over a cardboard box for two very good reasons: while the metal staples in the bottoms of some cardboard boxes can scratch furniture, plastic won't; just as important, if you spill some turpentine or stain in the bottom of a plastic dishpan, it isn't going to soak through and ruin your carpeting.

Your first aid kit isn't going to include many tools, but it is going to have an assortment of small quantities of refinishing supplies. You don't need to buy all of them at once, but you ought to gather the basic ingredients before you get too deep into your Saturday afternoon touch-ups. You may already have some in larger containers in your garage or basement, but since you won't need a gallon of turpentine or a quart of varnish for any of your first aid projects, I would recommend that you use small metal or plastic containers to keep the liquid supplies in your kit. Glass containers may work fine in your workshop, but I would discourage you from using them elsewhere. All too often I drop, kick, step on, step in, knock over, and stumble into my kit, and more than once those plastic containers have saved my life—not to mention my carpeting, my hardwood floors, and the upholstery on my couch.

The same principle also applies to your dry supplies. Instead of keeping a box of one hundred cotton swabs in your kit, wrap a rubber band around a dozen, toss them in your kit, and store the rest in your workshop. Slip a couple of pads of steel wool in self-sealing sandwich bags to keep them from unraveling; an assortment of crayons in traditional furniture colors—i.e., red, brown, black, and yellow—can be kept in an empty prescription bottle. You can use any number of unusual, but practical containers in your first aid kit; but if you haven't been a saver of empty prescription bottles and plastic spice jars, you can buy a variety of unbreakable, child-proof storage bottles at your local drug store.

Your First Aid Kit for Furniture

Wet	Dry
__ Turpentine	__ Rags (2–3)
__ Denatured alcohol	__ Plastic drop cloth
__ Lacquer thinner	__ Cotton swabs
__ Varnish	__ Masking tape
__ Shellac	__ Clean, shallow can
__ Lacquer (aerosol)	__ No. 000 steel wool
__ Tung oil	__ No. 0000 steel wool
__ Lemon oil	__ No. 600 wet/dry
__ Paste wax	sandpaper
__ Mineral oil	__ Artist brushes (2)
__ Wood putty*	__ Toothpicks
__ White glue	__ X-Acto knife
__ Shoe polish*	__ Felt-tipped pens*
__ Wood stain*	__ Crayons*
__ Acrylic paints*	__ Small screwdriver

*In basic wood-tone colors (black, dark brown, tan, yellow, red, etc.)

◄ Waxy Buildup

It doesn't seem to take long for everyone's favorite rocking chair or recliner to begin to get a case of sticky arms, especially during summer months, when the humidity gets as high as the temperature. The stickiness is the result of too much wax, furniture polish, or, on many antiques, linseed oil, rising to the surface.

The solution is rather simple and will only take a few minutes following these steps:

Steps	Materials
1. Place the chair on a plastic drop cloth.	plastic drop cloth
2. Protect any upholstery.	plastic drop cloth masking tape
3. Dip a clean rag in a can of turpentine and begin rubbing the dirty area.	can with lid turpentine clean rags
4. If the buildup is thick, lay a rag moistioned with turpentine over the wax until it softens, approximately 15–20 minutes	
5. On extreme cases, dip a pad of no. 000 steel wool in the turpentine and gently scrub the buildup.	no. 000 steel wool
6. Wipe dry and either polish with lemon oil or apply a protective layer of paste wax.	lemon oil or paste wax

Why go back to wax if wax was responsible for the stickiness? There is a very good chance that the finish on the arms of your chair has either worn down or completely off. Wax offers the finish and the wood more protection than just lemon oil, but doesn't demand the work or the time required to apply a fresh coat of varnish or even tung oil. The drawback to wax, as I will discuss in greater detail later, is that it is not a permanent finish. Under heavy use, it will wear off and may require fresh coats every six months. Too many coats, however, brings you right back to the same problem you just attacked: waxy buildup. Thin coats, applied only when needed and buffed until each is dry and hard, are the secret to a successful wax finish.

Scuff Marks ▶ Like most people, you probably spend more time and energy cleaning and polishing the tops of your furniture than any other part. But when was the last time you took a close look at the legs and feet? How many times has your coffee table, rocking chair, or desk been banged by the vacuum sweeper, sloshed with a mop, or crashed into by a miniature Mack truck? Chances are the lower six inches of your dining room table look a lot worse than the top six—but it only takes a few minutes to change that.

Steps	*Materials*
1. Slide a piece of cardboard under the foot to protect the floor.	cardboard or drop cloth
2. Wash the damaged area with a rag dipped in turpentine. Wipe dry.	rag turpentine
3. Dip a pad of no. 000 steel wool in dark paste wax for dark woods, clear paste wax for light woods.	paste wax no. 000 steel wool
4. Rub the wood gently with the wax and steel wool in the direction of the grain.	
5. Let the wax harden for 5–10 minutes, then buff off the excess.	clean rag
6. Let the wax harden another 15–20 minutes, then buff vigorously.	clean rag

You may find that most of the scuff marks were simply dirt imbedded in the finish. What the turpentine doesn't wash out, the steel wool will. And the paste wax? It's providing protection so that the next time your son or your cat mounts an assault up the leg of your dining room table, he won't leave any footprints behind.

Strange as it may seem, wood is always in motion, constantly expanding and contracting with changes in temperature and humidity. Wood finishes must also be flexible, which accounts for their vulnerability to abrasions. Fortunately, what goes into a finish—namely, scratches—can also come back out. And what won't come out, we can disguise, but more on that a little later.

◄ Shallow Scratches

Scratches in an Oil Finish

Steps	*Materials*
1. Protect any nearby carpeting and upholstery.	plastic drop cloth masking tape
2. Clean the damaged area with a rag dipped in turpentine. Wipe dry.	clean rags turpentine
3. Dip a pad of no. 000 steel wool in a dark furniture oil for dark woods or a clear furniture oil for light woods.	furniture oil or Old English Scratch Cover
4. Rub the damaged area lightly with the steel wool in the direction of the grain.	
5. If the scratch persists, switch to no. 600 wet-dry sandpaper dipped in furniture oil. Sand lightly with the grain, keeping the sandpaper wet at all times.	no. 600 wet-dry sandpaper
6. Wipe off the oil, then apply clean oil to the sanded area. Let dry 5 minutes, wipe off the excess, then let harden overnight. Reoil the following day if necessary.	furniture oil rags

An oil finish is easy to repair, revive, and touch up, for until it is completely saturated, the wood will continue to absorb all the oil you give it. Many times a dull, lifeless teak table, maple serving tray, or hand-carved burl walnut bowl won't have to be refinished; it just needs a good drink of oil to jump back to life.

Shallow ▶
Scratches in
a Shellac
Finish

If you have inherited your grandmother's rocking chair—or have bought some other grandmother's rocking chair—it may well have the kind of shellac finish that was common a hundred years ago. It may also have picked up an unsightly scratch on the way in from the car. If that is the case, then you may want to know how to get rid of some of those scratches:

Steps	*Materials*
1. Protect any nearby carpeting and upholstery.	plastic drop cloth masking tape
2. Clean the damaged area with a rag dipped in turpentine. Wipe dry.	clean rag turpentine
3. Dip a small artist brush in denatured alcohol.	denatured alcohol artist brush
4. Carefully brush a small amount of the solvent into the scratch.	

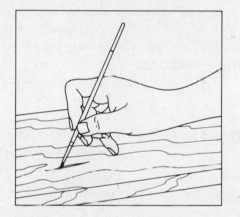

5. Continue to gently run the tip of the brush the length of the scratch as the solvent dissolves the finish surrounding the scratch.

6. When the scratch has disappeared, let the finish reharden.

7. If necessary, buff smooth with no. 0000 steel wool and lemon oil or paste wax.	no. 0000 steel wool lemon oil or wax

If you have a large number of scratches in a relatively small area, you can increase the size of your brush. If the entire piece is covered with small scratches, dings, and dents, I would recommend that you first read Chapter 3 on how to revive old shellac finishes.

Shallow ▶
Scratches in
a Lacquer
Finish

Lacquer, like shellac, has the added advantage that you can dissolve it temporarily with a common solvent, namely lacquer thinner. As we know it today, lacquer was first used commercially in this country around the turn of the century. By the 1920s, all of the major furniture factories in America were spraying lacquer on their furniture. It dried as quickly as shellac, but had as much resistance and durability as varnish. If you have a piece of furniture that was made since the twenties and has never been refinished, chances are very good that it has a lacquer finish. If you are not sure, you can test the finish on any piece of furniture using the Solvent Test explained in Chapter 3.

Shallow scratches in a newer Heritage coffee table or a recent Henredon armchair can be removed simply by dissolving the finish around them. It takes a steady hand and good-quality artist brush, but in just a few minutes time you can return your furniture to its original unblemished condition.

Steps	*Materials*
1. Protect any nearby carpeting and upholstery.	plastic drop cloth masking tape
2. Clean the damaged area with a rag dipped in turpentine. Wipe dry.	clean rag turpentine
3. Dip a small artist brush in lacquer thinner	lacquer thinner artist brush
4. Carefully brush a small amount of the solvent into the scratch.	
5. Continue to gently run the tip of the brush the length of the scratch as the solvent dissolves the finish surrounding the scratch.	
6. When the scratch has disappeared, let the finish reharden for an hour.	
7. If necessary, buff smooth with no. 0000 steel wool and lemon oil or paste wax.	no. 0000 steel wool lemon oil or wax

Be careful not to use too much solvent or to dissolve any more finish than absolutely necessary. You don't want to remove any of the finish; you just want to use it to fill in what the cat took out.

If your friendly feline, however, left numerous scratches on your table leg or if the movers put a long, wide scrape along an arm of a chair, you have a faster option than the brush, but only if the damage is shallow and the board narrow, such as a table leg or the arm of a chair—not a four-foot-wide tabletop.

After cleaning the damaged area with turpentine and letting it dry, reach for a can of aerosol lacquer rather than an artist brush. Make sure, however, that the can clearly says "lacquer" and not varnish or shellac. The lacquer has enough lacquer thinner in it to dissolve the shallow scratches before it dries; varnish does not. Protect the wood and upholstery around the scrape, then mist the area carefully. Too much lacquer will run; too little will dry before the original finish has time to dissolve and melt the scratches. You will know immediately if you have enough lacquer on the surface, for if you do, the scratches will begin to disappear before your eyes.

Afterward, let your new coat of lacquer harden, then rub out any roughness—or runs—with a pad of no. 0000 steel wool thoroughly moistened with lemon oil.

◄ Shallow Scratches in a Varnish Finish

While varnish has been heralded as the toughest furniture finish to yet be developed, it is also the most difficult to repair. One of the most popular variations on the standard formula—polyurethane varnish—leaves a finish similar to a thin sheet of Plexiglas. Unfortunately, like Plexiglas, once either standard or polyurethane varnish is scratched, it is difficult to buff out or touch up. Unlike shellac or lacquer, additional coats do not form a chemical bond with each previous coat. Rather than dissolving them, subsequent coats actually magnify the scratches.

Removing even shallow scratches from varnish is similar to removing them from wood, for the only way you can make them disappear is to lower the level of the surface of the finish around them until it is below the depth of the scratch. The deeper the scratch, the more varnish that has to be removed. To complicate the procedure, the scratches left by the sandpaper must also be removed.

But don't despair. It can be done; it just isn't as easy as it is with either lacquer or shellac:

Steps	*Materials*
1. Protect any nearby carpeting and upholstery.	plastic drop cloth masking tape
2. Clean the damaged area with a rag dipped in turpentine. Wipe dry.	clean rag turpentine
3. Dip a piece of no. 600 wet-dry sandpaper in either water, turpentine, or lemon oil.	no. 600 wet-dry sandpaper can or jar of water, turpentine, or lemon oil
4. Keeping the sandpaper wet at all times, gently sand the damaged area. Wipe dry to check progress.	clean rag
5. Buff sheen back with no. 0000 steel wool and lemon oil or paste wax.	no. 0000 steel wool lemon oil or wax

Disguising ▶
Scratches

No matter how well stocked my first aid kit is or how long I work on a piece of furniture, I invariably end up facing scratches that I simply cannot remove without also removing the finish. They may be too deep, the original finish around them may be too valuable, or they may be located in a spot that makes any repair too noticeable or too risky, such as the scratch left in the middle of a wonderful eight-foot-long mahogany table when the cleaning lady knocked one of the glass prisms off the chandelier hanging above it.

Fortunately, when you discover a scratch that is too deep to easily remove, you still have a couple of options besides resigning yourself to living with it. First, remember that all wood contains natural blemishes and abnormalities, such as tiny knots, insect borings, and grain variations. In addition, older nicks and scratches and other signs of age give an older piece of furniture ''character.'' What you cannot make disappear, then, you can often disguise as either being a natural part of the wood or an acceptable sign of age.

Let's assume that your daughter, the future neurosurgeon, has started practicing lunchtime incisions on the top of your oak table, leaving a three-inch scratch in the finish and the top layer of wood. What do you do?

First, you need to change the color of the scratch back to the color of the wood.

Second, you need to replace the missing finish.

You have several different types of materials to choose from, some of which are designed to take care of both steps at once. Among them are:

- Felt-tipped pens—blacks, browns, and reds are excellent for blending in scratches in oak, walnut, and mahogany, but must be followed with clear paste wax to fill the scratch.
- Crayons—they not only change the color of the scratch, but also fill the void.
- Shoe polish—again, several colors to choose from and it dries hard.
- Tinted paste wax—a limited number of colors, but dries even harder than shoe polish.
- Touch-up sticks—available at paint stores in more than a dozen colors, but not much better than crayons.
- Acrylic paints—have the advantage of a variety of colors that can be mixed to create a limitless number of other colors; if you don't like what it looks like after it dries, you can wipe it off with a rag dipped in water.
- Wood stains—naturally, dozens of different colors, but more expensive to buy than touch-up sticks or felt-tipped pens, and must be sealed and the scratch filled afterward.

Regardless of which material you choose, the important thing to remember is that the color should be the same as the other pores, knots, grain lines, and old scratches in the wood. If you look closely at most oak furniture, for instance, you will see that the pores are actually black; the wide ribbons or "flakes" of grain are what give it either a reddish or a golden oak color. A long scratch passing through numerous pores and flakes may require two or three different color combinations to really disappear from view, but that's what makes it a challenge—and fun.

And when touching up nicks and scratches, remember that neatness counts. While the tip of your finger may be the most convenient brush you will ever have, I have found that a toothpick, a matchstick, an artist brush, the point of a hobby knife, or even a sliver of wood provide more accuracy and less mess to clean up afterward. Some blending materials can even leave a semipermanent stain in the surrounding wood, so turn up the lights, get down next to your wood, and very, *very* carefully turn that fresh scratch into one that looks as old and as natural as the table itself.

Steps	*Materials*
1. Protect any nearby carpeting and upholstery.	plastic drop cloth masking tape
2. Clean any dirt, food, etc., out of the scratch. Wipe dry.	clean rag turpentine
3. Choose the appropriate blending material from the list above.	
4. Apply the material to the scratch.	toothpick, artist brush, etc.
5. Immediately wipe off any excess.	rag
6. Let dry.	
7. If necessary, fill with paste wax, let dry, and buff.	paste wax

I was lucky with the scratch left by the glass prism on the mahogany table. The scratch it left ran in the same direction as the dark grain of the wood, so I simply mixed the same color using my acrylic paints, brushed in an additional grain line, and later, after it had dried, sealed it with paste wax. No one, including the cleaning lady, was able to find it when I was done.

Raising Dents ▶ Though often small, dents can be among the most frustrating of all minor furniture problems to repair. The solution is somewhat drastic and can, if you are not careful, cause additional problems.

The best way anyone has yet discovered to raise the compressed fibers in a dent is with water or steam. The problem, of course, is that the water threatens certain finishes, especially old shellac and lacquer. Oil and varnish finishes are less likely to react to water, but both shellac and lacquer have been known to turn white if they have the opportunity and the time to absorb moisture. One way you can help prevent this from happening is to first protect the undamaged finish surrounding the dent with a heavy coat of paste wax.

Steps	*Materials*
1. Protect any nearby carpeting and upholstery.	plastic drop cloth masking tape
2. Clean the damaged area with a rag dipped in turpentine. Wipe dry.	clean rag turpentine
3. Puncture the finish in three or four places in the bottom of the dent.	straight pin

4. Fill the dent with water.	
5. If, after 24 hours, the dent remains, cover with a wet cloth and carefully touch with the tip of a hot iron until steam is produced.	wet rag hot iron

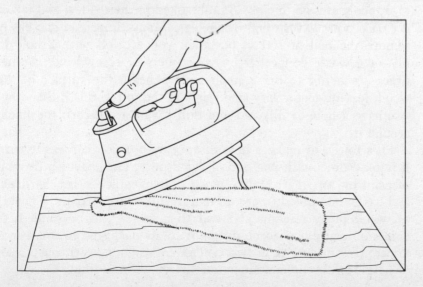

Steps	Materials

6. Check the dent; repeat if necessary
   until the fibers swell back to their
   previous level.

7. Let dry, then touch up finish.   artist brush
                                     finish

Now that you know how to raise a dent, let me offer this bit of advice. If you have an authentic antique that you are not stripping, consider carefully if you can live with the dent. I say this because the old finishes are the most apt to react to water and turn white. If that happens, the damage may be worse than the dent was.

But if your small son decided to take his toy hammer and club your new coffee table, then I would be more apt to say, "Take a shot at it." Newer finishes are less apt to react adversely to water. In either case, any time you have stripped off the finish, that is the perfect time to swell a dent back to its normal level. Until that time comes, you may just want to touch it up with stains, waxes, or paints to make it less noticeable.

Filling ▶ Small Holes
There is something about the nature of wood that lures people into drilling holes and pounding nails into it—whether it needs it or not.

Rolltop desks end up with pencil sharpeners screwed to their tops; bookcases get memos thumbtacked to their sides; and tables get nails pounded through their legs. Many times you can easily remove the nail or screw, but then you are left with a hole to fill—or a worse gouge left by your pliers or screwdriver. Sometimes it's better to drive small nails beneath the surface of the wood, leaving just a very small hole at the top to fill. Either way, you have a hole to fill, and you don't want to disturb the finish around it.

It's tough to make a hole disappear, but you can easily turn it into a "dot" with just dab of wood putty and maybe a tiny bit of paint on top of it. Unlike wood dough, which dries, hardens, and has to be sanded (more on that in Furniture Repairs, Chapter 4), wood putty remains soft and so never has to be sanded. It comes in nearly two dozen different colors packaged in small containers costing less than two dollars each. Unless you have a lot of holes to fill, one container can last you a long time.

Steps	*Materials*
1. Remove any dirt or old wax from the hole.	toothpick
2. Select the matching color of wood putty.	wood putty
3. Carefully insert the putty into the hole.	small screwdriver or wood scrap
4. Wipe off any excess.	rag
5. (optional) Cover with a drop of stain and/or finish.	artist brush stain or finish to match wood

The only real problem with wood putty is that it can be wiped off with a vigorous dusting, especially if it has not been sealed. If that happens, just add a little more to the hole.

Be especially careful not to smear excess putty across woods with open pores, such as teak, oak, mahogany, or walnut, for the putty will catch in the pores just as it did in the nearby hole. Instead of a small spot of putty, you will end up with an unsightly smear; but if it does happen, don't panic. You can just wash it all off with turpentine and start over.

Splinters are tempting. You're going along, dusting a piece of furniture or wiping off one you just stripped, when suddenly your rag snags. A splinter has reared up and grabbed it. It seems so easy just to snap it off, but don't. That fragile point sticking through your dust rag is but the tip of a dangerous iceberg; give it a pull and you'll probably see three more inches of wood follow it.

◄ Repairing Splinters

Splinters are actually very easy to fix and don't require any tools. More often than not, the hardest part is just restraining yourself from breaking it off.

Steps	*Materials*
1. Remove any threads or dirt from beneath the splinter.	toothpick or dental floss

Steps	*Materials*
2. Insert a few drops of glue.	toothpick Tite-Bond or 　Elmer's 　Carpenter's 　Wood Glue
3. Press the splinter back into place with your thumb.	
4. Wipe off any excess glue.	damp rag
5. While applying pressure with your thumb a second time, secure the splinter and maintain the pressure with masking tape pulled tightly across it.	masking tape
6. Let dry 12 hours, then carefully remove the tape.	

There are now at least two types of masking tape available: the standard household masking tape and a special painter's masking tape that has less sticking power. I would recommend that you keep both in your kit, the sticky version for use over tough, new finishes and the less sticky type for use on fragile, old finishes that might peel off with the other type of tape.

Regardless of which you use, always remove the masking tape as soon as possible after the glue has dried. This will reduce the risk of pulling away the finish with the tape. Also, peel the tape off slowly and by pulling directly across rather than straight up from the surface. Think of the wood as if it were your arm and you were about to take a Band-Aid off a cut.

Veneer Chips ▶ While many people assume that a veneered piece of furniture is automatically worth less than a solid piece, that simply is not the case—as long as none of the veneer is missing or badly damaged.

The new furniture you spend several hundred, if not thousands, of dollars on is more apt to have veneer than much of the furniture made a hundred years earlier. Unfortunately, from the 1920s through the 1960s, veneered furniture was produced at an astonishing rate by American furniture companies using inferior glues, veneer, and construction techniques. By the time you and I find it at an auction, in our mother's attic, or at a garage sale, it is likely to need some attention. If you can get to any of the loose veneer before it's swept up by dusting cloths and vacuums, your furniture can maintain all of the value it would have otherwise lost.

The best time to fix a loose piece of veneer is when you find it. Nothing is more important at that particular moment, for one veneer chip the size of a dime out of the top of your teak dining room table will permanently reduce its beauty and its value. If the chip is lost, you'll find several alternatives in Chapter 4. Right now, however, you're going to fix what hasn't yet disappeared into the jaws of the vacuum.

Steps	*Materials*
1. Remove any threads, dirt, or splinters from beneath the loose veneer.	tweezers or toothpick
2. Insert glue as far into the veneer as possible.	Tite-Bond or Elmer's Carpenter's Wood Glue disposable syringe or toothpick
3. Press down on the front of the veneer with your thumb, forcing glue back into any air pockets.	
4. Wipe off any excess glue.	wet rag
5. While applying pressure with your thumb or fingers, secure the veneer tightly in place.	masking tape, books, weights, etc.
6. Allow twelve hours to dry, then carefully remove.	

When applying masking tape, start at the back of the loose veneer and stretch it across and down the side of the furniture. When removing the tape, start at the back again, pulling it across and down the veneer rather than up and against it. The latter only increases the stress on the new glue joint and may cause it to break loose again.

If an entire edge along the top of a dresser or table has come loose, insert or inject glue into all loose areas, then lay a thin strip of wood on top of the freshly glued area before attaching the masking tape. The wood will spread the pressure from the tape to all of the veneer beneath it, reducing the amount of taping you will have to do.

One warning: Masking tape can damage fragile finishes. Before using it to clamp a repair, test an inconspicuous spot to make sure it will not remove the finish when you peel it off. If it does, use books, padded bricks, or any suitable weight to hold the veneer in place while the glue dries.

Repairing ▶
Water Damage

Given enough time, water can cause as much damage to wood as can fire. Unlike a burning cigarette, however, you can spill a drink, overwater a plant, or leave a wet umbrella lying on your dining room table for a few hours and not have a catastrophe on your hands. Let water remain undisturbed for several days though, and you'll need to reach for your furniture first aid kit.

Small amounts of water generally evaporate, but often leave behind a mineral deposit that has attached itself to the finish. Larger amounts of water may be absorbed by the finish, especially if it is shellac or lacquer, turning it white in the process. The real problem, one we will discuss in Chapter 4, is when the water is given enough time to penetrate the finish and cause a chemical reaction with the wood itself. That's when you find black rings under your flowerpots—and they are serious business.

Right now, however, we are going to take care of the first two levels of problems: mineral deposits and white rings.

Mineral Deposits

Steps	Materials
1. Cut or fold a soft cloth to cover the mineral deposit.	absorbent rag
2. Dip the rag in mineral oil, wring out the excess, and lay over the deposit.	mineral oil

Steps   *Materials*

3. Check periodically to see if the
   minerals have come loose. Remoisten
   if necessary.

4. Remove mineral deposits with a rag,   clean rag
   then wipe dry.

5. (optional) Wax the area for added   paste wax
   protection and to restore the sheen.

Any clear, lightweight oil can be substituted for mineral oil, including paraffin oil, lemon oil, baby oil, or vegetable oil, but avoid wood finishing oils, such as linseed oil, Danish oil, or tung oil. Many of these oils now have drying agents added to them, causing them to harden when they come in contact with the air and leaving you with a sticky, gooey mess to deal with.

Removing White Rings

The first step in removing fresh white rings is simple: do nothing. Nothing, that is, except to remove both the source of the water and any excess water remaining on the wood surface. Then wait.

One Monday morning the phone was already ringing as I unlocked the door to our shop. On the other end of the line was a frantic woman who had just that morning discovered a fresh white ring beneath the glass that had sat on a bookcase over the weekend.

"I tried wiping it off," she explained, "but when that didn't work I sprayed some wax polish on it to see if that would take it off. But that didn't work either."

What she had assumed was that the white ring was something that could be wiped off. White rings are not mineral deposits, but are evidence of moisture trapped in the finish. When she sprayed it with furniture polish, she not only wasted her efforts, but she provided the white ring with a barrier that would prevent it from evaporating on its own. Instead of releasing it, she had locked it in.

In some instances, fresh white rings will disappear if simply given the time to be absorbed by dry air. High humidity will slow the process, but when warm, dry air is present, it can happen. A hair dryer, set on low and used with discretion, can speed the process. Do not, however, presume that if a little heat is good, more will be better—and reach for a heat gun. The white ring may disappear, but only because you have just succeeded in melting the finish around it.

If the white ring refuses to leave on its own, then consider the following:

Steps	*Materials*
1. Protect any nearby carpeting and upholstery.	plastic drop cloth masking tape
2. Clean the damaged area with a rag dipped in turpentine. Wipe dry.	clean rag turpentine
3. Sprinkle damaged area with fine ashes or rottenstone.	ashes or rottenstone
4. Dip a coarse cloth in mineral oil, then lightly rub area in direction of grain.	coarse cloth mineral oil
5. Check progress frequently, adding more oil and abrasive as needed.	
6. Lightly rub out entire top to insure a uniform sheen.	
7. Wipe dry and rewax.	paste wax

As you no doubt realize, you have to be careful any time you are using even a fine abrasive on a furniture finish. Too much pressure for too long a period of time will remove all of the finish, leaving you with a tougher problem to solve than simply a white ring. If a light rubbing doesn't work, then brace yourself: you may have to live with it until the time comes when you decide to refinish it.

CHAPTER 3
Saving Old Finishes

I discovered not long ago a new reason why I like going to antiques malls. I was roaming through the aisles of a dealer cooperative in southern Ohio when I was stopped short—not by the sight of a piece of Gustav Stickley furniture, as is usually the case, but by a fragment of conversation that drifted over a tall display cabinet behind the mall desk.

"He claims it's eighteenth-century Philadelphia," one dealer was whispering to another, "but I swear it's the same one I saw at the Norton estate auction—and there wasn't anything there older than my grandmother."

I should have moved on, since the conversation obviously was not intended for my ears, but suddenly I was fascinated by an authentic reproduction of an imitation Ming dynasty vase. By mere coincidence it just happened to be in the same tall display case. Besides, I wanted to know what piece in the mall they were talking about.

My problem is that I'm an eavesdropper. I love to listen in on antiques dealers talking shop. They know every dealer's inventory, the ages of his children, whether or not his wife works, what he bought last weekend, what he shouldn't have bought last weekend, where he goes on vacation, whom he calls—in some instances, even, what his bank balance is.

Eavesdropping on antiques dealers may seem a little weird, but it's the best way I've discovered to really find out what's going on in the antiques business. So I listen, and what I'm hearing antiques dealers talk about today are original finishes.

It doesn't matter whether its a two-hundred-year-old Philadelphia lowboy or a twenty-year-old teak table, if the original finish is still there and still in usable condition, it's considered more valuable.

As a former "strip-sand-thank-you-ma'am" refinisher, I know I spent hours scraping off original finishes that, had I known how to restore and revive them, would not have had to be removed. Now, too many years and too many Hoosier cabinets later, I know better—and I know what to do with a tired old finish to bring it back to life, to give it vitality, strength, and more value.

And believe me, it's a *lot* easier than stripping.

Restoring vs. ▶
Refinishing

Today's collectors are making a fine, but clear distinction between ''refinishing'' and ''restoring a finish.'' You won't have any trouble distinguishing between the two if you remember that:

- REFINISHING implies that the existing finish is to be chemically or mechanically removed before a new finish is applied.
- RESTORATION refers to the process in which the original finish is cleaned, revived, and protected.

There are five very good reasons for restoring rather than refinishing an original finish:

1. It's easier. You won't need neoprene gloves, harsh removers, mechanical sanders, or gallons of sweat.
2. It's faster. You can save an old finish in half the time it takes to strip one—and you don't have to sand, stain, or refinish it.
3. It's cheaper. By using only a fraction of the solvents, sandpaper, and stripper required to strip and refinish a piece, you can save money as well as your finish.
4. It's more valuable. As every piece of quality furniture grows older, it grows more valuable—and experience has proven that an antique with a good authentic finish is worth more than the same piece refinished.
5. It often looks better. Unless the original finish has been ruined, a revived authentic finish looks more natural than a new finish simply because it and the piece are the same age. When a couple who have been married for fifty years walks down the street, they look natural together. Put an eighteen-year-old bride next to a seventy-year-old groom, however, and everyone starts whispering.

   The same goes for furniture. Put a young finish on an old piece of furniture and everyone starts whispering.

How, then, can you distinguish between an authentic, original finish and one that has been added years later? ◄ **Is It an Old or New Finish?**

First, you have to realize that just as there is no such thing as the perfect crime, there is no such thing as the perfect refinishing project. Once you realize that it is impossible for anyone to strip, sand, stain, and finish a piece of furniture without leaving behind some clues, you will be halfway toward being able to spot a non-authentic finish. It may be as obvious as swirling scratches left by an orbital sander or as subtle as a strand of steel wool snagged in a carving. In either case, the discovery of one suspicious clue is reason enough to look for another. Find enough of them and you'd probably be right in concluding that the finish on this particular piece of furniture is not the original one.

You should begin your search for clues on the exposed surfaces, such as the top, sides, and legs. Watch for any of the following:

- traces of darker finish in carvings,
  corners, and around the hardware
- sanding scratches, especially at the joints
- suspiciously uniform color throughout
- lack of signs of normal wear
- runs in the finish, especially on the legs
  and outsides of drawers
- new hardware

Even a lazy refinisher may disguise his work on a tabletop, but if you turn the piece over or crawl under it with a flashlight, you are apt to be surprised by what you will find. Instead of old gum, cobwebs, and rusty screw heads, you may discover:

- dried stripper residue
- partially dissolved finish
- trails of stripper rinse
- runs and drips of a new finish
- powdery lacquer overspray
- unnatural light or dark areas
- new screw heads

Be sure to inspect:

- the sides and bottoms of drawers
- the backs of large pieces

- underneath bottom boards and shelves
- around decals, carvings, and trim
- under the lips of tables
- the undersides of arms
- beneath the hardware

So what does this mean to us, especially if we come to the conclusion that it has already been refinished?

If it is an antique that you are considering buying, it means that the authentic finish is missing, and this should be reflected in the price.

If it is a piece that you already own, it means that you can refinish it completely—strip, sand, stain, and new finish—without endangering its present or future antique value. A second refinishing is not going to further decrease that value; in fact, if the first refinisher did such a poor job that even the casual observer can see it, then a second and proper refinishing by you is only going to increase its value.

I once had to listen to an antiques dealer proudly describe in glorious and gory detail how just the previous week she had meticulously stripped, sanded, bleached, and varnished a dark Mission Oak table until it finally—and relunctantly—became Golden Oak. When she finished, I quietly paid her seventy-five dollars for the table, took it home, and promptly stripped off her fresh varnish; the next weekend I stained it a more appropriate dark walnut, applied four coats of shellac, and rubbed it out with no. 000 steel wool dipped in paste wax; a week later I sold it to another Arts and Crafts collector for two hundred and fifty dollars. Later, I returned to the dealer's shop and asked that in the future she call me before, rather than after, she refinishes any more Mission Oak furniture.

But, if you do *not* find any evidence of a previous refinisher's work, chances are very good that your piece of furniture still has its original finish. If that is the case, you must identify the finish before moving on to the restoration process.

Identifying ▶ a Finish

Before you can attempt to save a finish, you first have to know what it is you are saving: oil, shellac, lacquer, or varnish. Just as every house, apartment, cottage, and condominium has within it a number of different types of furniture woods, each also has a number of different furniture finishes. Your grandfather's oak

Morris chair has an old shellac finish that is entirely different from your newly lacquered Baker dining room table in the next room. And the varnish on your daughter's dresser won't react the same way your oiled teak bedroom set will to the same solvent.

Each major furniture finish has its own particular solvent; using the wrong solvent could turn a simple restoration into a major disaster.

Identifying a furniture finish isn't difficult and doesn't require a degree in chemistry. The age of a piece of furniture will give you a good clue to the type of finish it has:

Era	Popular Finishes	Remarks/Techniques
1700–1850	linseed oil paint beeswax	Major museum curators have estimated that fewer than 1 percent of these original eighteenth-century finishes have survived without being refinished.
1800–1930	shellac	First introduced through the technique of French polishing with a pad; by the twentieth century was being brushed or sprayed on.
1900–present	lacquer	By 1930 the major furniture firms were spraying on lacquer almost exclusively; most widely used finish today in furniture factories and refinishing shops.
1900–present	varnish	Dries too slowly to ever become a factory finish; brushed on by refinishers.
1950–present	tung oil Danish oil	Reintroduced with Scandinavian-style furniture; popular with refinishers and custom furniture designers.

**Finishes and ▶
their Solvents**

Identifying shellac, varnish, or lacquer simply by sight or feel is difficult, for once they have dried, they look very much alike—especially after each has been used for several years. An oil finish (tung oil, linseed oil, Danish oil, mineral oil, etc.) is generally easy to distinguish from the others since it is absorbed into the wood rather than coated over it. A wood finished with oil will look more natural than with any of the others. If you stand with a piece of furniture between you and a bright light, such as a window on a sunny day or a table lamp, you will be able to see that the pores of the wood remain open under an oil finish and that the finish is dull rather than glossy, as you'll see in Scandinavian teak or walnut furniture that has been oiled rather than finished with shellac, varnish, or lacquer.

The best way to identify the major surface finishes—varnish, lacquer, and shellac—is by using the solvent test. Each has one particular solvent that will immediately start to dissolve it; under most of the other common solvents, nothing will happen. As soon as you know what the solvent is for each finish, you can determine in a matter of seconds what the finish is on nearly any piece of furniture you own.

Finish		*Solvent*		
	Mineral Spirits (Turpentine)	Denatured Alcohol	Lacquer Thinner	Methylene Chloride*
Shellac		X		X
Lacquer			X	X
Varnish				X
Paint				X
Paste Wax	X	X	X	X
Linseed Oil**				
Tung Oil**				
Danish Oil**				

* Methylene chloride is the active ingredient in most commercial paint and varnish removers.
** Once an oil has been absorbed by the wood fibers, it cannot be dissolved or removed. Turpentine will dilute most oils and take them deeper into the wood, but it will not enable you to identify them. Most oil finishes have a distinctive odor that will help you tell one from another.

Steps	*Materials*	◄ **The Solvent Test**
1. Lay the piece on its back or side.	padded surface	
2. Locate a section of finish that cannot normally be seen.		
3. Thoroughly clean an area no larger than two inches square.	turpentine rag	
4. Dip one end of a cotton swab in denatured alcohol, then squeeze out the excess.	cotton swab denatured alcohol	
5. Rub the dampened end in a one-inch circle in the cleaned area.		
6. If the finish immediately begins to dissolve, becomes sticky, and turns the cotton swab dark, the finish contains shellac.		
7. If none of the above occurs, dry the spot, take a fresh swab, dip it in lacquer thinner, and repeat the process. If the finish begins to soften, it contains lacquer.	rag cotton swab lacquer thinner	
8. If neither lacquer thinner nor denatured alcohol affects the finish, then it most likely is a modern, varnish-based finish.		

Now that you know what kind of finish you have in front of you, how do you decide if it can be restored?

◄ **Restoring a Finish**

For starters, there has to be a finish. If the arms on your rocking chair have worn down through the finish to the wood itself, then they need a new finish, not a restoration. If the back of the rocker still has its original finish, but is simply dirty or has started to develop tiny cracks in the surface—a condition called ''crazing'' or ''alligatoring''—you can restore that section without stripping it.

Next, the wood beneath the finish has to be in good condition. Deep black rings, large ink stains, and deep scratches or gouges cannot be removed or repaired easily without involving stripping or sanding—or both. In most instances, you will find that the condition of the wood and the condition of the finish will be the same. When the wood is in bad shape, the finish will have suffered as well. If the finish is in good condition, then the wood most likely will be, too.

And when that is the case, why strip it—especially if you can make it just as attractive and far more valuable in a fraction of the time by restoring it?

Step I—▶
Preliminary
Cleaning

Even though everyone knows that wood and water don't get along together well, a moderate amount of warm water and mild dishwashing soap can remove a good deal of dirt with very little expense. If your current project didn't come from the far corner of someone's basement or beneath a pigeon roost, you can skip to Step II, but if you've never pulled a gem out from a chicken shed antique shop along a country road, then you haven't lived a full life yet.

Steps	*Materials*
1. Protect any nearby carpeting, upholstery, decals, or labels. Remove hardware.	plastic drop cloth masking tape screwdriver
2. Set the piece on several layers of newspaper (or an old blanket) on top of the plastic drop cloth.	newspapers or an old blanket
3. Dip a sponge or rag in a bucket of warm, soapy water. Wring out the excess.	sponge or rag bucket of water mild dishwashing soap
4. Starting at the top, gently wash the piece, one section at a time.	
5. As each section is completed, wipe dry with a clean rag.	clean rag

If you find any damaged areas during your cleaning, don't make them any harder to repair. A long, jagged break is actually very simple to reglue, provided you don't mash or break off the exposed wooden "teeth." If necessary, keep your sponge and water away from any damaged areas until after you have made your repairs.

And if you think water and regular wood don't get along, just hope you don't have to see what it does to thin veneer. I once spent four weeks with a rosewood piano that had been stored in a leaky garage. It only took one week to do the work; the first three I spent staring at it, trying to decide where to start.

If the veneer is secure, a careful cleaning with a damp cloth should pose no problem. Loose edges, however, are easily snagged and should be glued and clamped before the area is cleaned. Water will also dissolve the old animal glues that were used to attach the veneer—an even better reason to reglue any loose pieces before you clean. Keep a dry rag close by and use it often, wiping toward the edge of any board to avoid snagging the fragile veneer.

If you count the number of times you wax, oil, or polish your furniture each year and multiply that number by the age of the piece—ten, fifty, or one hundred years—you will begin to understand why what may look to be a dead or dark finish is actually several decades accumulation of dirt trapped between hundreds of layers of wax and polish.

◄ Step II— Removing Old Wax and Polishes

These old waxes and polishes have not harmed either the wood or the finish beneath them; in fact, they have protected them very effectively. Granted, 487 coats of lemon-scented Pledge may have distorted the grain a little, but you can remedy that much easier than you can remove the finish itself.

Steps	*Materials*
1. Protect any nearby carpeting, upholstery, decals, or labels.	plastic dropcloth masking tape
2. Set the piece on several layers of newspaper (or an old blanket) on top of the plastic drop cloth.	newspapers or an old blanket
3. Dip a sponge or rag in a clean coffee can containing turpentine.	sponge or rag empty can turpentine
4. Starting at the top, gently wash the piece, one section at a time.	

Steps   *Materials*

5. As each section is completed, wipe   clean rag
   dry with a clean rag.

You should completely remove the old waxes and polishes as soon as they are softened; if you let them dry, they will reharden into a hazy film, leaving you no choice but to repeat the process. Change rags and turpentine as often as necessary to insure that you are actually removing the old wax and not merely moving it from one section to another.

Step III— ▶
Reviving an
Original Finish

Once you have identified and cleaned the finish, you are now ready to revive it. Up to this point your materials and techniques were the same regardless of the type of finish. Now the restoration process depends on the type of finish you're dealing with. It is important that you *don't* substitute one solvent for another.

Reviving ▶
an Original
Oil Finish

Oil finishes are perhaps the easiest to restore, for when most of the oil has either been absorbed into the wood, evaporated into the air, or been worn away by daily use, all you have to do is apply more oil.

In the last few years, though, researchers have determined that not all furniture oils are as beneficial to wood as we once believed. Neither raw nor boiled linseed oil is now recommended as a finish, even if the piece had been treated with this traditional favorite. Time and experimentation have revealed that both raw and boiled linseed oil will darken most woods—some, such as mahogany and rosewood, to the point where their grain is barely visible. Neither ever completely dries, but instead remains tacky, especially when the humidity is high, attracting dust and dirt, and making regular cleaning a chore. To make matters even worse, once applied, they are also both nearly impossible to remove.

Fortunately, you have a wide range of alternative oils. Among the natural and pure oils (those to which no toxic thinners or driers have been added), you have the following, all of which are suitable for use on cutting boards, chopping blocks, and wooden bowls used to prepare or serve foods:

mineral oil	soybean oil	sunflower oil
olive oil	vegetable oil	walnut oil

Some of these oils, though, most notably olive oil and vegetable oil, do turn rancid, and none of them provide long-term protection for the wood. Of these six, mineral oil is my choice for wooden serving utensils, chopping blocks, and cutting boards.

Chemists have also taken various natural oils and, through the use of synthetic additives, developed penetrating oil finishes that harden when exposed to air. Among the most common polymerizing oils today are:

tung oil   Danish oil
teak oil   Antique oil

Experience has shown that, unlike shellac, lacquer, and varnish, you can switch from one type of oil finish to another without fear of creating a chemical reaction. A table that had previously been treated with linseed oil can be cleaned and reoiled using tung oil or any of the other oils without any problem. I still recommend that you first thoroughly clean the piece with turpentine and let it dry completely before you apply the new oil; it only takes a few minutes and may insure a successful bond.

Steps	Materials
1. Protect any nearby carpeting and upholstery. Remove and label any hardware.	plastic drop cloth masking tape screwdriver
2. Clean the worn area with a rag dipped in turpentine. Wipe dry.	clean rag turpentine
3. Thin the appropriate amount of oil with an equal volume of turpentine.	oil clean can or jar turpentine
4. Using either a rag or brush, apply a liberal coat of the oil to the wood.	rag or brush oil
5. Allow to penetrate until it becomes tacky, then wipe off the excess.	clean rag
6. Let dry a minimum of 2 hours.	
7. Repeat at least once more using unthinned oil.	

It's a little tricky judging how many coats of oil will be enough. When the wood has absorbed all that it can, you will find yourself wiping off just as much as you brushed on thirty minutes earlier. The more you use a piece of furniture, the more coats it should have. Although you can always add more oil later, it is easier to give it that third, fourth or fifth coat now—while it's ready and you're in the mood.

Reviving a ▶
Shellac Finish

For most of the nineteenth century and well into the twentieth, shellac was the cabinetmaker's choice. Originally rubbed on (French polishing), later brushed on, and early in this century even sprayed on, shellac was the most durable, fastest-drying finish that had ever been developed.

Shellac, however, has three major flaws: it is vulnerable to heat, alcohol, and moisture. A dressing of paste wax could build its resistance, but chemists continued their search for the perfect finish. Once a spraying lacquer and a brushing varnish were developed, shellac was almost forgotten, but not before hundreds of thousands of pieces of Golden Oak and Mission Oak furniture had been produced and finished with shellac.

Since you are apt to encounter shellac quite often, you will need to know how to revive what may simply be a tired, thin, or alligatored shellac finish. Fortunately, this is almost as easy to restore as oil.

Steps	*Materials*
1. Protect any nearby carpeting and upholstery. Remove and label any hardware.	plastic drop cloth masking tape screwdriver
2. Clean the worn areas with a rag dipped in turpentine. Wipe dry.	clean rags and can turpentine
3. Scuff the old finish lightly. Wipe clean.	no. 220 sandpaper rag
4. In a clean jar combine one part commercially prepared shellac with four parts denatured alcohol.	clean jar liquid shellac denatured alcohol
5. Brush the solution over the finish in the direction of the grain, working only on one horizontal section at a time.	brush

Steps	*Materials*

6. Allow the solution to dissolve and revive the old shellac. Let dry from 2 to 4 hours.

7. Rub out with no. 000 steel wool dipped in paste wax. Buff to desired sheen.

no. 000 steel wool
paste wax
clean rag

If the alligatoring of the finish is severe, a second application of denatured alcohol and shellac may be necessary to dissolve it completely. In any case, never forget the paste wax in the final rubbing out, especially if you can ever imagine any water, alcohol, nail polish remover, or hot coffee mugs coming near the piece. Even new shellac can suffer from a spilled drink, overwatered plant, or midmorning cup of coffee.

If all of the furniture made in the twentieth century were put into two piles, the one of pieces finished with lacquer, the other finished with anything else—the lacquered furniture would tower over the other. Lacquer has been developed into the near perfect furniture factory finish: it sprays easily, dries quickly, remains durable for years, and is resistant to water, alcohol, and heat.

◀ **Reviving a Lacquer Finish**

And when it does begin to wear out, you have an important solvent on your side that will enable you to revive a tired lacquer finish—namely, lacquer thinner. The procedure isn't difficult and works well regardless of the age of the piece.

Steps	*Materials*

1. Protect any nearby carpeting and upholstery. Remove and label any hardware.

plastic drop cloth
masking tape
screwdriver

2. Clean the damaged area with a rag dipped in turpentine. Wipe dry.

clean rags and can
turpentine

3. Scuff the finish lightly. Wipe clean.

no. 220 sandpaper
clean rag

4. Into a clean jar pour approximately one cup of lacquer thinner.

lacquer thinner

Steps	*Materials*
5. Brush the lacquer thinner on the finish in the direction of the grain, working only on one horizontal section at a time.	brush
6. Keeping your brush wet at all times, continue brushing until the scratches, nicks, and blemishes disappear, then let dry 4 to 6 hours.	
7. Buff out any roughness with a pad of no. 000 steel wool dipped in either paste wax or lemon oil. Buff to desired sheen.	no. 000 steel wool paste wax or lemon oil clean rag

If you have a large number of shallow scratches on either a small piece of furniture or a large piece with numerous small sections, such as table legs, drawer fronts, or short shelves, but not dining table tops, you can try using an aerosol can of lacquer rather than a brush and lacquer thinner. An aerosol can of lacquer contains enough lacquer thinner to dissolve small scratches before the fresh lacquer hardens, enabling you to both revive the old finish and apply a new finish in one step. Follow the same steps as outlined above, but substitute several careful mistings of lacquer in place of the brush and lacquer thinner.

Reviving a ▶
Varnish Finish

Modern varnish is tougher than the older shellacs and lacquers, but the trade-off is that it is not as easy to repair or revive. Whereas shellac and lacquer can be easily respread and recoated, varnish cannot. If alligatoring occurs in varnish, it cannot be dissolved. If the finish begins to chip or flake, additional coats will not "melt" into the surrounding original finish as shellac and lacquer do.

Oftentimes a varnish finish will be intact, but through aging it will lose its ability to ward off heat, moisture, and the bruises of everyday use. Small bumps begin leaving impressions in the finish; coffee cups leave hazy heat marks; and a water glass left sitting on it overnight leaves a ring that won't wipe off. The most you can do at this point is to remove as many of the surface scratches as possible, put some new life into the finish, and provide it with additional protection.

Steps	*Materials*
1. Protect any nearby carpeting and upholstery. Remove and label any hardware.	plastic drop cloth masking tape screwdriver
2. In a fresh can mix a 50/50 solution of turpentine and mineral oil (or any pure, lightweight oil).	clean can turpentine mineral oil
3. Dip a pad of no. 000 steel wool into the mixture and lightly scrub the surface in the direction of the grain. Wipe clean as each section is completed.	no. 000 steel wool clean rag
4. Thin an appropriate amount of polymerizing oil with an equal amount of turpentine. Rub into the surface, let stand until it becomes tacky (approximately 15–30 minutes), then wipe off.	clean jar tung oil, Danish oil, etc. turpentine clean rags
5. Let dry overnight, then buff with lemon oil or paste wax to desired sheen.	paste wax or lemon oil

If your furniture is made from a dark wood or has been stained dark, you can use a tinted polymerizing oil, such as Minwax's Walnut Antique Oil, to disguise any white scratches or dents that cannot be removed using the steel wool.

◀ **Reviving an Original Painted Finish**

Although it took us nearly a hundred years finally to figure it out, woods that were originally painted were meant to be painted. This is as true for modern furniture as it is for 1920s Hoosier kitchen cabinets, 1820s Pennsylvania corner cupboards, and 1720s Windsor chairs. Up in that Great Workshop in the Sky those old cabinetmakers must be having a good chuckle over those fools (present company included) who worked their fingers to the bone stripping off stubborn milk paint, only to discover that it had been disguising a mixture of bland or unappealing woods.

What you and I have to realize is that these old cabinetmakers were pretty darn smart. They weren't going to build a cabinet out of imported mahogany and then paint it, at least not if they could avoid it. They'd only use paint on common pine, bland poplar, or a mixture of less expensive, secondary woods. In fact, what makes this furniture valuable, especially antique furniture, is not the wood, but the finish. Rather than stripping the paint off, we should be reviving and preserving it. It's easier, faster, cheaper—and more fun.

Steps	*Materials*
1. Protect any nearby carpeting and upholstery. Remove and label any hardware.	plastic drop cloth masking tape screwdriver
2. In a clean can mix a 50/50 solution of turpentine and mineral oil (or any pure, lightweight oil).	clean can turpentine mineral oil
3. Dip a rag into the mixture and lightly scrub the surface. Wipe dry as each section is completed.	clean rag
4. Let the surface dry completely, then seal with paste wax. Buff to desired sheen.	paste wax clean rag

With antique painted pieces, the original paint, like an original shellac finish, acquires a patina over the years that adds to its value. While a thorough cleaning is only going to improve the appearance of a piece of painted furniture that is only a few years old, if you are fortunate enough to discover a two-hundred-year-old painted blanket chest, anything more than a gentle cleaning and a coat of paste wax might lower its value.

Step IV—▶
Protecting a
Revived Finish

Remember when I made the comparison between taking care of your furniture and taking care of your car? Let's return to that idea.

Your car needs to be washed, so you wash it. It looks great while it is still wet, but what happens to the color just as soon as it dries?

It's dull. Clean, but still dull.

And what happens when it rains the next day? Do the water and the dust slide right off—or do they stick to the paint? Does your car need a new paint job? Of course not, just a coat of wax.

And, as you have guessed by now, wax (though not car wax) will do the same for your furniture as it will for your car: bring out the beauty of the finish and protect it at the same time.

Unfortunately, wax has gotten a dirty name. Television commercials tout floor polishes and furniture oils "with no waxy buildup." We equate waxing furniture with tennis elbow. The problem isn't with the wax, though, but with our misconceptions regarding it.

First, wax doesn't have to turn yellow and become sticky. It only does that when layer after layer after layer is applied without first removing the old wax with turpentine or a commercial furniture cleaner.

Second, wax doesn't have to be hard to apply. Most people put too much on and then let it stand too long before buffing it. One thin, hard layer of wax is better and easier to apply than several soft layers.

Finally, wax is a good preservative. It used to be considered a furniture finish of its own right, but now it is more like a former starting pitcher who has been relegated to the bull pen. When the starter begins to tire, we can bring in the reliever to save the game—or our furniture.

After any finish has been cleaned and, if necessary, revived, follow these steps for added protection and beauty:

Steps	*Materials*
1. Dip either a rag or pad of no. 0000 steel wool in a can of clear or tinted paste wax.	no. 0000 steel wool clean rag paste wax, such as Minwax or Briwax.
2. Lightly apply a thin coat of wax in small, light circles, working the wax into any open pores. Work on one section at a time.	
3. No more than 5 minutes after the wax has been applied, buff lightly with a soft cloth, in a circular motion, removing only the excess wax.	soft cloth

Steps	*Materials*
4. Wait 10 more minutes, then buff again, but with more vigor and only in the direction of the grain.	soft cloth
5. At the end of an hour, give the piece a vigorous final buffing with the grain to bring out the sheen on the hardened wax film.	soft cloth

New tinted waxes designed for darker-colored woods can hide minor scratches and fill open pores. Minwax has an excellent tinted wax, as does Briwax, which, in addition to a dark wax for walnut, has a reddish wax for woods such as mahogany and cherry. And avoid liquid waxes and waxes intended for cars or floors; they'll bring you nothing but grief.

Summary ▶ Regardless whether the original finish was oil, shellac, lacquer, varnish, or paint, it is almost always better to restore it than refinish it. Not only is it easier and faster, it can, especially on antiques, enhance the value of the piece. A final application of paste wax will give any finish, new or old, additional protection against water, heat, and alcohol.

The Shopping List

__ denatured alcohol

__ lacquer thinner

__ turpentine

__ shellac

__ mineral oil

__ lemon oil

__ paste wax

__ clean rags

__ sponge

__ drop cloth

__ masking tape

__ mild soap

__ cotton swabs

__ cans and jars

__ assorted brushes

__ no. 200 sandpaper

__ no. 000 steel wool

__ no. 0000 steel wool

CHAPTER 4
Furniture Repairs

◄ **Index to Repairs Section**

Burns ▶ As all of us have discovered while living with wood furniture, regardless of whether its new or old, people are not the only ones who suffer the consequences of cigarette smoking. One careless smoker can do more damage in sixty seconds to your magnificent eighteenth-century inlay desk or brand-new Thomasville table than a room full of Super Bowl partiers. Add to that the damage caused by hot cooking utensils and house fires and you begin to understand the need for information on repairing burns.

Special Problems

Burns range in severity on wood as much as they do on the human body. First-degree surface burns do little more than scorch the finish and can be buffed or wet-sanded out. Second-degree burns penetrate the finish, but stop short of ruining the wood. Third-degree burns, however, are characterized by charred, blackened wood and require a wood graft for a full recovery.

Third-degree burns must be treated just as you would treat a deep gouge, for that is what will remain after you have carefully cut away the charred wood. *(See Gouges for steps)* Second-degree burns will require a new patch of finish, not wood. You can only hope that all of your burns will be only first-degree, requiring only a minor repair to the existing finish.

First-Degree Burn

Steps	*Materials*
1. Clean the damaged area.	turpentine clean rag
2. Rub lightly with mild abrasive.	either: (a) fine wood ashes and mineral oil (b) pumice or rottenstone and oil (c) automotive rubbing compound (d) no. 600 sandpaper and water clean rag
3. Polish entire top.	lemon oil or paste wax clean rag

Second-Degree Burn

Steps	*Materials*
1. Clean affected area.	turpentine rag
2. Scrape away and/or sand off charred material.	hobby knife or razor blade no. 120 sandpaper
3. Bleach any darkened area. Repeat if necessary.	cotton swab Clorox (shallow marks) commercial wood bleach (deep marks)
4. Stain damaged area.	cotton swab wood stain or artist paints
5. Build up finish with several thin coats, allowing each to dry completely before adding next.	finish artist brush
6. Rub out leveled finish.	automotive rubbing compound
7. Polish entire top.	clean rag lemon oil or paste wax

> TIP: The key to blending a new section of new finish with the old is to rub out or polish the entire top rather than just the new patch. Without it, the color and grain may match, but the gloss of the two finishes won't. Rather than let all of your previous work go for nothing, rub out and polish the entire surface for a nearly invisible repair.

◄ **Chair Backs, Regluing**

As an old, grizzled refinisher once told me, "Show me a chair without arms, son, and I'll show you a chair with a loose back."

It didn't take me long to discover how right he was. While the backs of armchairs enjoy the additional support provided by the arms, the backs of side chairs must go it alone. The better the quality of the chair, the longer it can go between regluings, but sooner or later the joints between the back posts and the seat will need your attention.

Special Problems

Chair back designs fall into two categories: (1) those that are independent of the rear legs and (2) those that are formed by two continuous rear legs extending from the floor up to the head rail. Side chairs of the latter style were more expensive to produce, but offer a great deal more strength than the type whose back posts were simply inserted into holes drilled in the seat.

Their Achilles' heel, however, appears where a small hole was oftentimes drilled through the back of the post for a screw or dowel to be attached to the seat. When these posts do break, it is generally at this point and with little warning. Such breaks are difficult to repair without weakening the structure of the chair.

With the weaker style of chair back design, the one in which the back posts are simply glued into holes in the seat, the posts tend to loosen before they break, giving you ample warning of trouble. Before pulling these backs apart, inspect the rear of the

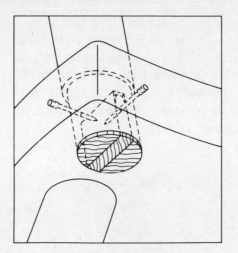

seat for hidden nails and the bottom for wedges driven into the end of the back posts. If you don't remove them, you are apt to split the chair seat taking them apart.

Steps	*Materials*
1. Remove any nails and wedges.	diagonal and/or standard pliers
2. Tap loose joints apart.	padded hammer
3. Remove old glue from tenons and inside holes.	no. 120 sandpaper, metal file, or strips of cloth soaked in vinegar
4. Apply glue to all surfaces.	woodworker's glue narrow putty knife, old table knife, or tongue depressor
5. Apply pressure.	pipe clamps, web clamp, or rope tourniquet
6. Remove excess glue and let dry 24 hours.	rag dipped in water warm room

TIP: Since chair backs were most often positioned at a comfortable angle to the seat, two pipe clamps work best: one exerting pressure from the head rail to the rear of the seat and the other exerting pressure from the head rail to the front of the seat. Although a single web clamp may suffice, the adjustments in pressure and angle offered by two pipe clamps are far more effective.

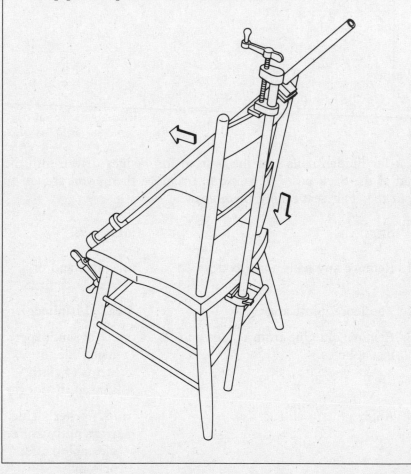

Chair Rungs, ▶
Regluing

Without a doubt, the most common furniture problem—and one of the easiest to correct—is loose chair rungs. Rocking chairs, side chairs, armchairs, Morris chairs, baby chairs: they all have rungs—and most have one or two loose joints. Dry winter air is especially hard on glue joints, but then, so are movers, guests, and teenagers. Given the choice between having a joint come loose under stress and having a rung snap in two, choose the loose joint. It's easier to fix.

Special Problems

When one rung becomes loose, another must bear additional stress. When the joints holding that rung also give way, a third joint must bear three times the stress intended for it. Eventually, one by one, each joint will surrender until finally the chair falls apart—or, worse yet, one of the rungs splits. For that reason, then, it is important to reglue a chair rung as soon as it becomes loose and not wait until they are all ready to pop.

Regluing one loose joint when all the others are still tight, however, can prove to be difficult. Rough dismantling can result in broken rungs rather than loose joints, since the surrounding wood will often splinter before the glue joint will surrender. Rather than force otherwise strong joints apart ("If it ain't broke, don't fix it"—a motto my auto mechanic just laughs at), the trick is to insert the needle of a syringe into the one loose joint without pulling it completely apart. If necessary, you can even drill a tiny hole through the exposed rung into the joint cavity to insert the needle and inject the glue.

Steps	*Materials*
1. Pull or tap any loose joints apart.	padded hammer
2. Clean off the old glue.	no. 120 sandpaper, metal file, or strips of rag soaked in vinegar.
3. Coat both surfaces with glue.	narrow knife or disposable syringe woodworker's glue
4. Apply pressure.	web clamp, pipe clamp, or rope tourniquet
5. Wipe clean and let dry 24 hours.	rag dipped in water heated room

TIP: Snug-fitting joints are essential to a successful regluing. If the rung has either shrunk or had wood removed along with the old glue, insert strips of freshly glued veneer alongside it as it is pulled back into the hole. Trim off any protruding veneer after the clamps have been tightened.

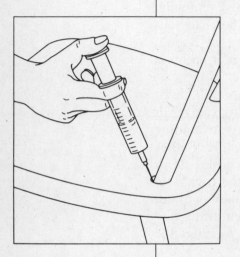
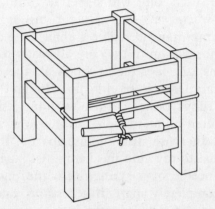

If you have tried unsuccessfully to reglue your chair rungs using woodworker's glue, substitute epoxy next time. The steps are the same, except that lacquer thinner must be used to wipe off the excess glue after clamping—but be careful: lacquer thinner will also remove a new lacquer finish.

Rungs, ▶
Replacing

At some point, you may be faced with a chair, footstool, or library table with a rung that is either missing or broken beyond repair. That may also be the first time you will need to insert and disguise a new piece of wood among several old ones. The care you take in removing the damaged rung and in matching the old wood will greatly affect the value of your antique.

Special Problems

A rung often breaks because the glue joint refuses to give under extreme pressure. It may even refuse to surrender when you want to remove a splintered portion to make way for the new rung. A number of steady, yet gentle taps with a hammer at various points on the broken segment may release the glue, but if it doesn't, consider steaming the joint apart. An old teapot with a length of rubber hose leading from the spout will direct the steam into the joint, and dissolve the old glue.

Installing a new rung may also be difficult if you don't want, or have, to disturb the other joints. You may need to shorten the tenon on one end of the new rung slightly to slip it into place without dismantling the entire chair. I learned to spread the two legs apart carefully by cutting a piece of soft pine slightly longer than the new rung and gently tapping it between the legs until I could slip the rung in the holes.

Steps	*Materials*
1. Remove remnants of broken rung.	hammer and pliers or possibly a drill and bit, vinegar and syringe, and/ or boiling teapot and hose
2. Clean old glue and wood fragments out of hole.	vinegar narrow chisel or drill and bit
3. Cut and sand new rung.	wood saw nos. 120 and 240 sandpaper
4. Duplicate worn areas and age marks on new piece.	no. 120 sandpaper
5. Stain and finish to match.	wood stain finish brushes and/or rags
6. Install new rung.	web or pipe clamps woodworker's glue
7. Remove excess glue, then let dry 24 hours.	rag dipped in water

TIP: Before forcing a damaged rung out of its hole, inspect the joint closely, looking for a finish nail that may have been driven through the joint from either side and then hidden under a small spot of wood putty. Before digging it out, consider using a punch (or nail with a flattened point) to drive it through the other side before pulling it the rest of the way out.

Chair Seats,▶ Regluing

The earlier they are detected, the easier chair seat splits can be repaired. Unless the chair has been subjected to extreme dryness, splits almost always start at either the front or rear edge and follow one of the original glue joints. Repairing them at this point is simply a matter of injecting glue and applying pressure with a pipe clamp overnight.

Special Problems

Curved or tapered seats can pose a bit of a problem when it comes to convincing your pipe clamp to stay in a position without slipping off as you tighten it. The solution is simple—if a second clamp is available. Use the extra pipe clamp to hold a two-foot length of pine two-by-four along either side of the chair seat. If necessary, insert a wedge of softwood in the space between the two-by-four and the tapered chair seat, then place the remaining pipe clamp across the ends of the pair of two-by-fours and tighten (see illustration). The resulting pressure will be transferred through the parallel softwoods to the seat and the joint being reglued.

Steps	*Materials*
1. Clean dirt out of split.	Hobby knife, toothbrush, or dental floss.
2. Clamp without glue to check fit.	pipe clamp scraps of softwood
3. Remove clamp and insert glue.	woodworker's glue narrow putty knife or syringe

Steps   *Materials*

4. Replace clamp and tighten.   pipe clamp and
                                            scraps

5. Remove excess glue and let dry for rag dipped in water
    24 hours.

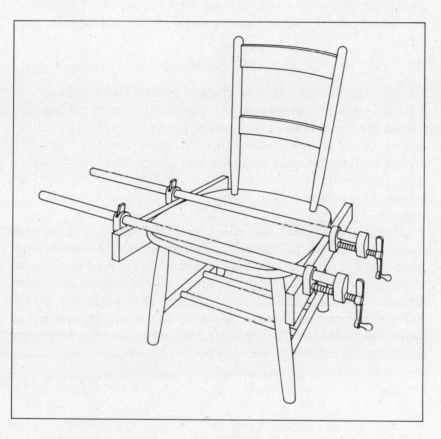

TIP: It may be helpful to insert a small screwdriver carefully into the split from the underside of the chair to spread
the gap in the wood slightly to both remove any accumu-
lated dirt and to inject glue deeply into the joint. Try not
to mar the wood.

    If the joint or crack has been unsuccessfully glued be-
fore, use epoxy instead and lacquer thinner on a rag to
remove any excess after clamping.

Chair Spindles, ▶
Repairing

If ever the phrase "strength in numbers" had an application in the world of furniture, it would refer to chair spindles. Square or round, turned or tapered, these decorative soldiers form an impressive rank, but once they are isolated and placed under pressure, most will bend only slightly before they break. When grouped tightly together, a row of slender spindles can support the weight of a grown man leaning back in his chair; but when one does break, this same tight formation can interfere with your repair.

Special Problems

You may discover a broken or cracked spindle that you can't—or may not want to—remove before making the repair. While the spindle may be broken in the middle, both ends will often still be securely glued in their holes. In these cases you must gingerly inject glue into the split, bring the two pieces back together, and apply pressure in whatever way space permits: tiny C-clamps, alligator clips, rubber bands, strips of inner tube, or tightly wound string.

If the small amount of exposed wood surface will not insure a strong bond, additional strength may be supplied through a miniature metal dowel—a finish nail minus its head. By using one of two identical nails as a drill bit, first drill the proper-sized hole into which you can then tap the other nail. If you snip the second nail slightly shorter than the depth of the hole, you can tap it below the surface of the wood and disguise the tiny hole with tinted wood putty.

Steps	*Materials*
1. Clean out any dirt or splinters from break.	hobby knife, toothbrush, or dental floss.
2. Insert glue.	woodworker's glue syringe or toothpick
3. Apply manual pressure.	fingertips
4. Wipe off excess glue.	rag dipped in water

Steps	*Materials*

5. Apply clamp pressure.

wax paper under
either
(a) C-clamps and
scrap pads
(b) tightly wound
string
(c) rubber bands

6. Let dry 24 hours.

TIP: Before winding string, rubber bands, or strips of inner tube around any cracked or broken spindle, wrap the
glued area with wax paper to prevent any excess glue from
bonding your clamp to the wood.

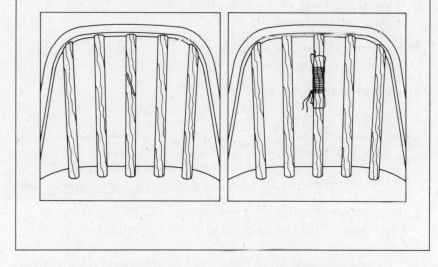

Problems with drawer bottoms in dressers, desks, buffets, and
library tables can range from shrinkage cracks and water damage
to improperly repaired or even missing bottoms. Whenever possible, the original bottom should be repaired rather than replaced,
but when a new bottom must be cut, you can still make it appear
authentic.

◄ **Drawers,
Bottoms**

Special Problems

The majority of the furniture made since 1900 contains thin wood panels of either solid wood or an early form of plywood as drawer bottoms. Until recently, replacement panels have been difficult to find, but increased demand for quarter-inch oak and maple veneer plywood in modern cabinet shops has now made it readily available. However, you should first attempt to locate wood the same age as your piece from which to cut your new drawer bottoms. The backs of badly damaged dressers, chests of drawers, and kitchen cabinets of the twenties and thirties can provide thin panels similar to those used as drawer bottoms. Each month community auction houses and used furniture stores throw away enough badly damaged pieces to keep a weekend refinisher stocked with a year's worth of wood for repairs and replacement parts.

Steps	*Materials*
1. Turn the drawer over and inspect for nails along back and sides.	
2. Remove any nails holding drawer bottom in side grooves.	diagonal pliers
3. Slide bottom out of grooves.	
4. Either: (a) repair original (b) cut replacement	woodworker's glue clamps metal ruler utility knife or saw
5. Slide repaired or new bottom in place and nail along back edge.	hammer brads

The easiest and neatest way to cut quarter-inch plywood panels is with a long metal straightedge and a utility knife (also called a box-knife or razor blade knife). Place the plywood on a thick sheet of cardboard or scrap plywood, then hold or clamp the metal straightedge firmly in place. Don't try to cut all of the way through the plywood with the first or second pass; a series of passes with the knife held under firm, steady pressure will be safer and leave you with a cleaner edge than that left by a saw. I have used this method to cut wood as thin as veneer and as thick as half-inch plywood—and with no noise, no dust, and no stitches.

> TIP: Don't overlook the obvious. You may be able to re-
> move a badly stained or abused drawer bottom, turn it
> over, and slide it back in its grooves. Not only is this
> method fast, easy, and inexpensive, but it retains the au-
> thenticity of the piece as well.

While not actually a difficult repair, musty smells in old drawers   ◀ **Drawers, Musty**
certainly pose a perplexing problem. It stems from the fact that
most cabinetmakers left the interior woods, including drawer sides
and bottoms, unsealed. The open pores act like a sponge, absorbing whatever odors they come in contact with—including those in
musty basements and stale attics.

Solutions fall into two categories: those that attempt to remove
the odors and those that, failing the first, attempt to solve the
problem by trapping the pungent smells under a coat of sealer.

Special Problems

One of the most recommended solutions is that of sealing the
interior woods with either oil, shellac, or thin varnish, but in the
eyes of those concerned with preserving the authenticity of old
furniture, this raises a serious dilemma: Should a finish be applied
where there originally had been none?

In the case of a legitimate antique, perhaps not. It may be that
you simply need to adjust your attitude toward the peculiar odors
often associated with antiques and resign yourself to disguising
rather than entombing them. When faced with the same problem
in what should be accepted as a piece of used furniture and not a
true antique, then you are probably increasing both the attrac-
tiveness and the usefulness of the piece by sealing interior wood
surfaces.

Steps	*Materials*
1. Remove any old newspapers and liners.	
2. Clean thoroughly.	mild soap and warm water vacuum

Steps	*Materials*
3. Set outdoors in shade and gentle wind for 1–3 days or place an absorbent in each drawer.	perfect weather baking soda
4. Reassemble in house and disguise any lingering odors.	cedar chips, herbs or spices
5. (optional) Seal any raw wood surfaces on the drawers or interior.	thinned furniture oil, shellac, or varnish brush or rag

---

TIP: Do not discard any old newspapers until you have carefully searched for items of historical importance. Old papers of only local interest may be eagerly accepted by area historical societies or libraries.

Drawers, ▶ Regluing

Over the centuries furniture makers have experimented with a variety of types of joints in drawer construction. As a result, you will likely find examples of nearly every style in need of regluing. In many instances, nails may have been added to reinforce a weak joint, but nails have never been an acceptable substitute for glue.

Special Problems

One drawer joint will sometimes loosen while the others remain intact. If you must dismantle a weak, yet intact, joint, do so using a hammer and a block of softwood cut to span the entire length of the joint. A series of gentle taps along the entire length of the softwood block will gradually release the remaining glue without breaking any fingers of wood (see illustration).

More than one refinisher has taken the clamps off a reglued drawer only to discover that it no longer fits the opening in the case. Since it is impossible to check the fit while the clamps are still in place, the best means of insuring that you won't have to disassemble your freshly glued drawer and start over again is with a tape measure. To determine if your drawer is perfectly square, as soon as the last clamp is in place, measure diagonally from each front corner to the opposite back corner. If the diagonal distances are the same, the drawer is square. If they differ, the pressure or the position of the clamps will have to be adjusted before the glue hardens.

Steps	*Materials*
1. Remove any nails in joints.	diagonal pliers
2. Disassemble loose joints.	hammer softwood block
3. Clean out old glue.	narrow chisel, sharpened screwdriver, or vinegar
4. Glue and clamp.	woodworker's glue narrow putty knife clamps
5. Compare diagonal measurements.	tape measure

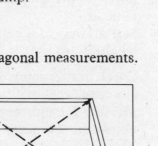

6. Remove excess glue and let dry 24 hours.	rag dipped in water

TIP: Do not glue drawer bottoms in the side grooves. If the four corner joints are properly glued, the drawer does not need this extra reinforcement. The bottom panel should remain unrestrained in the grooves to allow it to expand and contract without splitting.

Drawers, ▶
Stubborn

While stubborn drawers, like long stoplights, may have been created just to test your patience, they are often a sign of a developing problem—a problem which, if left unsolved, could become costly to correct. As with many small repair problems, bigger ones loom ahead, such as breaking off the pulls when you struggle with the drawer. The list of problems associated with stubborn drawers is lengthy, but few are difficult to solve. More often than not, the biggest hurdle is simply identifying the problem at hand.

Special Problems

Problem	Solution
Swollen drawer side	Use warm sunshine or hair dryer on low setting to free drawer. Place in sunshine for gradual drying or in 200-degree oven for faster results. Check every 5 minutes. Seal drawer sides with furniture oil afterward.
Sides rubbing	Check drawer joints for looseness; reglue if necessary. Measure for squareness; reglue if necessary. (See inset A.) Wax sides.
Framework no longer square	Reglue case.
Drawer no longer square	Reglue drawer.
Warped drawer side	Soak concave side with damp towel until able to clamp back into place without splitting; let dry in clamps; release clamps, then reglue.
Guide loose	Reglue guide in correct position. (See inset B.)
Guide worn	*See Drawers, Worn Guides.*
Runner worn	*See Drawers, Worn Runners.* (See inset C.)

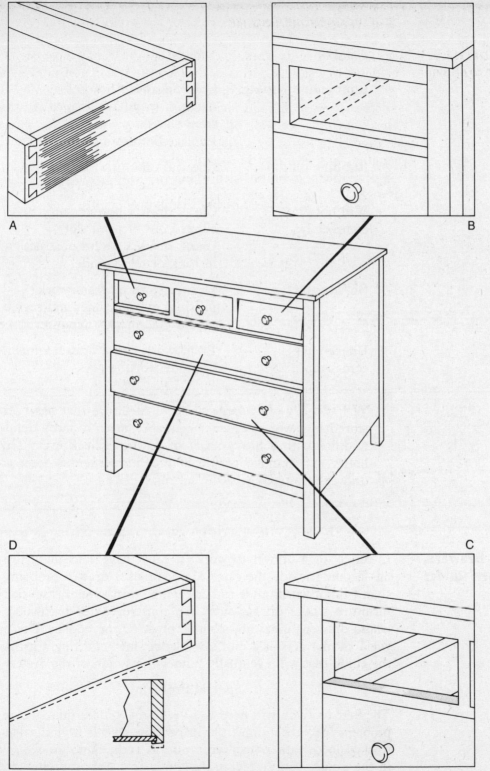

A

B

D

C

Problem	*Solution*
Rubbing on bottom	Check drawer bottom for sagging; may have slipped out of front slot. Replace bottom if necessary.
Rubbing on top	Check framework for sagging; may need to be reglued.
Will not close completely	Check drawer bottom; may have slipped out of front slot. Check inside case for obstruction in back or loose guide.
Goes in too far	Drawer stops on framework missing; cut new ones and reglue on old glue mark. (See inset D.)
Uneven gap across top	Framework loose; drawer runner or guide worn.

TIP: To dry out a large piece of furniture that has been stored in a wet basement or garage, cover it and a dehumidifier with a heavy sheet of plastic. Check every few hours and remove plastic and dehumidifier as soon as drawers are freed.

Drawers, ▶
Worn Guides

In order for a drawer to work, it must have something to slide on—a guide inside the case. Many times a drawer problem will stem from a worn guide rather than a worn runner, especially in furniture whose drawer sides are constructed of hardwood and whose drawer guides are a softer pine, fir, or poplar. The hardwood runner acts as a dull saw blade, slowly cutting a groove in the guide that will eventually hinder the action of the drawer.

Special Problems

The first tool you will need is a flashlight to determine where the problem lies. Oftentimes the inspection reveals a guide that has worked loose rather than worn out. If there is no groove carved in the guide, simply reglue the guide in its appropriate spot. If the loose guide is going to require additional repairs, it may be easier to first remove it from the framework.

Strips of veneer—sliced, glued, and clamped in the groove, then sanded flush the following day—make excellent patches. While appearance is always a consideration, it is not as essential as a smooth, snag-free path for the drawer runner. Finish any inspections and subsequent repairs with a liberal application of paste wax to reduce friction.

Steps	*Materials*
1. Inspect the worn area.	flashlight
2. Determine the dimensions of the worn area.	tape measure
3. Cut buildup material.	hobby knife thin strips of hardwood
4. Trim and glue material in groove.	woodworker's glue C-clamps
5. Let dry twelve hours.	
6. Sand smooth.	no. 120 sandpaper
7. Lubricate.	paste wax

TIP: If the guide has shrunk to the point where it does not come in contact with the back of the case, you may want to insert a wood screw through the back of the case into the end of the guide to give it the required support. If this is necessary, mark and drill the pilot hole from inside the case.

When you consider (1) the fact that most drawer sides are constructed from thin softwoods and (2) the number of times an ordinary drawer is opened and closed (e.g., if a dresser drawer made in 1900 were opened and closed only once each day, the runners would have been used 64,240 times), is it any wonder that they

◄ Drawers, Worn Runners

eventually wear down to the point where the drawer bottom rubs on the case?

Special Problems

Practical solutions to worn drawer runners range from the extremely simple (thumbtacks) to the extremely complex (splicing in new sections complete with matching dovetail joints). The first consideration to be made involves the age and authenticity of the furniture. A fine pre–1860 case piece should not be subjected to shortcut solutions, but if a strategically placed thumbtack is going to solve the problem on a five-year-old dresser, why not use it?

When a worn runner requires more than just a thumbtack, though, you may need to trim off the old and glue on the new—a new runner, that is.

Steps	*Materials*
1. Score a straight line the length of the drawer immediately above the worn area.	straightedge utility knife
2. Continue cutting this line until the blade removes the worn area.	
3. Measure and cut new splice to fit.	tape measure wood straightedge utility knife
4. Glue and clamp splice in place.	woodworker's glue clamps and pads
5. Remove excess glue and let dry 24 hours.	rag dipped in water
6. Sand the new joint and stain the splice to match the old portion of drawer.	no. 180 sandpaper stain rag
7. Apply a finish to the splice only if one exists on the remainder of the drawer.	finish brush or rag

TIP: Don't feel that you have to remove the worn area to make the repair. If you can build up the depressed area by gluing on strips of wood and then sanding it flat and smooth, by all means do so. Remember: the more of the original wood you can save, the more the piece will likely be worth someday.

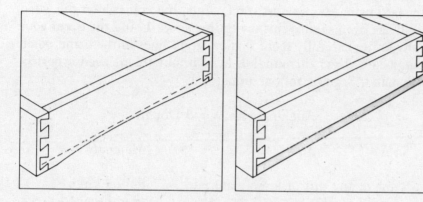

◀ Gouges

One of my assistants once observed, "You know, people really shouldn't get all that upset about gouges. They're only deep dents."

The fact that he had just knocked a bar clamp off the top of a dresser and onto a drawer sitting on the floor beside it, leaving a "deep dent" for me to repair, may have had something to do with his cavalier attitude. But the fact is, a gouge can't be steamed back into place. It has to be filled.

Regardless of what you want to call it, a gouge is still a problem, not so much in filling the crevice, but in blending your new patch with the surrounding wood. While wood dough is the most often used patching material, it does not absorb stain as well or in the same way as wood, nor does it have the texture of real wood. For those reasons, then, consider taking the time to select, cut, and sand a wood patch for any "deep dents" you may encounter.

Special Problems

Although the analogy may be painful, a refinisher preparing to patch a gouge with wood dough is similar to a dentist preparing to fill a cavity. First, any loose fibers or alien material (dirt, wax, old patches) must be removed, then the hole must be deepened or undercut to provide a niche in which the wood dough can anchor itself (see illustration). The wood dough is then packed firmly in the hole, allowed to harden, then sanded smooth. (Novocaine is optional.)

The secret to an inconspicuous patch is not just in the color selection of the wood dough, for that generally has to be altered afterward using stains or artist oil paints, but comes after the wood dough has been sanded flush with the wood. Using the tip of your hobby knife, carefully score shallow grain lines in the bland patch to duplicate those surrounding it. Without them, even a perfect color match is going to look unnatural.

Patching with Wood Dough

Steps	*Materials*
1. Remove any dirt or loose material.	hobby knife toothbrush
2. Undercut and/or deepen gouge.	hobby knife

3. Pack wood dough firmly in gouge, mounding slightly to allow for shrinkage.	wood dough small screwdriver
4. Allow to dry and harden for 24 hours.	

Steps	*Materials*
5. Sand flush with wood.	nos. 120 and 240 sandpaper

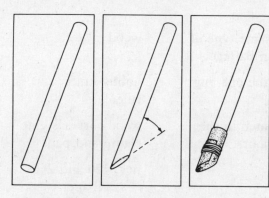 

Steps	*Materials*
6. Extend and duplicate adjacent grain lines.	hobby knife
7. Match color of wood. Let dry.	wood stains and/or artist paints
8. Apply finish.	finish artist brush

TIP: Once it hardens, wood dough can be as difficult to remove from the surrounding pores as it is from the gouge itself. Try not to smear the soft dough across the wood; either be neat, or, if that is impossible, protect the area around the gouge with a layer of masking tape. It will save you some unnecessary sanding afterward.

Patching with Real Wood

Steps	*Materials*
1. Remove any dirt or loose material.	hobby knife toothbrush
2. Trace the outline of a diamond or triangle around the gouge, or extend and taper the sides to meet at a common point.	hobby knife ruler

Steps	Materials
3. Trim the sides of the gouge until they are perpendicular to the surface of the wood.	hobby knife
4. Select a patch of the same type of wood and similar grain pattern.	wood
5. Trim the patch to fit the opening.	hobby knife ruler
6. Glue and clamp the patch in the opening. Let dry 12 hours.	woodworker's glue clamp and pads
7. Sand flush.	nos. 120 and 240 sandpaper
8. Stain and finish to match.	wood stain and/or artist paint finish artist brush

TIP: By tapering the sides of the patch slightly, so that they flair outward and beyond the sides of the gouge, you will get a near perfect fit when the patch is sanded. (see illustration).

For shallow gouges, you can glue together scraps of veneer to match the depth of the opening. It's fast, easy, and safer than trying to trim a one-eighth-inch-thick patch from a one-inch board.

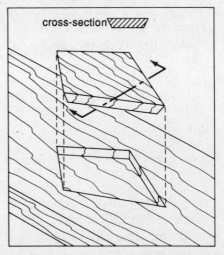

cross-section

Two of history's most common yet inappropriate means of repairing furniture, especially loose joints, are nails and screws. Graduates of the Hammer and Nail School of Furniture Repair still stalk the streets at night searching for a wobbly chair or defenseless table to assault. Some of their victims may seek refuge in your workshop, where you can do what's right: remove the foreign object, then patch the wound.

◀ **Holes**

Special Problems

Small nail holes can easily be patched using wood dough (*see Gouges*), but larger holes—those more than a quarter inch in diameter—are best filled using actual wood. Manufacturers now produce wood dowels in maple, oak, and walnut; if you cannot find dowels in the type of wood you need, seek out a local professional woodworker who is apt to have a three-eighths-inch or a one-half-inch plug cutter. All you need then is the wood and an electric drill. Once you have your plug, you simply enlarge the nail hole to the same size, glue in the plug, and sand it flush.

Steps	*Materials*
1. Remove the screw or nail.	screwdriver or diagonal pliers
2. Select a wood plug or dowel one standard size larger than the hole.	wood dowel or plug
3. Enlarge the hole to match the dowel selected.	drill and bit
4. Cut the plug or dowel.	hacksaw
5. Sand one end of the dowel.	nos. 120 and 240 sandpaper
6. Coat the inside of the hole with glue.	woodworker's glue cotton swab or toothpick
7. Tap the dowel into the hole, flush with the surrounding wood.	hammer and softwood scrap
8. Let dry and fine-sand if necessary.	no. 240 sandpaper.

TIP NO. 1: Cut the dowel or plug shorter than the depth of the hole to allow for excess glue and compressed air.

TIP NO. 2: By coating the inside of the hole rather than the outside of the dowel or plug, you will avoid the problem of excess glue oozing out onto the surface of the wood.

TIP NO. 3: If you discover screw holes on an antique made before 1850, whittle a plug by hand. Start with a standard dowel one size larger than the hole, whittle it down to fit the hole, then glue and tap it into place. The irregular sides of your handcrafted plug will look more natural than a machine-made, perfectly round dowel.

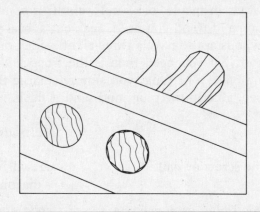

Panels ▶ What many refinishers, past and present, have failed to realize is that the thin panels in furniture doors and sides were intended to ''float'' in their grooves. The evolution from thick, solid sides to thin, paneled sides reduced both the weight and the cost of each piece of furniture, but it brought with it a need to understand that wood expands and contracts with changes in temperature and humidity. When these panels become locked in place, either with glue or several coats of varnish, they often split with the next change of season.

Special Problems

What makes split panels difficult to repair is the fact that clamping them while they are still surrounded by the framework is nearly impossible. If the joints of the framework are loose, you can tap them apart, remove the panel, repair it, and then reglue the panel.

If the framework cannot be disassembled, the panel must be repaired while still in place. First use a sharp hobby knife to free the panel from the channels in the framework—if the repaired panel cannot float, the problem will soon reappear.

One means of regluing a floating panel requires a minimum of four large C-clamps, which you may want to borrow rather than buy. Each pair of clamps is tightened on either side of the split, using softwood pads to protect the panel from the metal clamps. Each clamp is then connected to the one across the split from it with a double length of cord; this is done on either side of the panel (see illustration). By turning each cord into a tourniquet, you can pull the two panel halves together with the necessary pressure to enable the glue to form a strong bond.

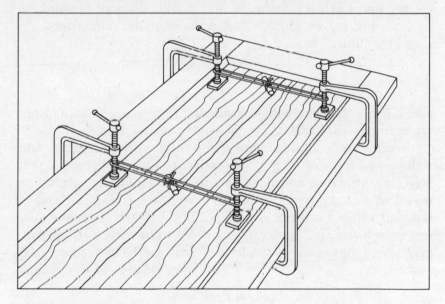

Steps	*Materials*
1. Free panels from channels.	hobby knife
2. Clean dirt from split.	toothbrush or dental floss
3. Attach two clamps on either side of split.	four C-clamps
4. Loop a cord between each pair of clamps, spanning split on both sides of panel.	four lengths of cord

Steps	*Materials*
5. Insert glue in split.	woodworker's glue syringe or toothpick
6. Tighten tourniquet cords, pulling panels together.	four short dowels.
7. Remove excess glue.	rag dipped in water
8. Let dry 24 hours.	

> TIP: The glue will not require extreme pressure. Moderate, undisturbed pressure is all that you will need to bond the panel halves, since it should not be under much stress in the future.

Rings, Black ▶ The rule for rings is among the simplest to remember: white rings are in the finish, black are in the wood.

When water comes in contact with certain woods, such as oak, walnut, and mahogany, it often produces a chemical reaction that leaves a semipermanent black or blue ring. Paint and varnish remover won't take it out, and it is generally too deep for you to sand out without creating a low spot in the wood. To make matters even worse, it is generally too deep to be bleached out with even several applications of Clorox. What you have to resort to is oxalic acid.

Special Problems

Don't panic. Oxalic acid isn't as bad as it sounds. You can buy it in crystal form over the counter from your local pharmacist; it doesn't require a doctor's prescription. The crystals pose no problem so long as you don't take them internally; even when dissolved in water, which you will do, they do not form a burning solution. When the water evaporates, however, leaving dried crystals on the now-bleached wood, you do have to be careful not to inhale the crystalline dust. A simple particle mask, a vacuum sweeper, and a fan (or, better yet, working outdoors) will prevent you from undergoing a coughing or sneezing fit caused by the crystals.

It's a good idea to wear protective glasses, a particle mask, and rubber gloves when working with oxalic acid.

Steps	*Materials*
1. Strip and sand the section to be bleached.	paint and varnish remover no. 0 steel wool and rinse no. 120 sandpaper
2. Stir oxalic acid crystals into two cups of hot water until a saturated solution is reached.	hot water oxalic acid crystals clean jar and spoon
3. Brush the saturated solution onto the wood, covering all sections completely.	old brush
4. Apply additional solution to darkened areas.	
5. Let the piece dry completely, preferably in mild sunshine.	
6. If the stains remain, apply a second coat over the dried crystals.	
7. Let the piece dry completely.	
8. Vacuum the dried crystals, then sand the wood until smooth.	vacuum nos. 120 and 240 sandpaper
9. Stain and finish to match.	wood stain finish brushes and rags

TIP: It is important to remember that you cannot simply bleach the stains themselves. If you do, you will end up with light spots in place of dark spots, which is like trading a lawnmower that won't start for one with a broken blade. Instead, bleach the entire section. It's easier to match the stain and finish on an entire section than try to blend in one spot within it.

Rocking Chair: ▶
Repairing
a Runner

Rocking chair runners generally break in one of two places: where they are attached to the back leg, and where two boards were glued together to form the rear curved portion.

My experience has shown that the larger the gluing surface (or, in other words, the longer the break), the more chance you have for a successful repair. Short, vertical breaks that occur where the runner is attached to the back leg are difficult to repair, since the amount of wood surface to be glued is much smaller. In such cases, the runner should generally be replaced. The longer breaks, those that run horizontal with the grain, can often be mended without reducing either the value or the usefulness of the rocker.

Special Problems

Clamping two curved pieces of wood together can test your ingenuity—and your patience. If you have tried it before, you know that either the clamps keep slipping off the curved pieces of wood or the curved pieces of wood start sliding as soon as pressure is applied by the clamps. Either way, its enough to make you think about having a new runner made.

If you have a professional assortment of clamps available, you may be able to equalize the pressure around the joint and make a successful repair.

If, on the other hand, you don't, then consider either of these options:

The Nailing Board

Steps	*Materials*
1. Lay the chair on its side with the broken runner atop a wide scrap board.	wide board
2. Position the broken pieces in their original position.	
3. Drive a series of construction-grade nails to the scrap board at four-inch intervals approximately 1/2 inch from the runner.	no. 10 nails hammer
4. Insert glue into the clean joint.	woodworker's glue syringe or toothpick

Steps	*Materials*
5. Force the two pieces together by tapping softwood wedges between the nails and runner.	3-by-¾-inch tapered wedges hammer
6. Use the wedges to adjust the pressure on the joint until glue oozes out. Wipe off.	rag dipped in water
7. Let dry undisturbed for 24 hours.	

TIP: If you feel additional support will be needed to hold the two pieces together, after the glue has dried and the chair has been removed from the nailing board, drill holes from the bottom of the runner up through the joint. Do not drill through the top of the runner. In each hole you can either tap in a dowel coated with glue or you can screw in a no. 10 flat-head screw. In either case, make sure the end is either flush with or slightly below the surface of the wood. Otherwise, it will snag on carpeting or scratch hardwood floors.

The Temporary Nail

Once in a great while it becomes necessary to create a small problem in order to solve a larger one. Such is the case when you are attempting to clamp together two boards that insist on sliding apart.

Steps	*Materials*
1. Have someone hold the two pieces of runner in their original position without using any glue.	extra pair of hands
2. From the bottom of the runner, drill a small hole through the lower piece, the joint, and into, *but not through*, the upper piece.	drill small bit or finish nail

Steps	*Materials*
3. Insert glue into the joint.	woodworker's glue syringe or toothpick
4. Pull the two broken pieces back together.	extra pair of hands
5. Tap a finish nail into the hole, letting the head protrude slightly.	finish nail hammer
6. Position the clamps and tighten.	clamps and pads
7. Wipe off any excess glue.	rag dipped in water
8. Let dry undisturbed for 24 hours.	
9. Remove the clamps, then carefully withdraw the finish nail.	pliers
10. Patch the hole.	wood dough or wood putty

TIP: This method can be adapted to solve a number of clamping problems, but only if the resulting hole is not going to be obvious. On larger pieces requiring additional strength, a quarter-inch or three-eighths-inch dowel can be used both to prevent the two pieces from sliding apart while being clamped and to provide greater permanent strength under stress.

Screws, Loose ▶ Although more than one refinisher has been accused of having a screw loose, if the truth were to be known, everyone probably has a few rattling around upstairs. Drop-leaf tables, fall-front desks, bookcase doors, and china cupboards are all likely to have hinges, pulls, and hardware hanging by a mere thread—that of a tiny screw bobbing around in its hold.

Special Problems

Those who scoff at the idea of loose screws being a real problem for refinishers have never experienced what one professional refinisher confessed to having done: he turned a square oak table over on his workbench to replace the loose screws holding the table together with longer ones. Twelve screws later he and his helper tried to lift the table—and found it firmly screwed to the workbench.

Moral of the story: It's safer to fix rather than replace a loose screw.

The particular procedure you select depends on two factors: the looseness of the screw and the amount of stress the screw must withstand. A simple matchstick wedged in the hole may work for low-stress screws, but a drop-front desk requires screws that won't pull out under the weight of one notebook, two history books, four volumes of the *Encyclopedia Brittanica*, and two teenage elbows.

Low-Stress Screws

Steps	*Materials*
1. Remove the loose screw.	screwdriver

2. Dip any of the following in glue, then insert in hole:
    matchstick
    toothpick
    softwood sliver
	hobby knife
	woodworker's glue

3. Replace screw snugly, but do not overtighten.	screwdriver
4. Let glue harden before subjecting to stress.	

> TIP: Although it has been recommended often, wood dough is not an acceptable means of repairing a loose screw. When subjected to stress, it often crumbles.

High-Stress Screws

Steps	*Materials*
1. Remove the loose screw.	screwdriver
2. Enlarge hole to next standard dowel size.	drill and bit

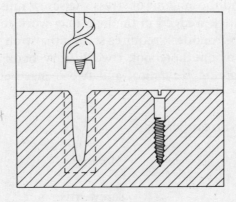

Steps	*Materials*
3. Cut, glue, and tap dowel into enlarged hole, flush with surface.	dowel saw hammer
4. Let dry six hours.	
5. Drill pilot hole for screw in end of dowel.	drill and bit

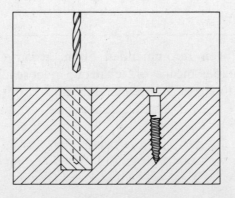

Steps	*Materials*
6. Install original screw.	screwdriver

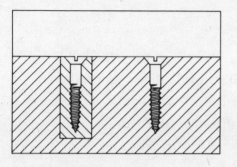

> TIP: It may be necessary to tap a small dowel into the original screw hole before enlarging it with your drill bit. If your three-quarter-inch drill bit has a point that requires more than just air space to guide it down the center of its intended path, tap a small piece of wood into the hole, then drill it back out. Sounds crazy, but it works.

Stubborn screws have left their share of scars on both furniture and frustrated refinishers. In some instances rust will have bonded the threads to the wood fibers. In others the green wood will have dried, shrunk, and tightened its grip on the steel threads. Whatever the reason, stubborn screws pose a problem that, if not attacked properly, can lead to serious injury—when the screwdriver slips and plows a three-inch gouge across the top of your table— or the back of your hand.

◄ **Screws, Removing**

Special Problems

Proper and safe removal of a screw begins with a perfectly clean slot. Use a small screwdriver to remove any old paint, varnish, wax, or dirt. If you encounter a raised screw whose slot has been ruined by earlier attempts to loosen it, you can deepen the slot with either a hacksaw or just a hacksaw blade with electrical tape wrapped around one end to fashion a handle.

If one side of the slot is broken off, use a hammer and a punch to carefully rotate the screw with a series of taps at one end of the former slot. When it rises above the surface of the wood, grasp the broken head with a pair of pliers or vise grips and continue rotating.

Steps	*Materials*
1. Clean out the slot.	small screwdriver
2. Select a screwdriver with a blade that completely fills the slot.	screwdriver
3. Alternate attempts to turn the screw both clockwise and counterclockwise to break it loose. —or—	
4. Strike the end of the screwdriver to jar the threads loose. —or—	hammer
5. Heat the head of the screw; let cool. (Unequal expansion and contraction of metal vs. wood should break bond.)	soldering iron

TIP: Select one screwdriver in your collection that has a sturdy grip to be your "designated screwdriver." This will be the screwdriver whose tip you can file or grind to fit any slot of any size. A snug fit will reduce the likelihood of the blade slipping out of the slot or enlarging the slot to such an extent that no screwdriver will fit properly.

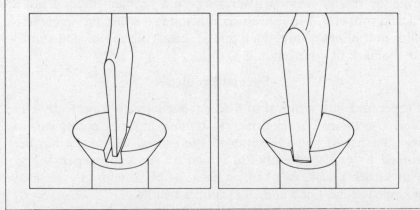

It is not uncommon for a joint in a dresser top, the side of a **◄ Splits**
bookcase, or a table leaf to begin to separate after several years
exposure to changes in heat and humidity. A small degree of
shrinkage in an antique is no cause for worry. Only when the
separation continues down the joint or when the two boards begin
to move independently of one another is your attention required.
If you discover a new separation, mark the distance of the opening
on the underside of the table with a piece of chalk, then check it
weekly to see if it is growing.

Special Problems

Complete splits are often easier to repair than partials, but I prefer
not to break two boards apart just to make my task a little easier.
If the joint is still too tight to slip a thin spatula or a syringe needle
into, then I would question whether or not it needs to be repaired.
A small screwdriver can be inserted in the split from the underside
of the table to wedge the two boards apart slightly. However,
don't take the easy way out and shove your screwdriver between
the ends of the boards. The depression it leaves will be obvious
to anyone who looks at the edges of your table.

Steps	*Materials*
1. Clean out split.	hobby knife or dental floss
2. Clamp the two boards together without glue.	clamp and pads
3. If a gap remains, trim a length of veneer to fill it.	veneer scrap

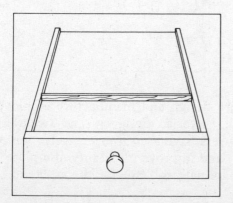

Steps	*Materials*
4. Coat the veneer with glue.	woodworker's glue
5. Coat both sides of the separation with a thin layer of glue.	spatula or syringe
6. Clamp, remove excess glue, and let dry 24 hours.	pipe clamp and pads rag dipped in water
7. Remove clamp, trim and sand veneer.	hobby knife no. 220 sandpaper

TIP: Long splits—three feet or longer—should be repaired using pipe clamps positioned no more than eight inches apart. Alternate placing the clamps above and below the tabletop to prevent the top from curling under the pressure (see illustration).

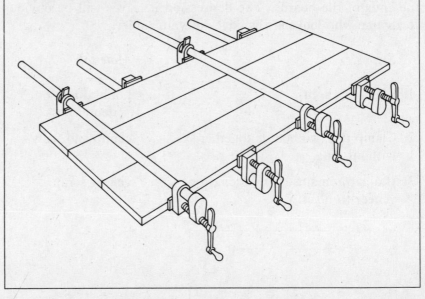

Veneer ▶ Nearly every era of furniture design and manufacture employed veneer in some form. Both Victorian designers and twentieth-century furniture manufacturers have used it extensively. Veneer can cut cost, reduce weight, and improve the beauty of a piece of furniture, but it also poses special problems for the weekend refinisher.

Special Problems

Most older veneer you encounter is held in place with hide glue, for centuries the most popular adhesive among cabinetmakers. But this type of glue is vulnerable to both heat and water. Several days of direct sunlight or water can gradually weaken the old glue and loosen the veneer, but many times it can be reattached by heating it with a household iron pressed over a thin, moist towel. Be careful not to damage either the finish or the wood by applying too much heat too quickly.

Reheating Loose Veneer

(not to be used on veneer with a shellac finish)

Steps	Materials
1. Clean out loose area.	long, dull knife
2. Lay a damp cloth over the loose area.	wet towel
3. Warm the area using an iron set at low heat. Press down firmly.	household iron

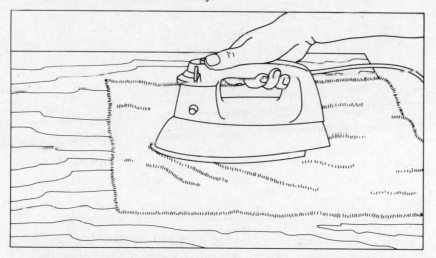

4. Check the finish often to avoid scorching.

5. When the glue beneath the veneer becomes tacky, remove the iron and press down firmly as it cools and rehardens.

Regluing Loose Veneer

Steps	*Materials*
1. Clean out loose area.	long, dull knife
2. Insert glue between veneer and framework.	woodworker's glue syringe and/or dinner knife
3. Spread glue by pressing on veneer with fingertips.	
4. Wipe off excess.	rag dipped in water
5. Cover with wax paper and board slightly larger than loosened area.	wax paper scrap wood
6. Apply pressure.	C-clamps or weights

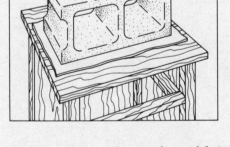

7. Remove excess glue again and let dry 24 hours.	rag dipped in water

TIP NO. 1: Granules of hide glue can be dissolved and/or removed by inserting a heated knife blade under the loose veneer.

TIP NO. 2: Keep a roll of wax paper near where you do any regluing, for if you place a piece between the wood and your clamp pad, it will prevent the two from sticking together.

Heat, moisture, shrinkage, and age can all cause bubbles in old veneer. When air gets between the veneer and the wood beneath it, it can continue to dissolve the old glue. Even when you cannot see or feel the slight rise in the surface of the veneer, you can hear the hollow sound of trapped air when you tap it with your fingertip. Small bubbles can sometimes be reglued using a warm iron (see preceding section), but more often than not fresh glue and pressure are required.

Special Problems

Veneer bubbles have an uncanny knack for appearing just out of reach of the jaws of your clamps. Before jumping into a bubble-popping project, decide exactly how you are going to apply pressure to the bubble after it is back in place. It may be a stack of weights, a long clamping board balanced like a teeter-totter over a smaller board and then clamped (see illustration), or a long two-by-four wedged between a ceiling rafter and the bubble. Regardless of what you devise, have it ready before you reach for the glue.

Steps   *Materials*

1. Press down on bubble with thumb to insure that it will lie flat.

2. If it will not, use a hobby knife to carefully slice the bubble along the path of the grain.   hobby knife

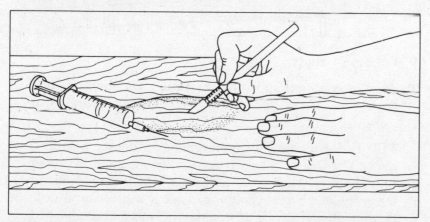

3. Inject the glue into the bubble.   woodworker's glue syringe

Steps	*Materials*
4. Spread glue by pressing on center of bubble with thumb.	
5. Press bubble or two halves of bubble flat (may be necessary to overlap halves).	
6. Wipe off excess glue.	rag dipped in water
7. Cover the bubble with wax paper and a softwood scrap.	wax paper scrap wood
8. Apply pressure.	clamps or weights

9. Let dry 24 hours.	
10. Trim or sand overlapped halves until flush.	hobby knife or no. 220 sandpaper

TIP: It doesn't take as much glue as it does pressure to reglue a veneer bubble. Go easy on the glue and heavy on the clamping. Make sure all excess glue is forced out of the entry hole before clamping, since it will be impossible to wipe off the excess glue after the wax paper and pad have been laid in place.

If veneered furniture has a place at which damage is most likely to occur, it is along the edges. This is where the glue is most vulnerable to water and where the veneer itself is most apt to be snagged on a sleeve, a dust rag, or a carpet thread. When the veneer chip is saved, it is simply a matter of gluing it back in place (see Chapter 2), but when the chip is swallowed by the vacuum cleaner, then the real work begins.

◄ **Veneer Chips**

Special Problems

The toughest—and most important—hurdle to overcome in patching a veneer chip is to find a piece of veneer (1) of the same type of wood, (2) of the same grain pattern, and hopefully, (3) of the same approximate age.

The best source may be the piece itself. Veteran restorers have been known to rob Peter to pay Paul, taking a patch of veneer from an inconspicuous part of the back, side, or bottom of the piece and transferring it to the crucial chip. Then they use a piece of new veneer to patch the donor spot. It may sound time-consuming and somewhat barbaric to do this, especially if it is an antique, but the logic is that a near perfect patch on the top is more important than a standard patch along the bottom; this has thus become a standard practice among professional refinishers and collectors.

Steps	*Materials*
1. Trim jagged edges of chipped area.	hobby knife ruler
2. Trim cardboard patch to fit missing section snugly.	thin cardboard
3. Trace cardboard patch on new veneer.	pencil
4. Cut and trim veneer patch to fill missing section.	hobby knife
5. Glue and clamp in place.	woodworker's glue wax paper softwood pad clamp
6. Remove excess glue and let dry 24 hours.	rag dipped in water

Steps	Materials
7. Sand, stain, and finish to match.	no. 240 sandpaper stain finish artist brush

TIP NO. 1: Save veneer chips as soon as they come off in sealed envelopes with the name of the piece of furniture from which they came clearly written across the outside. It is much easier to reglue the original than to replace a lost chip.

TIP NO. 2: Many of the annoying problems associated with patching veneer chips can be solved simply by starting each project with a new hobby knife blade. The handle style similiar to a surgeon's scalpel offers the best control; the long, tapered blades are ideal for removing damaged veneer and cutting new patches.

TIP NO. 3: Brittle veneer can be made easier to cut without splitting if it is dampened slightly. Wet the veneer, wipe off the excess water, then let it begin to dry. Before it completely dries, hold the veneer firmly in place between a metal ruler and a flat board, then make several light passes with a new knife blade. The veneer is less apt to split under several light passes than it is under one heavy pass.

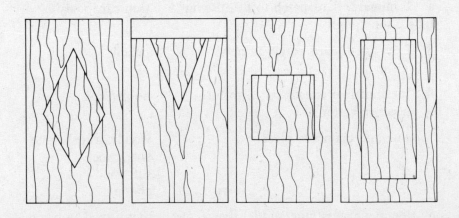

In some instances, particularly drawer fronts, table skirts, and raised decorative panels, an entire section of damaged veneer may have to be replaced with a sheet of new or antique veneer. If a portion of the ruined veneer remains intact, you can remove it in a variety of ways, from soaking it (using either wet sawdust or a wet towel), to a heat gun, or with a combination of water and direct sunlight. Regardless of which method you use, check the piece often to make sure no damage is being done to the wood underneath the old veneer.

◀ **Veneer Replacement**

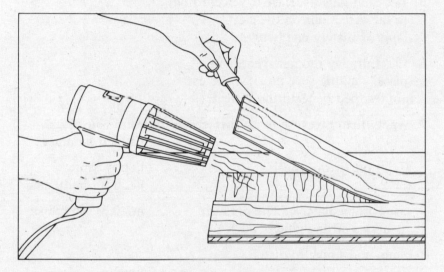

Special Problems

The problem of matching new veneer to old is one that still lacks a satisfying solution. Whenever possible, try to find old veneer from pieces of furniture that are considered worthless for reasons other than veneer problems. Turn-of-the-century and newer dressers, vanities, and library tables are excellent sources of large pieces of old veneer which you can carefully remove and use on the piece you are restoring.

Non-clamping Technique

Steps

Materials

1. Remove the ruined veneer from the area to be reveneered.

   wet towels or heat gun
   putty knife

Steps	*Materials*
2. Cut the new veneer to fit, leaving a one-inch overhang on all edges.	hobby knife straightedge
3. Sand the surfaces to be glued.	no. 120 sandpaper.
4. Apply contact cement to both surfaces.	contact cement inexpensive brush
5. Let each glued surface dry according to the directions on the can (approximately one hour).	
6. Carefully lay the new veneer in place, making sure no air bubbles are trapped beneath the veneer.	
7. Apply firm pressure to all surfaces.	softwood block padded hammer
8. Trim off extra veneer.	hobby knife no. 120 sandpaper
9. Sand immediately. (The pressure assures a strong glue bond.)	no. 220 sandpaper
10. Stain and finish to match.	stain finish

TIP: When using contact cement to attach large sheets of veneer or pieces of veneer that are difficult to clamp, keep a piece of wax paper between the two glued surfaces while you are positioning the new veneer. When the veneer is in position, slowly slide the wax paper out from between it and the wood, pressing out veneer bubbles as you proceed.

Clamping Technique

Steps	*Materials*
1. Remove the ruined veneer from the area to be reveneered.	wet towels or heat gun putty knife

Steps	*Materials*
2. Cut the new veneer to fit, leaving a one-inch overhang on all edges.	straightedge hobby knife
3. Sand the surfaces to be glued.	no. 120 sandpaper.
4. Apply a thin layer of glue to each surface.	woodworker's glue inexpensive brush
5. Immediately position the veneer, pressing out air bubbles.	softwood block
6. Cover the veneer with wax paper and clamping board slightly larger than veneer.	wax paper scrap wood

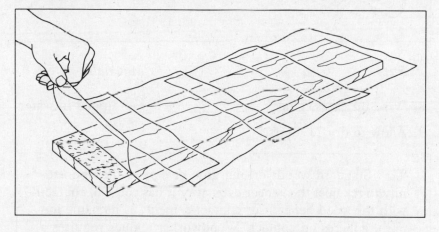

7. Apply pressure.	clamps or weights

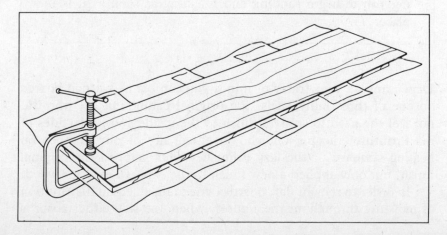

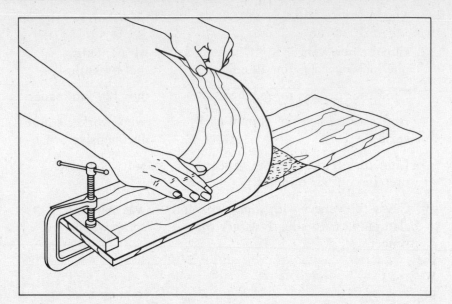

Steps	*Materials*
8. Wipe off excess glue.	rag dipped in water
9. Allow to dry 24 hours.	

TIP: Standard woodworking glue gives you the opportunity to readjust the veneer even after it has come in contact with the wood beneath it; contact cement, as its name implies, adheres on contact. Woodworker's glues requires a drying and bonding time; contact cement does not, allowing you to begin sanding and finishing as soon as it is in place.

Warped Boards ▶ Depending on your frame of mind, you can blame warped boards on one of three individuals: the original cabinetmaker, who did not feel the need to apply a finish to the inside and undersides of his furniture; the person who invented any of our dry central heating systems; or the lazy refinisher who stripped the original finish, but only applied a new finish to the exposed exterior wood.

In order to remain flat, boards depend on an equal distribution of moisture throughout their pores; when one side either absorbs or loses moisture faster than the other (as is the case in a board with a finish on one side only), the board is apt to either split or warp.

Special Problems

To correct a warped board, the old woodworker would simply take the board, cut it into three lengths, plane each edge, and reglue them. The resulting board was definitely flat, but it was also three-eighths inch narrower than it was originally. Perhaps this didn't pose a serious problem to the woodworker, who could always add a three-eighths-inch strip of wood to one edge, but to the weekend refinisher who values wide boards and doesn't want to buy a table saw and jointer, this method doesn't quite work.

The woodworker's compromise—scoring a series of closely placed, shallow saw cuts the length of the concave side of the warped board—often enabled him to force the board back into its original form, but not without its share of failures, a serious weakening of the board, and an obvious desecration of the furniture. Like its predecessor, this treatment bears mentioning only as a solution more damaging than its problem.

If you are like me, you would like to be able to correct warped boards without also having to refinish them. Some shallow warps will respond to the treatment prescribed below without disturbing the original finish, and you might try it before stripping the piece. The bottom line on a severe warp, however, is this: You may have to choose between living with a warp or living with the existing finish.

Remember: the key to correcting a warp is to equalize the moisture content by removing moisture from the raised (convex) side and adding it to the concave side. Then you have to keep it that way.

Steps	*Materials*
1. Remove the warped board from furniture; also remove any hardware from the board.	screwdriver
2. Place the warped board on a wet towel on a concrete floor with the humped side up. (Option: lay it on wet grass on a sunny day.)	wet towel

Steps	*Materials*
3. Pad the raised side, then stack enough weight on it to apply pressure, but not enough to cause the board to split under weight.	dry towel concrete blocks
4. To speed the process, direct heat to the raised side.	heat lamps or sunshine

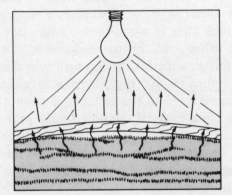

5. When combination of moisture, heat, and weights flattens the board, remove wet towel and heat; lay the board on a flat, dry surface, but maintain pressure from blocks.	
6. When board has dried, remove weights and immediately sand, stain, and finish both sides.	nos. 120 and 220 sandpaper stain finish
7. Reassemble.	screwdriver

TIP: The equalization process may take two or three days, during which time the warp should be checked often. Do not be alarmed if the warp reverses itself; simply remove the wet towel from beneath the board and place it on top of the board and beneath the weights until the board straightens itself.

Although, technically speaking, there is a difference between wood rot and dry rot—the first having been caused by water, the other by fungi or insects—the process for the weekend refinisher is still the same: First, you must remove the cause of the problem, and second, you must preserve and strengthen the weakened wood.

◀ **Wood Rot**

Special Problems

Before the problem can be treated, it must first be stopped. In the case of dry rot, the fungi or insects must be destroyed with an insecticide. In the case of wood rot, the moisture must be removed. Presuming the antique, often an icebox, tavern table, or any piece stored for a long period of time in a wet basement or on a dirt floor, is no longer in direct contact with water, you must thoroughly dry the affected area. If the humidity in the air remains high, a hair dryer can speed the process. Whenever possible, preserve rather than remove all of the original wood. If, as in the case of an icebox, the damaged portion must also support a great deal of weight, attach wooden braces to the inside of the weakened members to reduce the weight each must carry.

Steps	*Materials*
1. Dry out the affected area.	
2. Remove any dirt and loose particles.	bristle brush
3. Inject the weakened area with a hardening solution.	syringe carpenter's glue and water (50/50) or commercial product (Stop-Rot) from marine supply company
4. Let harden.	
5. Patch, rebuild, or strengthen damaged area.	wood dough and/or wood
6. Sand, stain, and finish to match.	sandpaper stain finish

TIP NO. 1: Weakened feet can also be strengthened by the addition of three-eighths-inch wooden dowels glued into holes drilled through the rotted area and up into unaffected wood. They can transfer the weight from the contact point with the floor up to a portion of the wood that has not been affected by the wood rot.

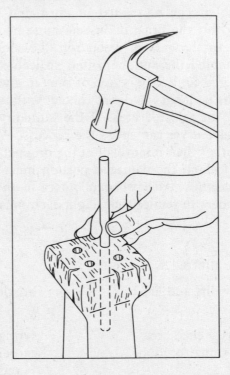

TIP NO. 2: Nylon glides attached to the bottoms of heavy case pieces will help reduce the friction and resulting stress on weakened and repaired feet whenever the piece is being moved.

CHAPTER 5
Removing Old Finishes

I stripped my first piece of furniture when I was sixteen and my most recent one last Tuesday. In between I can't imagine how many pressed-back chairs, oak ice boxes, and mahogany dining room tables I have stripped—all by hand—but from it all I have drawn one very definite conclusion.

Stripping has gotten a bum rap.

After experimenting with dozens of brands of paint and varnish removers and as many different techniques for removing the softened finish, I have decided that the most critical decision you have to make to insure a successful strip is deciding what NOT to strip.

Five years after I had stripped my first piece of furniture—a small walnut bookcase—I had the opportunity to buy a Hoosier-style kitchen cupboard at an estate sale in my home town of New Windsor, Illinois. I paid dearly for it, thirty-six dollars, but the two-piece cupboard featured a roll-top compartment and several doors above a porcelain counter. Below there were three drawers and a large storage area for pots and pans. The cupboard had been painted white some time after it had been purchased, probably when the previous owners had painted their kitchen. I tackled the stripping with more enthusiasm than experience.

The first layer crumbled under my paint and varnish remover, but instead of the gleaming quartersawn oak I had hoped for, I discovered another layer of paint. Disheartened but not discouraged, I brushed on another coat of remover, but the paint clung to the wood like a cat to a tree limb. I can recall actually chiseling off more paint than the stripper dissolved. Hours later I thought I had it all off and called a friend over to see it. He looked it over carefully and then spoke.

"See you got yourself one of those Friday cupboards."

"What do you mean?"

"On Friday morning they would gather up all the leftover wood and use it in the cupboards they made that day. Oak, walnut, cherry, maple—it all went in. Then, to disguise it, they painted them.

"Look," he pointed. "There's a piece of cherry, that door's

made of maple; you got some oak in the legs, but the sides are all birch. You got yourself a genuine Friday cupboard.''

Whether or not his theory was genuine—I never have been able to prove it—he was right about one thing. My cupboard was made of at least four different kinds of wood. And they all still had traces of paint lodged in their pores. Sanding didn't faze them and staining couldn't hide them, so I ended up with a refinished cupboard that should never have been stripped.

Since that time I have come across several ''Friday cupboards.'' Some I could've bought, but didn't. Others were brought to me by clients wanting to have them refinished. In every instance I convinced them that they would not be pleased with the final results. I told them that they still had two choices: they could either live with them as they were or repaint them.

Stripping is always an option, but it shouldn't be either your first or your last one. First you always want to see if the original finish can be cleaned and preserved. When it can't—say the original finish has turned black, someone has slopped on a coat of lime-green paint, or the old polyurethane varnish is now beginning to chip and peal—then stripping may be in order.

On the other hand, if, like my Friday cupboard, the piece was factory-painted or if—heaven forbid—someone stripped it and then painted it, taking off the old finish may require more time, energy, and money than you want to put in it—or than the piece is worth. If the piece has already been painted, adding another layer certainly is not going to decrease its value further. It may even increase it. A Hitchcock chair, a style that has been reproduced for over a century and is still available in new furniture stores, was always intended to be painted, even stenciled. If you find a set of four reproductions with pealing paint at a garage sale, it would be more appropriate for you to repaint them the original color than to strip and stain them to match your cherry table.

Another piece that should not be stripped is the Early American painted piece, but how late we were to realize it! For years painted tavern tables, corner cupboards, and bedsteads were numerous, especially in the New England area, where many of them originated. Not so long ago, it was still cheaper to strip, sand, and shellac one of these old pieces than buy a piece of new furniture, so antiques dealers, newlyweds, auctioneers, and scores of others hauled truckloads of painted pieces to dipping shops, where they were stripped and sanded until they were nearly white.

Today the few painted pieces that never made it into the dipping tanks are now bringing record-breaking prices, while their stripped and shellaced peers have been relegated to the "if only I had known" pile. An original and authentic eighteenth- or nineteenth-century paint—often made with milk, animal blood, plants, etc.—was put there for a reason. If you come across such a piece and you aren't taken with its worn appearance, whatever else you do, don't strip it. Chances are you can find someone who will appreciate it more than you just the way it is.

Between the pieces of furniture bearing an authentic home-made paint and those that were painted in the factories are hundreds that may warrant refinishing. When it is obvious that the existing finish, old or new, paint or varnish, will have to be stripped, then you have two choices: pay someone else to strip it, or strip it yourself.

If you are now expecting to hear a tirade of abuse heaped on professional stripping operations, brace yourself, for as a former professional refinisher, I stripped many pieces of furniture for people who wanted to do their own refinishing, but did not want to do their own stripping. I find that I often do not have the time or energy to undertake a stripping project. When I don't, I find a reliable stripper; if I didn't, I know the piece would simply get pushed to the back of the garage and buried behind some worn snow tires.

If stripping is what stands between you and your next project, then you need to make a choice: either take it to your favorite refinisher—or keep on reading. At the end of the chapter I'll give you some tips on selecting a reliable refinishing shop.

When I said earlier that I had drawn a conclusion from my years of refinishing furniture, I should have said that I've drawn two conclusions. The first involves deciding what not to strip. The second has to do with those pieces that you are going to strip. To wit:

◀ Do-It-Yourself Stripping

Just as important as knowing what not to strip is being prepared for stripping.

In other words, get it together—or you're going to get it all over.

To begin with, you need room. Paint and varnish remover can't distinguish between the paint on the bookcase you're stripping and the paint on your station wagon. And if you don't believe me, ask one of my former employees. I warned him, too, but he just didn't listen. Paint and varnish remover isn't like paint or varnish; it doesn't flow smoothly off the end of your brush. It springs off the ends of the bristles like a kid off a diving board. And unlike paint or varnish, it starts dissolving whatever it lands on—paint, leather, upholstery, carpeting, wallpaper, or plastic—the instant it lands. One errant flick of the wrist and your Saturday morning project could turn into a costly disaster.

Probably the safest place for the weekend refinisher to work is outdoors, preferably in a shaded area. Regardless of whether you are working on grass or concrete, I would still recommend spreading out a large plastic drop cloth and several layers of newspaper to catch the mess. Thick globs of dissolved paint and remover won't disappear in the tallest grass. They will remain to haunt you the next time you mow the lawn or walk barefoot across the yard. And if that isn't enough incentive, think about how terrified your toddler or cocker spaniel is going to be if either of them picks up a stinging gob of stripper and old varnish later in the day. When you're done, you can roll up your rags, brushes, steel wool, and mess in the plastic drop cloth and deposit it all in a tightly closed metal trash can located away from any buildings. Last week's paper had another story about a garage that burnt down when refinishing rags thrown in an open garbage can next to the building ignited and started the wall on fire.

The weather being what it is, you can't always work outdoors, so you need to think about what precautions you should take when stripping in the basement, garage, or on your kitchen floor. The first step is obvious: you need to protect everything. Floors, appliances, counters, and cabinets need to be draped with plastic sheets, old blankets, or newspapers. Bicycles, cars, and charcoal grills need to be wheeled outdoors. In short, anything within twelve feet should be covered.

Second, you need to make sure that the fumes from your paint and varnish remover won't have a chance to accumulate. Methylene chloride, the active ingredient in most paint and varnish removers, is the subject of much debate today. Ten years ago we presumed it was safe to use, but recent research has raised some serious questions about its safety. If I were stripping furniture daily, I would be more than a little concerned, but the thirty or so minutes it's going to take to strip a chair or table isn't going to place you in any serious danger. Until the final determination has been made on methylene chloride, though, it would be wise to use some common sense. Open the doors and windows and set up a pair of fans to remove the fumes and bring in fresh air. Wear a pair of heavy-duty neoprene gloves, a long-sleeve shirt, long pants, a work apron, and safety glasses. If you have any history of asthma or other breathing problems, be sure to wear a charcoal filter respirator.

Each year since the do-it-yourself craze got started in the sixties, manufacturers have introduced a number of different types of paint and varnish removers. A few have even packaged paint and varnish remover in an aerosol can; even though it is more convenient than the brush method of application, it certainly isn't cost-effective. The E-Z Way company recently came out with a pump spray called "Wood Prep," which claims to contain no methylene chloride. I must admit that I was doubtful at first, but it does work. The only problem I had was that the active ingredient, methanol tuluol, evaporates in seconds. Not only do you have to work on small sections, you have to work fast—but then, maybe that's not such a bad idea anyway.

Among the many different types of paint and varnish remover that you will find on the shelves are the following:

Semi-Paste Paint and Varnish Remover—This has been the most popular type of stripper for several years. The addition of wax to the methylene chloride slows both the evaporation rate of the remover and its tendency to run down the side of your furniture. While this wax must be rinsed off competely with mineral spirits, denatured alcohol, or lacquer thinner, the additional working time it provides for the methylene chloride cuts down on the amount of stripper required for most projects.

As the directions will generally indicate, turpentine or water can be used as a rinse once the old paint or varnish has been softened, but many firms also recommend the addition of detergent (Spic and Span, Borax, or a similar type containing trisodium phosphate) to warm water to help cut through the wax and sludge.

Liquid Paint and Varnish Remover—Whether it was intentional or not, this thin, runny stripper is best suited for clear finishes that do not require a strong, slow-acting solvent. It has the advantage of having little wax added to retard evaporation; thus, it both starts working and stops working quickly. It works best on horizontal surfaces, since it runs easily.

Like most strippers, it can be rinsed with water, but turpentine, denatured alcohol, or lacquer thinner will leave the wood cleaner and will require less sandpaper later.

Water-Wash Paint and Varnish Remover—It is impossible to determine from the list of ingredients on the backs of cans of paint and varnish remover whether water-wash stripper is any different from standard semi-paste stripper, but the directions state that water can be used to rinse off the sludge. They also warn that "water may loosen veneers and glued joints" and generally recommend the addition of trisodium phosphate to help dissolve any wax deposited by the remover. Personally, I have a problem with water-washes, but you'll hear enough about that a little later.

No-Rinse Paint and Varnish Remover—These bother me. If you have ever stepped out of the water without rinsing all of the shampoo out of your hair, you know what your wood feels like if you used a no-rinse paint and varnish remover. Sure, you saved a few minutes in time, but how did your head feel later when you start hearing those funny little noises and then you started itching? I never found rinsing to be so much of a chore that I was willing to risk leaving stripper in the wood to cause problems with my finish.

Solvent Refinishers—Several years ago an executive with a firm that manufactures refinishing products came up with a brilliant idea. "Why don't we invent a special name for the common solvents, like lacquer thinner and denatured alcohol," he suggested, "then package and sell them as alternatives to paint and varnish remover?" His idea worked, and while manufacturers will swear that their particular brand of "refinisher" is more than just denatured alcohol and lacquer thinner, the end results are just about the same.

If you don't believe me, run your own test. In one jar mix a solution of 50 percent denatured alcohol and 50 percent lacquer thinner. In another jar pour the same amount of a popular "refinisher." Use them both on the same board with the same old lacquer or shellac finish and decide for yourself if there is a difference.

I must admit, in one respect, there is.

Most "refinishers" cost twice as much.

Regardless of whether you buy it premixed or make your own, solvent refinishing is easier, less messy, and can be less expensive than using standard paint and varnish remover. It does not require a rinse, since the old finish is completely dissolved rather than merely softened. The only drawback is its limited effectiveness: it only works on shellac and lacquer finishes. Modern varnish, polyurethanes, paint, and oil finishes are unaffected by the solvents.

If the can states that it removes modern varnishes and paints, then it contains methylene chloride (or a similar substitute) and is actually a liquid paint and varnish remover rather than what we consider a "refinisher."

◄ **What About Uncle George's Secret Weapon?**

I'm almost afraid to even bring the subject up, since I might end up tempting you with a stripper you didn't even know about. But if I don't you might stumble across something Uncle George wrote years ago about stripping painted furniture with lye.

Back in the days when lye was a household staple and life spans were much shorter than they are now, someone discovered that lye dissolves paint. No doubt it happened one hot afternoon when they were making soap and splattered some lye on the side of the old shed. Regardless, the undeniable truth is that lye does dissolve paint, just as it will burn flesh and cause permanent blindness. It is fast and inexpensive, but the risk it poses to your furniture, your family, your pets—not to mention yourself—makes any advantage pale in comparison.

No doubt you've heard the saying "I wouldn't touch it with a ten-foot pole." My theory is that it came from using lye, for the traditional way of applying a lye-and-water solution to furniture was with a long pole with a rag wired to one end. You couldn't tie it on because the lye would eat through the twine. How's that for strong?

Even if you were to somehow protect yourself from the lye, your furniture would suffer just as much as you. In addition to burning off the paint, lye also burns out the life of the wood, raises the grain, removes the color from some woods, darkens others, such as oak, walnut, chestnut, and ash, and simply ruins cherry and mahogany. To make matters worse, once in the wood, lye doesn't stop burning until you douse it with vinegar.

Now, does that sound like your idea of a good time?

◄ **Rinses**

Paint and varnish removers don't actually remove any paint or varnish; they merely soften it. You and I end up doing the actual removing. It didn't take the first refinisher long to figure out that removing the sludge is easier if you can flush the surface with some sort of liquid; thus, the "rinse" was invented.

To be completely honest with you, any liquid can be used as a rinse: water, turpentine, lacquer thinner, denatured alcohol, beer, tonic water, soda, or champagne—though I wouldn't be quick to recommend these last four. They are more effective afterward. The point I am trying to make is that any liquid will help you remove the sludge created by the paint and varnish remover. The question is: Which liquid is the best?

Every rinse, like every type of paint and varnish remover, has its advantages and disadvantages. Rather than select and swear by only one, you need to know which is the best choice for your particular situation, whether that be determined by your budget, the type of finish on the piece you are stripping, or where you are working.

Here, then, are the four most popular rinses:

Water—Let's face it. Water is cheap and readily available. It can also be pressurized, if you have a garden hose. Those three reasons, plus the fact that it can be heated and will accept the help of a detergent, make it an undeniably popular rinse.

So what's the problem?

Water and wood don't get along very well. Water swells the pores of the wood, so you have to do some extra sanding. Water also can cause thin softwoods to warp, split, and buckle, leaving you with some real repair problems.

It also doesn't get along well with wax. In fact, it doesn't do much of anything to wax, unless you heat it and add harsh detergents containing trisodium phosphate. And if you don't, water alone won't remove the wax deposited on the wood by the paint and varnish remover. And what that means is that you will either have to wash it off with turpentine or sand it off afterward—or risk having your finish not stick to it.

Another problem with water is that it will dissolve the old glues used in joints and under veneer. Given the opportunity, it will loosen entire sheets of veneer and in the process will generally warp or buckle the wood beneath it to the point where simply regluing the veneer is not enough. The effect it has on glue joints is deceiving, for while it will soften the old glue, it also swells the wood, giving you a false sense of security. Your chair feels tight and looks tight, so you proceed with the sanding, staining, and finishing. A few months later, though, as the wood begins to dry out, you will hear a slight creaking in your chair, then a noticeable looseness, and finally the rungs start slipping out of their holes. And then it's back to the workshop.

Finally, water takes a long time to dry. If the weather is humid, it may take three or four days before the wood is dry enough to sand properly. Setting it out in the sun speeds up the process, but not without subjecting the bare wood to the risk of buckling, splitting, or bleaching under the rays of the sun.

I could go on, but I'll spare you the sermon. Just remember, water is cheap, but your time—and your furniture—isn't.

Turpentine (mineral spirits, paint thinner)—Turpentine is often recommended by the manufacturers of paint and varnish remover as a rinse because it will dissolve the wax their product deposits on the wood. It is also relatively inexpensive, especially if purchased in quantity from a discount store. And when it comes to stripper rinses, money is one consideration. It's just not the only one.

Turpentine will evaporate faster than water, though not as fast as either lacquer thinner or denatured alcohol. It will not dissolve old glue, nor does it swell wood as much as water does. What it also will not do is dissolve either shellac or lacquer finishes, which means that it will help flush off that finish which has been softened, but it will not dissolve any parts of the finish that you or your paint and varnish remover missed. In other words, if you didn't get it, the turpentine isn't going to cover for you.

Denatured Alcohol and Lacquer Thinner—As the solvents for shellac and lacquer, denatured alcohol and lacquer thinner make excellent rinses for most old finishes. Unlike turpentine or water, they will dissolve any of the finish that the paint and varnish remover may have missed. Denatured alcohol and lacquer thinner, though, are not as cheap as water. They cost about the same as turpentine and, like turpentine, can be captured, strained, and reused, helping to make your investment last longer.

The other advantage to using denatured alcohol or lacquer thinner as a rinse is that they both evaporate quickly, far more quickly, in fact, than turpentine. To give you an idea what that can mean to you, I once received a call late on a Friday afternoon, just as we were beginning to close up the shop and make our way next door to Fitzpatrick's to rinse the sawdust out of our throats. One of our best customers was on the phone, reminding us that his daughter would be arriving at noon the next day to pick up the table he had dropped off the previous month for us to refinish.

For whatever reason, we had completely forgotten about his table. I wasn't about to tell him that, so Mike and I raced to the storage room, uncovered his table, and quickly began dismantling it. As soon as the legs were off, I started brushing on the stripper while Mike continued taking the table apart. As each piece came off, I brushed on the stripper; by the time Mike was finished, the legs were ready to be scrubbed and rinsed. We were using lacquer thinner as a rinse and no. 00 steel wool to scrub off the softened finish.

As each piece emerged from the stripping pan, I quickly wiped it clean with a rag dipped in lacquer thinner and set it outside where a fresh breeze was blowing. Within an hour the entire table had been stripped and was dry enough for us to begin sanding the legs. The steel wool and lacquer thinner had left them smooth and clean, so it didn't take long to prepare them for a stain. As soon as the legs were sanded I started staining them, and by six o'clock, two hours after the call, the entire table had been dismantled, stripped, sanded, and stained.

Mike and I then made our well-deserved way next door to Fitzpatrick's. Later he went home to dinner and I went back to spray on the first coat of lacquer. Two hours later I was back for the second coat. By last call at Fitz's, the table was finished; and so was I. The next morning Mike came in early to see that it was rubbed out, reassembled, and ready to be loaded. By noon the table was on its way to Chicago. As for me, I was still home in bed.

Saving ▶ Your Rinse

One way you can justify the added expense of using turpentine, denatured alcohol, or lacquer thinner as a rinse is by capturing, straining, and recycling it. Depending on how much rinse you use and how often you strip, you can buy a one-, three- or five-gallon can, either a metal gas can or an empty lacquer thinner container, from an automotive paint shop. Regardless of the size, it needs to have a lid or the rinse will eventually evaporate and fill your workshop with dangerous fumes.

Naturally, to capture any liquid you must have a container to catch it as it flows off the furniture. Professionals often have shallow sheet metal pans constructed for them, some as large as six by eight feet and slanted for ease in draining. At the other end of the scale, you can recapture some of your rinse simply by placing the legs of your table or chair in empty coffee cans or discarded cake pans. Having used both, the large one when I was stripping furniture every day and the coffee cans when I was working atop my parent's picnic table, I now have constructed a simple two-by-three-foot sheet of metal nailed onto a piece of three-quarter-inch plywood for support. I nailed and caulked two-inch boards around the outside of the plywood and metal sheet, forming a shallow pan. In one corner I drilled a three-quarter-inch hole, in which I keep a cork until I am ready to drain it.

When stripping small pieces, such as footstools, shelves, or drawers, I simply set my stripping pan on top of my workbench or across a pair of sawhorses. When stripping large tables, desks, or case pieces, I lay the pan on the floor and set either one or two legs of the piece of furniture in it at a time. When I am finished, I simply pull the cork and let the liquid run into an empty coffee can. I generally let it stand in the coffee can for a day to allow the heavier particles to settle to the bottom, then strain the liquid through a large funnel lined with cheesecloth, panty hose, or an old towel, and into my metal can. The used rinse is never perfectly clean, so I only use it for a first rinse on my next project. Afterward I follow with a final rinse using fresh lacquer thinner, turpentine, or denatured alcohol, recapturing both to use again next time.

If there is a place in your work area for tools with plastic, rubber, or painted handles, it's not the stripping pan. While you won't need a large number of expensive tools, you will want to select them carefully; if you don't, you may find the red paint on the handle of your stripping brush dripping down onto the top of your oak piano bench.

◄ Stripping Tools

Your basic solvents—methylene chloride, denatured alcohol, and lacquer thinner—can each turn a plastic screwdriver handle into sticky goo, a rubber hammer grip into black sludge, and a foam brush into a limp noodle. Solvents require wood and metal tools. If that means cutting the rubber grip off an extra hammer or stripping the paint off a putty knife handle first, then do it before your remover does it for you—in the middle of an important project.

Perhaps the most practical tool in your stripping process is the two- or three-pound coffee can. I have never found that you can have too many of these. They hold stripper, clean rinse, dirty rinse, clean steel wool, dirty steel wool, hardware, tools, and brushes.

What is absolutely unacceptable is any type of glass container. One of the first things you will discover is how slippery stripper is. If you are anything like me, you'll soon be dropping one of your coffee cans—but at least you won't break it. Shards of glass can hide in stripper, sludge, brush bristles, and the bottom of cans, waiting for you to reach in so that they can jump out and bite you. Don't give them the chance; use only metal containers around stripper.

Before I start, then, I stuff pads of coarse and medium steel wool into one clean can. The medium I use when I'm stripping old shellac, lacquer, or varnish; the coarse works best for scrubbing off softened paint. In another can I keep my tools: a couple of screwdrivers, a pair of pliers, a small hammer, and both a narrow and a wide putty knife. It never seems to fail that as soon as I have my hands full of stripper, I discover a tack, nail, or screw that has to be removed. The screwdrivers also work well for scraping the old finish out of moldings, carvings, and joints, but a sharpened dowel is less apt to leave a gouge if you slip. If you can't find a wide putty knife, go to the kitchen and dig out one of the metal spatulas you haven't been able to use since they started making Teflon pans. Safer yet is an inexpensive wooden spatula. In either case, the rounded corners, flexible blade, and long handle make both types ideal for scraping off softened finishes.

A third can holds nothing but brushes: stripper brushes, natural bristle scrub brushes, a couple of toothbrushes, and even a brass bristle brush. The last I use to get the paint out of deep pores (more on that a little later). The toothbrushes are great for carvings, but they do dissolve quickly and they do tend to splatter stripper and rinse around the room if you aren't careful. A good scrub brush is ideal for carved legs on old tables, but don't settle for anything less than one with a wooden handle. The pretty ones with the fancy handles soon become indistinguishable globs of green plastic. I don't buy new paint brushes just for putting on stripper; instead, I buy new brushes for putting on finishes and assign my used finish brushes to the stripper can.

Another coffee can holds my favorite pair of tough rubber gloves. Thin surgical gloves and dishwashing gloves won't hold up under strong chemicals and rough steel wool. Buy a pair of high-quality, flexible neoprene gloves; the further they go past your wrist, the more protection they offer.

Not far away I keep what may be the two most important tools: a shop apron and a pair of protective glasses. I have a home-sewn apron made from tough denim; it has large pockets for holding small tools, parts, an extra rag, and whatever else I can't find a place for. The glasses are a literal lifesaver. Inevitably I forget to put them on, and inevitably my brush flicks stripper or lacquer thinner in my face. Before it happens to you, slip on your glasses. If it's too late, know where the nearest clean rag is (your apron pocket is a good place for one) and an eyewash bottle. It doesn't have to be a two-hundred-dollar OSHA-approved spray system; a simple one-quart plastic squeeze bottle with a special eye cup attached to the top will flush out the chemical before it can do any damage.

Buy one before you need it; if you don't, you can be sure you will.

◄ Step-by-Step Stripping

To those of you who haven't yet stripped a piece of furniture, it isn't as bad as people make it sound. To those of you who have had bad memories of a stripping experience, let me assure you this: it will be better the next time.

Most of us tend to recall the worst jobs first—the ones that would have been much easier if only we had taken the time to plan and prepare.

Before deciding to strip any piece, then, I now make sure that:

1. The finish (a) is not original to the piece, or
              (b) cannot be restored or revived.
2. I have prepared the best possible place to strip it.
3. I have assembled all of the materials and tools I need.
4. I am in the mood to do it right.
5. I am not wearing shoes I value highly.

When I am convinced, then, that I am ready, that my work area is ready, and that my piece of furniture is ready, I begin. Nine times out of ten, things go pretty well. But did I tell you about the time . . . ?

Semi-paste and Liquid Remover

Steps	*Materials*
1. Dismantle the piece.	screwdrivers
2. Remove and label all hardware.	cans or sandwich bags masking tape marking pen
3. Protect any upholstery and glass.	newspapers heavy plastic
4. Reglue any loose veneer.	woodworker's glue clamps and pads
5. Make any necessary repairs.	(see Chapter 4)
6. Position the piece so that the surface to be stripped is horizontal.	
7. Brush on a thick layer of stripper.	old brush stripper
8. Let stand undisturbed for 10–20 minutes, then test finish for softness.	old putty knife or sliver of wood
9. When finish has softened through to the wood, carefully scrape off and discard the sludge.	wide putty knife or spatula coffee can
10. (optional) If some of the old finish remains on the wood, apply another coat of stripper WITHOUT rinsing off the first coat. Do not apply only in spots, but brush across entire section to insure even removal.	
11. When all of the old finish has been softened, scrub off the remaining finish.	medium steel wool rinse
12. Rinse clean.	rag dipped in rinse
13. Wipe dry.	clean rag

Even though you will be wearing protective gloves, it never seems to fail that your hands come in contact with the stripper and sludge somewhere along the line. To help make cleaning them easier afterward, start the stripping process by working a liberal amount of hand cleaner into your skin, taking care to cover your cuticles and between your fingers, where it seems the most difficult to wash off later. The hand cleaner will do for your hands what cold cream does for an actor's face: it prevents the sludge from getting into your pores. Afterward another washing with hand cleaner will leave your hands clean enough to eat with.

◀ Stripping Tips

Among the most obvious signs of an amateur refinishing job are dried runs of either stripper or rinse down the sides of drawers or underneath tabletops and chair arms. When rinsing off your stripper, remember to both rinse off and wipe dry any of the spots where your stripper or rinse may have run.

The insides of drawers seldom need to be stripped, so I generally protect them by (1) covering the hardware holes on the inside with masking tape and (2) laying an old towel inside the drawer to catch any spills and splashes.

When stripping small doors from cabinets and buffets, it is easier, neater, and faster to strip both sides simultaneously rather than to try to strip only the outside while protecting the inside.

When you need to prevent stripper or rinse from running down the side of a case piece or a drawer, build a thin fence around the horizontal surface using masking tape. Two or three laps around the outside top edge will create a barrier that neither your stripper or rinse will be able to penetrate easily.

If you are called away from your project while you are waiting for the stripper to finish loosening the old finish and return later to find that it has dried on the wood, don't panic. Rather than attempting to scrape or chisel it off, simply brush on another thick coat of paint and varnish remover. In a matter of minutes it will reactivate your first coat.

If your solvent test reveals that the finish on your piece is either shellac or lacquer and you are satisfied that it cannot be preserved, then you may want to avoid at least some of the mess of a standard paint and varnish remover by using a solvent refinisher. Technically, all removers contain solvents, but by using either generic lacquer thinner and denatured alcohol or a commercial brand of "refinisher," you avoid the wax residue that can cause problems

◀ Solvent Stripping

later. In return, you do have to deal with a high rate of evaporation, especially on a warm and windy day, but you also get to control how much of the old finish you will remove. If, after dissolving the top layer of finish, you decide that you don't need to go any further, you can simply stop, wipe off the solvent, and the remaining old finish will immediately begin to reharden.

Many refinishers, both weekend and professional, prefer this method, since it cuts down on the amount of sanding and staining required afterward. What it does not allow you to do, when compared to a standard paint and varnish remover, is make any drastic changes in the color of the wood. Solvent refinishing leaves a thin layer of finish in the wood, which then acts as an effective barrier against penetrating stains. If you only want to lighten your piece slightly, though, or tint it one shade darker, solvent refinishing is a viable alternative.

Steps	Materials
1. Dismantle the piece.	screwdrivers
2. Remove and label all hardware.	cans or sandwich bags masking tape marking pen
3. Protect any upholstery and glass.	newspapers heavy plastic
4. Reglue any loose veneer.	woodworker's glue clamps and pads
5. Make any necessary repairs.	(see Chapter 4)
6. Position the piece so that the surface to be stripped is horizontal.	
7. Dip a pad of steel wool into the solvent and, starting at one end, begin scrubbing with the grain.	no. 00 or 000 steel wool empty coffee can solvent
8. Clean your steel wool often in the solvent, keeping the surface wet at all times.	

Steps	Materials
9. Check the progress by wiping with a rag dipped in solvent.	rag
10. Rinse thoroughly.	rag solvent
11. Wipe dry.	clean rag

If the wood remains tacky after rinsing, it is an indication that there is finish remaining on the surface. If you were only intending to remove the top layer of finish, fine; but if you were wanting to take it down to the wood in preparation for sanding, then you would be better off stripping it again with the steel wool and solvent now than wasting money trying to sand it off later.

When the manufacturers of the heat guns originally intended to remove paint from the exterior of buildings began advertising them as an alternative to paint and varnish remover on furniture, I balked. I had seen what they could do in the hands of an inexperienced operator: singed wood, warped panels, blistered veneer. ''More dangerous than a blowtorch,'' I once told an audience, ''because you can't see a flame.'' I still recommend extreme caution when using them, but after experimenting with several of the latest models, I have come to the conclusion that for certain refinishers in certain situations, they can be effective.

◄ If You Can't Stand the Heat . . .

For instance, if you react to the fumes or the chemicals in paint and varnish remover, but want to do your own stripping, a heat gun might be a wise investment.

And if the furniture you want to strip is painted but does not have any veneer or thin panels, a heat gun may be useful.

And if your work space simply will not accommodate liquid paint and varnish remover, sludge, or rinse, a heat gun may be the answer.

But remember: they don't call them ''heat guns'' for nothing. With one model I tested it took less than forty-five seconds for it to turn a pad of no. 00 steel wool into a ball of flame. Veneer can begin to dry up and curl in just about the same amount of time. A blast of two-thousand degree air coming from the end of the barrel will turn a putty knife, not to mention the barrel itself, into a branding iron.

Now that I've convinced you not to buy one, let me point out their advantages. Not too many months ago I discovered a Gustav Stickley rocking chair on the front porch of a Kentucky cabin. After some backwoods haggling I took the rocker, which had been painted battleship gray, home to my workshop. Somewhere beneath all that gray paint lay what I hoped to be an original Arts and Crafts finish and a Stickley decal. Traditional paint and varnish remover would remove the paint, but it would also remove the original finish and the decal as well. Perhaps, I thought, this was the time to experiment with the "new and improved" heat guns.

I discovered that heat guns do two things to paint. First, they dry it out. Second, given a little more time, they turn it into something between a paste and sludge. I soon realized that by watching the texture of the paint carefully, I could pinpoint the exact moment when I could withdraw the heat and, with a swipe of my steel wool, simply brush the brittle paint off the wood. When I caught it at just the right moment with my steel wool or scraper, the paint flew off the wood in dime-sized pieces; but if I waited too long, the heat turned the paint into a semi-liquid and it would smear into the pores under the pressure of my steel wool or scraper. By timing it carefully and working only on small areas, I was not only able to lift off the paint, but I was also able to leave the original finish beneath it unharmed. Afterward, all the chair needed was a light sanding and a careful scraping around a few of the joints and the now-exposed label. And to top it all off, cleanup just required a broom and a dustpan.

Perhaps the most important thing to remember about heat guns, next to their danger, is that to be effective they require some practice and a keen sense of concentration. Knowing when to stop, when to pull the heat away from the wood, is more important than knowing how to remove the brittle paint.

A high-quality heat gun and attachments will cost between fifty and ninety dollars, a sizable sum to be paid in one installment, but at fifteen dollars a gallon, you would only have to save approximately five gallons of stripper to pay for it—and a high-quality gun should last several years. In addition, they do have other uses. A gun with a low heat setting can be used to hasten the drying of your stain or finish on a humid day; I have also used it to speed-dry a stain color test on a scrap of wood. I have also found it can dissolve the old glue under old veneer I wanted to take from a damaged section of wood, either to be used as a patch or to be replaced with new veneer.

In short, you don't have to have a heat gun to refinish furniture, but if you can't use paint and varnish remover, it is an alternative.

Risky shortcuts.

◄ **What Shouldn't I Use?**

Such as any attachment on the end of an electric drill, including wire brushes, flapsander, or disk sanders; blowtorches, belt sanders, metal scrapers, shards of glass, or sandblasters.

Sandblasters?

I once received a letter from a bricklayer who loved to strip furniture on weekends using a sandblaster. He even sent me a photograph of his backyard setup: three six-foot-high plastic walls and a plastic floor with a peppered turntable sitting in the middle of it. He was quite proud of the fact that he could retrieve and reuse nearly eighty percent of his sand. I only wish that the percentage of his furniture that could be retrieved and reused could also have been that high.

Most of the risky means of removing old finishes also remove valuable wood or, as in the case of the open-flame torch, subject it to extreme risk. Some, such as belt sanders and any abrasive that runs in a circle, are going to leave cross-grain scratches in the wood. Old-timers used to swear by pieces of glass and metal they used to scrape off the old finish, but they also took a layer of wood and all of the great patina with them. Fortunately for collectors today, most of these old refinishers spent so much time stitching themselves up that they never got the chance to ruin too much furniture.

If you remember that your furniture, both old and new, will look better and will be worth more if you can remove the finish without removing any wood, then you should be able to determine which methods of removing old finishes are safe and practical and which are only going to endanger you and your furniture.

◄ **Paint in the Pores**

I receive so many questions from people wanting to know how to get paint out of the pores of the wood that I once held a contest for the best solution to this age-old problem. Along with the photograph from our sandblaster in Indiana I received numerous other suggestions, some of which made me laugh, a few of which made me nervous (like the one from the lady who recommends spray-on oven cleaner—but don't even consider it), and a few that made sense. Whether or not they will work in every situation, I have to wonder, but if we can win just a few battles with paint every now and then, I'll be happy.

First, I think 50 percent of the paint-in-the-pores problems could be solved if you simply let the stripper do its job. Too often refinishers stand over their freshly brushed stripper like an April gardener waiting for his freshly planted seeds to pop through the soil. As soon as we see those bubbles start to climb to the surface we begin poking at it, playing with it, testing it, teasing it, everything but simply walking away from it. Too often we begin scraping and scrubbing before the stripper has done all that it can. Too often we barely give it a chance to loosen the paint on top of the wood, let alone work its way down to the bottom of the pores.

When you are ready to begin stripping your next piece of furniture, brush on your paint and varnish remover thick and heavy. One thick coat is better than two thin ones—and takes half the time. Then, walk away. Go do something else. Clean the hardware, finish dismantling the doors, tape the insides of the drawers, have a cup of coffee, but leave the stripper alone. Give it a chance to soften the paint lodged deep in those pores. You've already paid for it, so why not let it work?

Second, the time to get the paint out of the pores is when it is soft, not two hours later, not tomorrow. As soon as the stripper is removed and the rinse begins to evaporate, the paint starts to reharden. Leave it until tomorrow and it's going to be just as hard as it was yesterday.

Third, if you have access to it, use air pressure to blow the softened paint out of the pores. It makes a mess, so you want to do it outside and away from any other painted surfaces (like the neighbor's car or the side of your garage), but it is the fastest, cleanest, and easiest way I have found to dislodge the soft paint. If you can borrow a small air compressor or even a portable air tank with a length of hose and a nozzle, you can blow that paint out so easily, you'll wonder why anyone bothered to buy a brass bristle brush.

Fourth, the reason refinishers do bother to buy a bristle brush is because you don't always have access to pressurized air. You may have tried water pressure, until you discovered that the water coming through your garden hose cooled and hardened the paint in the pores, making it nearly impossible to get out. Then you may have decided to force it out. If you used a standard wire brush, you found that it did more damage than good. The steel bristles can plow as many new pores into softened wood as they can clean out the old ones.

The solution, for me, at least, came in the form of a brass bristle brush. The individual wires are finer than those in a standard wire brush, are set more closely together, are more flexible, and are less apt to cause any damage. Dipped in the rinse and used as soon as the stripper is scraped off, a brass bristle brush can remove a high percentage of the paint lodged in the pores.

If a reasonable number of paint-clogged pores remain after you have rinsed and wiped the piece dry, I would recommend that you make yourself comfortable, with your board between you and a strong light, and begin picking out the flecks of paint. Your choice of tools is lengthy: a hobby knife, a nail, an awl, a sharpened length of coat hanger, a tiny screwdriver, or a long needle will each work. Again, however, let me stress that timing is important. While the paint is soft and unattached, all that it takes is a little pressure or a flick of the wrist to pop it out. Let it dry, though, and you'll find yourself digging, not flicking it out.

What happens when there are too many paint-filled pores to clean them out one by one? My first recommendation would be to repeat the stripping process. Brush on another coat of semi-paste paint and varnish remover, for this time it won't wear itself out on the surface paint. Let it sit until it has nearly dried and then scrub it off, using either coarse steel wool or your brass bristle brush.

Finally, there is a solution that, while at first glance would appear to make more work, actually is quite effective. After the wood has dried, brush on a solution consisting of equal parts liquid shellac and denatured alcohol. Let this dry, during which time it will penetrate the pores and attach itself to the flecks of paint. Afterward, restrip the piece. The shellac will strip easily and, believe it or not, will literally pull the flecks of paint out with it. When I first heard about this technique, I didn't believe it either—not until I tried it.

As a last resort—and this is not a solution so much as it is a disguise—you can cover many of the remaining flecks by using paste filler after the piece has been sanded and stained. The process is described in detail in Chapter 7, but briefly, it consists of rubbing into the pores a semi-paste filler that you let nearly harden before you wipe it off. All of the paste filler is removed except that which is lodged in the pores on top of the flecks of paint. You then let it dry, sand lightly, and prepare to finish.

**Choosing ▶
a Professional
Stripper**

Since sooner or later you will find yourself in a situation where you may want to consider hiring the services of a professional refinisher, even if just to strip a piece that you don't have the time, space, or enthusiasm to tackle, a few suggestions from a former furniture refinisher may be in order. Not long ago I received a letter from a new home owner who was ready to embark on her first refinishing project. She wanted me to tell her, in thirty words or less, no doubt, how to strip all of the painted woodwork in her house: floorboards, trim, windows, and stairway.

My advice was simple: Take off whatever would come off and have it professionally stripped.

In my mind there was no way she could safely, easily, or effectively (let alone quickly) remove three layers of paint and the original varnish from all of that woodwork without ending up putting her house back on the market. In my mind, it is better to have a professional take care of the stripping for you if that is all that is keeping you from starting or finishing a project.

To help you decide if you should undertake the stripping process yourself or turn it over to a professional, ask yourself the following questions:

- Do I have a space to deal with the mess?
- Does it have more than just adequate ventilation?
- Am I sensitive to fumes?
- Does my skin react to the chemicals in paint and varnish remover?
- Do I have the time, energy, and determination to see this step through to the end?

Let's presume, for example, that you don't have the proper space or adequate ventilation, that you do react to chemicals and fumes, and it takes you until late Sunday afternoon just to recover from your weekday job. What little space, time, and energy you do have will need to be reserved for the actual refinishing and not the stripping.

How, then, do you choose a reliable refinisher?

By following these steps:

1. Make a list of the professional refinishers who advertise in the yellow pages or your area newspapers.
2. Call your friends who have had any stripping or refinishing done recently and ask for their recommendations.
3. Call your area antiques dealers and ask for their recommendations.
4. Call the shop or shops that have received glowing recommendations and ask the following questions:
   (a) Do they dip or hand-strip their furniture?
   (b) Do they guarantee against warping, veneer damage, raised grain, and weakened glue joints?
   (c) How long would the job take?
   (d) (optional) Do they offer a pickup and delivery service? What is the charge?
   (e) Based on similar examples, what would an approximate estimate be of the stripping cost?
5. Visit the shop or shops you are considering, observing the following:
   (a) How safely is the furniture waiting to be stripped being stored?
   (b) How safely is the furniture that has been stripped being stored?
   (c) How organized is the operation?
   (d) How clean and safe does the shop appear?
   (e) Do they use dipping tanks?
   (f) How concerned do the owner and employees appear to be with their work?
6. Ask to see samples of their work, checking for:
   (a) unusual fuzziness
   (b) warped back or side panels
   (c) overbleached wood
   (d) cross-grain scratches from scrapers
   (e) runs down the sides of drawers
   (f) veneer lifting
7. Presuming everything thus far has met with your satisfaction, ask for a written estimate of

the stripping cost, including the completion date. (They will need to either see the piece or, in the case of large pieces, a sample drawer or door and a number of clear photographs.)

8. Make a decision and the arrangements necessary for the work to begin. Retain a signed copy of the estimate.

9. Call three days prior to the completion date to make arrangements to pick up the piece or to have it delivered.

10. Inspect the piece carefully before either leaving with it or paying for it. Make sure you are satisfied with the work.

Summary ▶ Stripping does not have to be the dreaded step in furniture refinishing. If you take the time to choose and prepare your work area carefully, pick the best remover for your project, have the proper tools assembled, and let the stripper do its job, you will find that watching a wonderful piece of walnut or a magnificent mahogany grain emerge from beneath a coat of green paint is the most rewarding step in the entire refinishing process.

Shopping List ▶

— paint and varnish remover
— denatured alcohol, lacquer thinner, or turpentine
— plastic drop cloth
— newspapers
— masking tape
— coffee cans
— no. 2 steel wool
— no. 0 steel wool
— rags
— work apron
— safety glasses

— rubber gloves
— eyewash
— screwdrivers
— pliers
— hammer
— putty knives
— assorted brushes
— toothbrush
— scrub brush
— brass bristle brush
— hand cleaner

CHAPTER 6
Surface Preparation

I don't like sanding, but it took me a few years in the business to find a good reason not to do it.

I don't think I'm lazy or a tightwad, and I know I'm not allergic to dust. I don't even blame it on my seventh-grade shop teacher, who saw sanding as an ideal form of punishment for young boys who misbehaved in his class. As messy as stripping might be, I find that far more rewarding than sanding blemishes out of an oak tabletop. And while stripping does signal the demise of the old finish, it does not remove any wood. We can replace an old finish, but we haven't yet discovered a means of replacing a 150-year-old patina.

Patina.

Despite what many antiques buffs would like you to believe, there isn't anything mysterious about patina. Technically speaking, everything has a patina—wood, metal, glass, pottery, paint, varnish, even human skin—for patina is simply the observable evidence of the aging process. On skin it may take the form of wrinkles, brown spots, or blemishes; on wood it is the gradual muting of the colors, mellowness brought on by years of exposure to everything from the ultraviolet rays of the sun to dusting, cleaning, handling, and polishing. The worn edge of a desk, the rounded corner of a table, the light areas on the arms of your favorite rocking chair, the hazy crazing of the finish, the soft wear around a dresser knob—these are all examples of furniture patina.

The aging process starts the moment a piece of furniture leaves the workshop and continues so long as it exists. For the first few years the change may not be noticeable, but it is taking place. Microscopic scratches—and some not so microscopic—begin to appear, the high-gloss shine gradually becomes a satin sheen, and the sharp, distinctive colors begin to fade. After a hundred years a piece of black walnut begins to look a little like cherry, red oak like golden oak, and yellow pine like soft maple.

The patination process takes place at two different levels on furniture. Both the finish and the wood beneath it acquire their own separate patinas: the finish from dusting, polishing, cleaning, and daily use; the wood from the rays of the sun and, as the finish grows thin, from mild abrasions. The changes, though, both in the finish and in the wood itself, are most noticeable in exposed surfaces. The protected recess of a table apron or the sides of a drawer are not as apt to reflect the effects of time as dramatically as the top.

Patina, like beauty, is only skin-deep. As the finish disappears, either slowly through hard use or quickly under fire from stripping solvents, its patina disappears. What remains afterward, however, is the patina of the wood. That, too, is very shallow; the effects of time cannot penetrate but a tiny fraction of an inch into the pores of the wood. One casual pass with a sharp scraper can erase one hundred years of patina. Ten minutes with a sheet of no. 80 grit sandpaper can turn a century's worth of slow aging into a pile of dust on the floor.

To an antiques lover, patina equals beauty—and beauty equals value. Manufacturers of new furniture recognize this and employ researchers whose task it is to devise ways of achieving an instant patina: satin finishes, fake wormholes, distress marks, paint speckling, and false tarnishing are but a few of their more common attempts to duplicate the signs of age and authenticity in new furniture.

As a refinisher, you control the fate of the patina, as little or as much as there may be. In some instances, the patina of the finish may have to be sacrificed in order to save, preserve, and better present the beauty of the patina of the wood. I always try to save both the patina of the wood and the finish, but if that is not possible, I strip the piece carefully, yet thoroughly, without removing the patina of the wood or requiring excessive sanding afterward. A proper stripping does destroy the patina of the finish, but it leaves the patina in the wood intact.

Sanding, however, sounds the death knell for both.

Many refinishers oversand simply out of habit. Woodworkers and cabinetmakers must do a good deal of sanding to remove production marks left by their saws, planers, and shapers. Most refinishers either took early classes in industrial arts or grew up watching a woodworker make furniture; we were taught that sanding is a necessary part of the cabinetmaking process. While sanding does play a role in refinishing, it should be a minor role, not a major one. Unless the original woodworker failed to remove unsightly saw marks, you and I shouldn't have to resort to but a fraction of the sanding cabinetmakers undertake.

Barring repairs or damage to the wood, any more than a

**light sanding in the refinishing process is not only unnecessary
and wasteful, it can, in the case of an antique or a potential
antique, permanently affect the value of the piece.**

The first day I went to work in a refinishing shop that was
being managed by a former cabinetmaker, I was told to sand a
mahogany rocking chair "until it's all as light as the arms."

Like most mahogany rocking chairs made in the twenties, this
rocker had one imported mahogany board—the wide back slat;
but the rest was American hard maple that had been stained burgundy to imitate the more costly mahogany. The stain on the arms
had worn off, exposing the natural light color of the maple. With
the arms as my model, I went to work. Two days, six Band-
Aids, and too many sheets of sandpaper later, the chair looked
terrible. I was able to break through to light wood on the flat,
open spaces, but the carvings, the joints, and the turned legs were
still as dark as the solitary mahogany board in the back.

Jim stood looking at it thoughtfully.

"Stain it," he announced.

"Stain it what?"

"Stain it dark mahogany."

And with that he left the room.

I found a can of dark mahogany stain on the shelf, pried it
open, and stirred up the heavy pigments on the bottom of the can.
Ten minutes later the mahogany rocking chair looked nearly identical to the rocker I had started sanding two days earlier. A subsequent six coats of lacquer made the chair look as good as the
day it was made, and the gentleman who picked it up on Friday
was pleased.

The shop owner was not. The bill for the chair barely covered
my wages. I was just as upset, but it had nothing to do with
money. I had just wasted two days of my time.

I did not leave House of Wood thinking that old furniture
never needs to be sanded. I just came to the realization that it
needs to be sanded for a good reason. Not, as in the case of the
mahogany rocker, to try to remove the remains of the old finish
and the original stain. Old wood does often need to be sanded,
but most sanding done by refinishers arises not out of a need to
remove any wood, but out of a failure to remove all of the old
finish and stripper residue.

To make an extreme point, consider this: If properly stripped,
a piece of furniture should not need to be sanded.

If you:

1. choose a reliable brand of paint and varnish remover,
2. use lacquer thinner or denatured alcohol rather than grain-raising water as a rinse,
3. employ medium to fine steel wool rather than a wire brush or scrapers to remove the sludge, and
4. take the time to wash and wipe away traces of old finish, stripper, and wax thoroughly,

then the wood should emerge smooth, clean, and ready for a stain or finish. At the very most, all that should be required is a light once-over with a pad of no. 000 steel wool or fine steel wool substitute to remove any film left after the final rinse and drying.

But what about the exceptions?

For example, if the wood is in poor condition, or has a splintered edge, an improper repair, or a rough surface, sanding will be required. What is called for in these situations, though, is sanding as a means of repair rather than a follow-up to a sloppy stripping.

Rather than raking the entire edge of the table with a metal file or a piece of sandpaper wrapped around a block of wood, loose splinters should be glued and clamped in place with masking tape. After they have dried, use a folded edge of sandpaper to carefully blunt any jagged edges. A few harmless gaps are far less noticeable than an edge that has lost all of its natural color by being rounded with a sandpaper block. As you may have already discovered, convincing a rounded edge to accept a wood stain is one of the most frustrating aspects of refinishing.

In a similar situation, sanding is not the best solution to an improper repair that has left one board protruding above the adjoining one, such as in a reglued tabletop. Here again, once the protruding edge is sanded, it loses its natural color and patina—and you are faced with a light streak in the middle of a darker table. Rather than sand the offender, you need to attempt to dissolve the repair and reglue the two boards. It may at first seem to take longer than simply sanding off the error, but after having spent an entire day trying to duplicate the original color on a freshly sanded edge, I can promise that it won't.

When does a dent or a scratch go from being part of the patina to being an eyesore?

To a purist, never.

To a perfectionist, immediately.

To a refinisher, it depends.

The question you must ask yourself before reaching for the sandpaper is "Will my solution be worse than my problem?"

Very shallow surface scratches can oftentimes be removed or disguised without causing any damage to the patina (see Chapter 2), but unfortunately, these are not the scratches that could be considered an eyesore. The type that are the easiest to remove are generally the type that are the least objectionable and actually impart a sense of authenticity and age to the piece. It is the deeper cross-grain scratches and annoying dents that dare you to reach for your sandpaper.

Desks, tabletops, buffets, and servers especially seem to exhibit distracting scars as evidence of their usefulness. Attempting to sand them out, however, can actually cause a worse problem—that created by a larger depression or, at the least, an area lighter in color than the remainder of the piece. Like ice on a pond, once you have broken through the thin layer of patina, it can never be the same again. As hard as you may try to patch it, the scar will remain. Even Nature, given another hundred years, cannot erase the damage your sandpaper has done.

As a rule, spot-sanding can only spell trouble for the weekend refinisher. You need to remember the general refinisher's rule: Whatever you do to one area, you must do to the entire board. If you forget, you end up with blemishes, shallow depressions, and light spots.

Given the choice to

- sand off the patina from the entire top,
- sand off the patina from just one spot, or
- seek another solution,

your choice should be obvious. If it is, indeed, a shallow dent or scratch, then I would still recommend using an appropriate stain to make it look older and less objectionable. If it is a gouge, then I would recommend filling it rather than attempting to sand it out (see Chapter 4).

The Exceptions ▶ In spite of all I've said to the contrary, you're still going to have to do some sanding. If you have a new piece made, such as a runner for a rocking chair, a leaf for a table, or a rung for an armchair, you may have to assume the role of a woodworker and sand off some lingering saw marks.

You may also discover a damaged section with a jagged edge that must be smoothed. And of course, you may have to correct someone else's error, such as smoothing a top that had been stripped, rinsed with water, and left unprotected. If you attempt to straighten a warp, you may cause some grain raising yourself, or if you have a drawer that is rubbing, a veneer patch that is raised, or a glue stain that is causing problems, you will need to know what types of sandpaper are available and which is the best for your particular problem.

Sandpaper ▶
Grading System In the past, at least three different grading systems for sandpaper have been used, but in recent years the grit or "mesh" system has emerged as being the most popular.

On the back of each sheet of sandpaper you will find a number indicating how many holes per square inch there were in the mesh used to determine the size of the granules that were attached to that particular backing. The lower the total number of holes per square inch, the larger each hole in the screen will be, thus the larger the granules are on that piece of sandpaper. The higher the total number of holes per square inch, the smaller each hole will be, meaning the granules on papers with higher numbers will be finer.

In the end it comes out looking like this:

Mesh Number	Description
50	Coarse
80	Coarse
100	Medium
120	Medium
180	Medium-Fine
220	Fine
240	Fine
320	Very Fine

Manufacturers also indicate on the back of each sheet the relative weight of the paper. Generally speaking, the heavier the granules, the heavier the paper must be to support them; thus, you will find that coarse grits often correspond with the heavier papers. The lightest weight is "A" paper, with "C" and "D" being heavier. The heavier papers cost more than the "A" papers, but last longer. Only in well-stocked paint and hardware stores will you get the opportunity to decide which weight of paper you will buy, since most stores generally offer only one weight of paper per grit.

Types of sandpaper vary almost as much as the various grits. It is important that you know not only how to recognize each type, but that you be able to compare the cost of each type to its durability.

◄ **Varieties of Sandpaper**

FLINT PAPER is made using a natural mineral, a yellow-white sand; thus, it is less expensive than the other types, but wears out much faster. Cost-conscious woodworkers and refinisher's don't buy it.

GARNET PAPER is also made using a natural mineral, but it is more durable than flint, costs more, and lasts longer. It is recognized by its reddish-yellow color and used most often for fine sanding.

EMERY CLOTH is also made using a natural mineral, but it is much finer and harder than either flint or garnet; thus, it is most often found on a flexible cloth backing ideal for cleaning metal and smoothing wood spindles. It is generally black.

ALUMINUM OXIDE PAPER uses synthetic abrasives, and, though it costs more than garnet paper, is a popular choice among woodworkers and refinishers as an all-purpose sandpaper, since it is durable and has excellent cutting abilities. It is reddish-brown in color and is often referred to as "production paper."

SILICON CARBIDE PAPER is also made from a synthetic abrasive. This blue or black paper is waterproof and ideally suited for extremely fine sanding between coats of finish.

Guide to Sandpaper Selection

Material	Type	Grit
New rough lumber	Aluminum Oxide	50–80
New planed lumber	Aluminum Oxide	100–125

Material	Type	Grit
Stripped hardwoods	Aluminum Oxide	125–180
Stripped softwoods	Aluminum Oxide	180
Final wood sanding	Aluminum Oxide	220–400
	Garnet	220
Spindles	Emery Cloth	Fine
Sanding Sealer	Aluminum Oxide	220
Between coats of finish	Silicon Carbide	320 wet
Smoothing old finish	Silicon Carbide	400 wet
High-gloss finish	Silicon Carbide	1200 wet

Each grit of sandpaper is designed only to remove scratches equal to or smaller than those created by the next coarser granule size. Therefore, jumping from no. 80 sandpaper directly to no. 220 will only result in the finer sandpaper wearing out before it is able to remove the scratches left by the no. 80 grit. Proceed in steps: 80, 100, 120, 180, 220. The cost and the time involved will be less than that required in making large leaps.

Sanding ▶ Techniques

Just as various means of removing old finishes have evolved over the years, so have various means of removing wood. In most instances, however, refinishers have attempted to borrow from the woodworker's shop a number of tools and methods that were not intended to be used on old wood with a valued patina. What little time or money any of these may have saved—and it is difficult to imagine how a sixty-dollar belt sander wearing out three-dollar sanding belts in a matter of seconds could ever actually save you money—is outweighed by the lost value directly attributed to the permanent damage done by the machine.

Nevertheless, you and I both know that power sanders, like hot dipping tanks, do exist, and we must also know why we neither want nor need to invest in them.

The four most common types of power sanders are:

orbital sanders   belt sanders
disk sanders   flap sanders

A FLAP SANDER consists of a series of strips of sandpaper attached to a bit designed to be inserted in an electric drill. They, along with disk sanding attachments, wire brush attachments, and a host of other gadgetry, evolved about the time portable electric drills became affordable for most households. It was as if manufacturers were attempting to convince hobbyists that they could have the equivalent of an entire workshop just by buying an electric drill and forty-seven different attachments.

Fortunately, flap sanders failed to become as popular as disk sanders, for they show no respect for fine carvings, delicate turnings, or, for that matter, wood in general. It is impossible, simply by its design, for a flap sander to exert equal pressure at all points while simultaneously sanding only in the direction of the grain. In short, they don't sand wood, they beat it to death.

DISK SANDERS have gouged a trail of antiques and fine furniture all across the country. I am still amazed and appalled by the number of so-called ''knowledgeable'' antiques dealers and professional refinishers who will use a disk sanding attachment on the end of their electric drills to remove paint. They seem oblivious to the fact that disk sanders leave deep, circular cross-grain scratches in the wood, permanently scarring and disfiguring unfortunate furniture.

Only slightly less offensive, the BELT SANDER can at least be run in the direction of the grain, but it cannot be used in corners, around joints, on curved surfaces, along edges, over veneer, on spindles, and in tight situations. On the one place where it can be used, namely, tabletops—it eats through the patina in seconds and leaves grooves, low spots, and irregular patches which can be seen and felt, and which stain unevenly. By the time we eliminate all of the places where a belt sander cannot be used, it is difficult to be able to justify either the expense or the risk involved in owning one.

When first introduced, ORBITAL SANDERS seemed to offer the solution to the problem of how to eliminate cross-grain scratches while speeding up the sanding process. It was soon discovered, though, that if any grit coarser than no. 220 was used with it, the orbital sander would leave thousands of tiny, swirling scratches in the wood. Sometimes these scratches will escape notice until the first coat of finish is applied, then they practically jump off the wood at you.

Like a belt sander, an orbital sander can quickly round corners, dull edges, ruin veneer, and flatten carvings—and all for a fairly hefty sum of money.

When all is said and done, then, your choices look something like this:

	Advantages	Disadvantages
Hand Sanding	complete control inexpensive excellent in corners, on turnings and irregular shapes low dust low risk	slow
Orbital Sander	moderate control high speed lightweight	rounds edges tears paper swirling scratches expensive ineffective on spindles, carvings high dust moderate risk
Belt Sander	high speed	poor control flattens edges leaves grooves and deep scratches expensive ineffective on spindles, carvings ruins veneer high dust high risk
Disk Sander	high speed	poor control flattens edges leaves grooves and deep scratches expensive ineffective on spindles, carvings ruins veneer high dust high risk

	Advantages	*Disadvantages*
Flap Sander	none	poor control
		flattens edges
		leaves grooves and
		deep scratches
		expensive
		ineffective on spindles,
		carvings
		ruins veneer
		high dust
		high risk

Now that you have a good idea what methods and machines you may not want to use, the key question is: What can you do to make hand sanding more efficient?

◄ The Refinisher's Choice: Hand Sanding

First, buy quality sandpaper with a heavy paper backing. It lasts longer and provides more strokes per sheet.

Second, select a grit that will be large enough to remove surface roughness without leaving deep scratches in the wood.

Third, cut each sheet into fourths before using it. The smaller pieces (4½ by 5½ inches) will be easier to handle, will give you more control, and, since they are less apt to tear, will last longer.

Fourth, before using, grasp each section of sandpaper at both ends, then pull the length of the paper, smooth side down, over the edge of your workbench. Turn the paper one quarter turn and repeat. By flexing the back of the paper, you actually increase its durability and decrease the likelihood that it will tear prematurely.

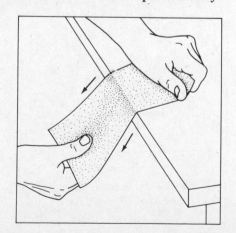

Fifth, find an old shoe with a crepe sole to use to clean the sandpaper as it becomes clogged. Spots of old finish on the sandpaper can actually mar the surface of the wood if they are not promptly removed.

The Sanding ▶ Block

Some refinishers prefer to use a sanding block whenever possible—and for two very good reasons. A block applies more pressure and more surface of the sandpaper to the wood than your fingertips do. In addition, sanding blocks don't develop blisters or get splinters.

Several styles of sanding blocks are available at paint and hardware stores, but it is easier, cheaper, and more comfortable to make your own. Start by selecting a block of either one- or two-inch-thick softwood. It should be 5½ inches in length to accommodate a standard sheet of sandpaper cut into fourths. Begin experimenting with different widths to fit your hand. The sanding block can be no wider than 3½ inches to allow for the 4½-inch wide paper to extend up either side, where it will be held in place by your thumb and fingertips. If you have small hands, it can be as narrow as you like.

Ideally, the bottom of the sanding block should be covered with a piece of thin cork or felt to protect the furniture from the block and to extend the life of your sandpaper. File or sand the top edges and corners of the block to fit comfortably into the palm of your hand. Finally, label the block clearly to prevent anyone from mistaking it for a piece of scrap wood.

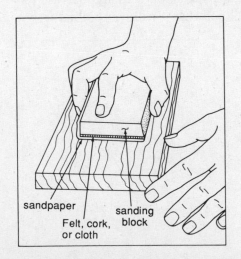

sandpaper   sanding block

Felt, cork, or cloth

The key to effective sanding—with or without a sanding block— **◄ With the Grain** is moderate, equal pressure, always in the direction of the grain. Overzealous sanding in one area will change the color of the wood, lower the level of the surface, and risk permanent damage to edges, carvings, turnings, and the patina. Letting your sandpaper run across rather than in the same direction as the grain of the wood will leave scratches that are difficult, if not impossible, to sand without changing the color of the wood.

The most difficult spot to maintain the discipline required to always sand in the direction of the grain seems to be where two boards meet at right angles to one another. The temptation is to let the sandpaper glide from one over the other, especially if it is in a tight corner or next to a spindle or slat. Resisting means your task will take a little longer and your knuckles may occasionally get bruised, but they will quickly heal—and cross-grain scratches never do. Even on flat areas you need to watch what your sanding hand does when it reaches the peak of each stroke. Do you pull it straight back? Or do you find yourself making an oval turn, leaving scratches running at an angle across the grain of the wood?

On some particular woods, most notably burled walnut and bird's-eye maple, the direction of the grain is difficult to distinguish. Since for that same reason these woods also show their scratches well, you must be careful to only use extremely fine sandpaper. If at all possible, avoid sanding altogether, and return to a rag dipped in lacquer thinner to remove any troublesome stripper residue. Fine steel wool may also be substituted for sandpaper, but if you must sand, start with nothing coarser than no. 320.

As dust accumulates on the wood, in the pores, and between the **◄ Dust** granules on your sandpaper, it acts as tiny roller bearings, effectively reducing the friction between the granules and the wood. Once the dust builds up between the sandpaper and the wood, you end up working twice as hard to get half the results.

While you can go out and buy an expensive shop brush, I prefer to keep a cheap paintbrush hanging nearby. A few swipes with it is all it takes to keep the area I am sanding free from dust. Better yet is one of the popular hand vacuums, for it eliminates the dust altogether. While the lightweight, cordless models are fine for a refinishing shop, the ungainly, old-fashioned canister-style vacuums with a hose and half dozen clinging attachments are even more versatile. If there isn't one lost in the back of your closet, check with any vacuum repair shops or secondhand stores in the area. Twenty dollars may buy a sturdy, dependable machine with more suction than any of the expensive plastic models.

If you use a canister vacuum in your work area, there are two easy and inexpensive ways you can improve its performance. First, when vacuuming up general workbench dust, slip either a panty hose leg or a small wire screen over the end of the hose to prevent it from gobbling up any small screws, washers, or chips of veneer you may have dropped.

Second, if you ever need a great deal of suction in a very small area, such as when you are cleaning out the inside corners on drawers and case pieces, select a rubber cork that fits snugly inside the opening on your vacuum nozzle. In the middle of that cork, drill a hole to fit a two-foot-length of flexible rubber hose (approximately one-half or five-eighths inch, depending on the size of the cork). Force the small hose into the cork and, when needed, simply insert the cork into the end of the hose. The smaller hose will give you added flexibility, accuracy, and suction.

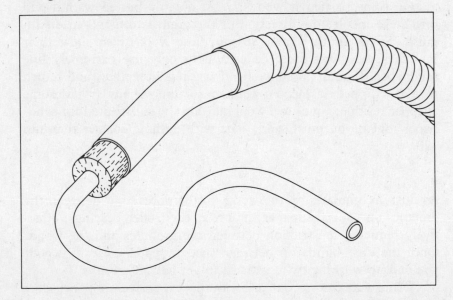

Wet Sanding ▶   If refinishers would borrow a little less of the power-sanding technology from professional cabinetmakers and a little more of the hand-sanding technology from the automotive industry, furniture refinishing could take a giant leap forward.

In 1907, L. & J. G. Stickley were the first to adapt the newly developed spring seat from the fledgling automobile industry for their Mission Oak Morris chairs and settles. Since then furniture manufacturers have closely watched advances in the automotive industry and have continued to borrow ideas and adapt them for their own use, for it was the automotive industry that made major advances in modern finishes, drying additives, and spray equipment. The auto industry also developed a durable, noncrumbling steel wool substitute and sandpapers with grits running beyond no. 1200. While not all of their advancements have a direct application for the weekend refinisher, wet-sanding can enable you to save finishes that you previously would have stripped.

To be effective, sandpaper depends on friction. But not too much. Too much friction removes more material and leaves more scratches than you want, especially on a clear finish. We knew for years that most liquids, from thin oils to plain water, can reduce friction, but until a waterproof backing was developed for sandpaper, we couldn't take advantage of this knowledge. Pumice and rottenstone, sprinkled over a thin oil, had been the most popular fine abrasive for smoothing out furniture finishes, but they have been all but forgotten in the rush to waterproof silicon carbide sandpaper.

Waterproof sandpaper opened the door to a technique commonly called wet-sanding, in which the sandpaper is dipped in water, furniture oil, furniture polish, turpentine, or mineral oil in the course of the sanding process. This reduces the friction and allows you to remove surface irregularities—dust, sags, and runs—without scratching or sanding through the finish.

The two grits of silicon carbide sandpaper that you will be most apt to need are nos. 400 and 600. If you are attempting to save a rough original finish or smooth out the last coat of a new finish, either grit can be dipped in water, lemon oil, mineral oil, or any thin furniture oil while sanding. It is important to keep the sandpaper thoroughly wet at all times, using the liquid both to wash away the sludge that accumulates and to reduce the friction between the granules and the finish. Keep a rag close by to wipe away excess liquid and sludge as they accumulate, for the fine-grit sandpapers clog easily. Given enough time and pressure, they, too, can sand through a finish if you aren't carefully checking your progress.

You can also wet-sand to prepare an existing finish for the next coat. In general, you should use water or mineral spirits—

NOT oil—to keep the sandpaper wet, unless the finish is an oil finish. If you make the mistake of using oil to lubricate your sandpaper, the next coat of varnish, lacquer, or shellac may react to traces of it clinging to the surface. If you are applying an oil finish, you should use a light furniture oil or clear mineral oil to lubricate the sandpaper.

Wet-Sanding Chart

Surface	Grit	Lubricant
Old Shellac Finish	600	Mineral oil
Old Lacquer Finish	600	Mineral oil
Old Varnish Finish	400–600	Turpentine, water, or mineral oil
Old Oil Finish	600	Furniture oil (tung oil, mineral oil, etc.)
New Shellac Finish		
sealer coats *	400	Water (minimal)
final coat	600	Mineral oil
New Lacquer Finish		
sealer coats *	400	Water
final coat	600	Mineral oil
New Varnish Finish		
sealer coats *	400	Turpentine or water
final coat	600	Mineral oil
New Oil Finish		
sealer coats	400	Furniture oil
final coat	600	Furniture oil

* Base coats may also be sanded with dry no. 220 sandpaper.

> TIP: To achieve a perfectly smooth surface, such as that found on buffets, tabletops, and servers, wet-sand between coats using a sanding block. To wet-sand rungs and spindles, cut your sandpaper into long, thin strips before dipping it into the liquid.

Bleaching ▶ For many years it was presumed that the only way to remove dark rings, spots, and blemishes from wood was by sanding. The frustrations that arose from trying to sand out these stains may have driven many people to belt sanders. In any event, the attitude toward such surface imperfections has changed, as have the means for dealing with them (also see Chapter 4).

Today an authentic antique furniture finish is held in higher regard than an unblemished new surface. Given the choice between a stained original finish and a perfect new finish, serious collectors will almost always pick the original finish. If removing a stain in your furniture requires the destruction of the original and otherwise fine finish, then you should learn to live with it. A strategically placed desk blotter, lamp, or piece of pottery will often do more to improve the appearance of the piece than a complete refinishing.

Pieces, though, which have been stripped yet which have severe or even light stains can be treated without the excessive use of sandpaper. Several varieties and strengths of bleaches are available which may be able to lighten or eliminate unsightly stains, such as black water rings, ink stains, oil marks, or rust residue. Most, however, require that the finish be removed in order for them to attack the stain; where the finish is thin, it may be possible for you to lighten a stain without having to remove the finish. In the case of a severe stain beneath a fine, authentic finish, it may be worthwhile to try bleaching only the stained area through the finish using a cotton swab as an applicator.

The following bleaching agents are readily available:

Liquid Chlorine Bleach   Hydrogen Peroxide
Oxalic Acid   Commercial Wood Bleaches

◄ Liquid Chlorine Bleach

Nearly every house in America has a bottle of liquid chlorine bleach under the sink, which can often work as well on stains in wood as it does on clothes. You don't need to dilute this rather mild bleach, though you certainly won't consider it mild if you haven't first protected your clothes, your eyes, or any nearby upholstery.

If the piece to be stained has been stripped, you need to make sure that all traces of wax and stripper residue have been removed before you brush on the bleach. I thoroughly wash the section to be bleached with one of the solvent rinses, such as turpentine or lacquer thinner, and follow that with a light sanding with no. 120 sandpaper to open up the pores to the bleach.

If the stain is small and shallow, you can apply the bleach

with a cotton swab to that area only. If the piece has numerous deep stains, then you should brush the bleach over the entire section, protecting other parts, such as the legs, apron, and sides, with masking tape and thick plastic. Attempting to bleach a half dozen spots rather than the entire section will leave you the unenviable task of later trying to restain those spots to blend in with the wood around them. Your critics (also known as your family) are much more apt to attribute a slight variation in color between two entire boards to natural irregularities than they are four or five distinctively different spots scattered about your tabletop.

The bleaching process is one of the few refinishing steps that works better in direct sunlight than in the depths of a cool basement. The bleaching agents work faster and penetrate deeper into wood when the rays of the sun are warming both the wood and the bleach. I recently stripped and sanded an oak library table that had several moderate stains—ink and water—scattered about the top. I set the table in the sunshine for about an hour after brushing on the bleach. In about thirty minutes most of the bleach and about half of the stains had disappeared, so I brushed on another coat, and in another thirty minutes all but a few faint stains were gone. Those I chose to leave, for I didn't want my table to look like a genuine reproduction.

If you don't see any change after the first application of bleach has evaporated, I would suspect that the wood still has an invisible layer of wax or finish that is keeping the bleach from penetrating the pores. Scrub it down thoroughly with denatured alcohol and no. 00 steel wool, let it dry, then repeat the process. If it begins to lighten but does not disappear after one treatment, additional coats may be immediately applied without risk to the wood. When the last of the bleach has evaporated or the stains disappeared, rinse the bleached area thoroughly with water to remove any traces of the bleach remaining in the pores.

Hydrogen ▶ Peroxide

Before reaching for the bottle of hydrogen peroxide in your medicine cabinet to remove a black water stain on your end table, you have to realize that the type of hydrogen peroxide intended for minor scrapes and irritations is only a 3 percent solution and thus is ineffective for removing wood stains. A stronger solution marketed as a bleach for hair is available under various well-known brand names and can be effective for removing shallow stains in your refinishing projects.

The process for using hydrogen peroxide is the same as that for using household bleach, though it is not recommended for bleaching anything other than small, shallow stains. What it will remove from wood, however, are fresh bloodstains. Although that bit of information won't be uppermost on your mind as you tear your workshop apart looking for the Band-Aids, when the pain stops, the refinishing will start again—and those tiny bloodstains will be waiting for you and your hydrogen peroxide.

As I said earlier, it's not as bad as it sounds. Oxalic acid crystals are available at most drugstores and, when dissolved in hot water, make a most effective and inexpensive wood bleach.   **◄ Oxalic Acid**

Like most refinishing products, oxalic acid is poisonous if swallowed, but neither the crystals nor the solution will burn your skin. I do strongly suggest that before using oxalic acid you take some important precautions, including wearing rubber gloves, glasses, and a particle mask and making sure that your work area is well ventilated. Although it may not be considered an extremely dangerous acid, you can never be completely sure how you might react to it.

Oxalic acid is only effective when the finish over the stain has been removed and the wood lightly sanded to open the pores. Begin by adding crystals to one cup hot water until the water reaches a saturated solution—there will be undissolved crystals in the bottom of the jar or can. I use an old brush to stir the mixture and work it into the wood, heaping extra crystal-laden water onto the worst stains. The bleaching solution will also lighten any other woods it comes in contact with, so be sure that you don't flick any of it onto other pieces of furniture or any sections of wood other than the one you are bleaching.

Once the entire section is covered with the oxalic acid solution, let it sit undisturbed in a warm room or in the sun until the water has evaporated. If the stains remain, repeat the process. If a stubborn stain appears to be resisting the oxalic acid, dip a pad of no. 00 steel wood into the solution and scrub the stain lightly to aid in the penetration.

Once the stains have disappeared and the water has evaporated, the crystalline residue should be removed. The dried crystals, though, should not be inhaled, unless you like severe sneezing and coughing fits. It is best to wear a particle mask and vacuum off the crystals—brushing them off only distributes them into the air. After most have been removed, rinse the bleached area thoroughly with a gallon of warm water to which three ounces of Borax, Spic and Span, or any detergent containing trisodium phosphate have been added.

The wood will then have to dry, but I don't recommend leaving it in the direct sunshine while it does. Rapid drying can cause either warping or splitting; it is better for the wood to dry gradually where you can keep an eye on it. If it begins to buckle, remoisten it and weight it down with concrete blocks as it continues to dry.

Commercial ▶
Wood Bleaches

Two-part commercial wood bleaches, available at paint and hardware stores as well as most restoration supply firms (see Chapter 12), are considered a last resort when all else has failed. They not only require particular care in their use—including safety glasses, protective clothing, and rubber gloves—they may remove more color from the wood than you'd like.

The commercial bleaches involve a two-step process. The first application is brushed on and left to sit for an amount of time specified on the directions. A second part is then applied, and this starts the actual bleaching. When the wood is bleached to the desired color, it is rinsed with white vinegar.

Don't use these bleaches for spot bleaching or for use on fine antiques. They present serious risks to both the user and the furniture. While I have used oxalic acid on a continued basis for the past seven years with regular success and no health problems, I have yet to be as satisfied with either the cost, the risk, or the results of commercial wood bleaches.

Shopping List

__ assorted steel wool	__ turpentine
__ no. 120 sandpaper	__ household bleach
__ no. 180 sandpaper	__ oxalic acid crystals
__ no. 220 sandpaper	__ crepe sole
__ no. 320 sandpaper	__ inexpensive brushes
__ no. 400 sandpaper	__ cotton swabs
__ no. 600 sandpaper	__ strong detergent
__ sanding block	__ rags
__ vacuum	__ cans or jars
	__ safety glasses

CHAPTER 7
Staining

The summer before I left for my sophomore year of college I worked for a carpenter who helped me build a large maple bookcase. I was going to be majoring in English and was already discovering that English majors never have enough room for books. After the last nail hole had been filled and sanded, I decided that I wanted a walnut bookcase, so I bought a can of a popular wiping stain called Danish Walnut, awoke the heavy pigments asleep on the bottom of the can, and started brushing it across the top of my maple bookcase.

In an instant the sleek maple boards I had spent countless hours sanding to a satin smoothness were suddenly transformed into a murky, muddy mess. The subtle grain lines I had come to know so well disappeared under a flood of dark pigments. In a panic I fought to save them with rags, turpentine, even sandpaper, but they were gone. Through my tear-swollen eyes I could see that my custom-made bookcase now had a dime store finish.

The lesson I learned as a nineteen-year-old has lasted a lifetime: Don't try to turn a piece of wood into something it isn't. If I wanted a walnut bookcase, I should have built a walnut bookcase—and left the can of stain on the shelf.

After years of working with nearly every type of native American and foreign wood, I have yet to find a single board that I could call unattractive. Subtle variations in grain pattern, pore size, and overall color distinguish not only one variety from another, but one tree from another. As a refinisher, I've learned to preserve the natural color of the wood, not change it.

Many times, though, we have to play the cards we've been dealt. If the piece of poplar has been stained to look as if it were cherry, then you may have no logical choice but to live and work with it as it is. During the twenties and thirties a great deal of soft maple was stained to look like walnut, cherry, and dark mahogany—with varying degrees of success. Much of the furniture produced then would feature one prominent hardwood board, such as a walnut top on a small table, a mahogany back slat in a chair, or cherry sides in a magazine stand, while the rest would be made from a less expensive wood stained to imitate it.

This didn't seem to pose as much of a problem for the original owners as it does for me and you. By the time Aunt Edith's walnut end table finally makes its way from her attic to your living room, a complete refinishing may be in order. Your paint and varnish remover won't have any problem with the old lacquer finish, but in the sludge you may also find the walnut stain that was disguising the soft maple in the base. If you don't restain the base to look like walnut again, your table is going to look worse than it did the day the ceiling collapsed in Aunt Edith's living room.

With each piece of furniture you refinish will come the decision of whether or not you need to stain it. Some of your decisions will be easy, such as staining Aunt Edith's table base or not staining a new, unfinished cherry cupboard; others may require some careful consideration or perhaps even some research. Knowing not only what color of stain would be most appropriate for the piece, but what type of stain to buy—these have as much effect on the value of that piece as any other step in the refinishing process.

And the way I see it, there's no sense in us both having to learn about stains the hard way—one thing this world doesn't need is another murky bookcase.

Uniformity—▶ or Conformity?

Refinishers have a real power over wood. You can strip it, sand it, and then decide what color it's going to be. Do you want it as light as a piece of birch, a more mellow golden oak, a reddish cherry, a rich burgundy mahogany, a dark walnut, or even a fumed ebony? What you have to realize in all this is that this new-found power does not justify making every piece look like the rest of the furniture in your house.

Long before the current Arts and Crafts movement revival had begun, a good friend led me to his basement workshop, where he had on display two magnificent dining room tables he had just refinished. Each underside still bore the unmistakable Charles Limbert trademark and remnants of a rich, fumed Mission Oak finish. The tops, however, he had belt-sanded, bleached, stained, and polyurethaned to match four pressed-back Golden Oak chairs. At the time I marveled at his perseverance and envied his son and daughter, each of whom was to receive one of the tables as a gift. Now I know that his efforts had been misdirected by the reigning fashion. As fine examples of a modern Golden Oak finish, they were without equal; had they been carefully restored, however, they would have been worth several times their present value.

One of the advantages of using a methylene chloride paint and varnish remover, rather than a homemade brew of lye, trisodium phosphate, or toilet bowl cleanser, is that it is less inclined to remove either the natural or man-applied color of the wood. The total refinishing process, however, especially if it involves harsh scrubbing, excessive sanding, or deep bleaching, can lighten or completely remove the original color. On severe cases, by the time you are done stripping, sanding, bleaching, and repairing a piece, the wood's reservoir of authentic color may have been nearly depleted. In instances such as these, it will be necessary for you to replenish the authentic color of the wood.

◄ **Staining Stripped Wood**

Ethically, the choice of color for the wood was made long before it arrived in your workshop. Regardless of which magazine cover your living room looks like, you are obliged to restore each piece to its authentic color. Just because your 1840 Country living room desperately needs a "Williamsburg Blue" corner cupboard, that doesn't mean a 1910 Golden Oak version should be made to assume that role. If an original piece is unavailable or beyond the reach of your paycheck, then rather than do irreversible damage to a piece from another era, I would recommend that you go shopping for a new, unfinished reproduction to transform into an authentic-looking replica (see Chapter 10).

Selecting the proper color for your stripped or bleached piece of furniture requires a bit of enjoyable detective work. Start with the piece itself, for somewhere on it, regardless of how many times it has been previously painted or stripped, there is going to be a clue to its original color. It may be as obvious as the top of a leg that was protected from the ultraviolet rays of the sun or it may require searching under the hardware, inside the framework, or beneath the border of the upholstery.

I was once asked to refinish a mahogany chest of drawers which the owner confessed to having painted during what she called her "blue mood." Despite her state of mind, she had been thorough, painting even the insides of the drawers a deep Mediterranean blue. It wasn't until we started removing the hardware—*nothing* escaped her blue funk—that we were finally able to find a sample of the original color. After setting one drawer aside, we proceeded to strip and refinish the remainder of the piece, staining and finishing it to match the mahogany oval on the unstripped drawer. Only when we were satisfied that we had restored the chest to its original color did we strip the final drawer.

Additional research may lead you to the public library, local bookstores, the historical society, area museums, or antiques shops and shows where furniture similar to yours is displayed or pictured. Museum curators, conservationists, and authors take pride in presenting accurate examples of furniture styles, colors, and finishes. Even if yours is only a reproduction of an eighteenth-century Windsor chair manufactured by the Johnson Chair Company in Chicago in 1928 or an unfinished model made by the Great American Furniture Company in 1988, knowing what color an authentic Windsor chair would have been will give you a good idea what color of stain you should pick out for your project.

Types of Stains ▶ There are many different ways in which you can change the color of wood. I know woodworkers who still insist on gathering walnut hulls each fall to make next year's supply of walnut stain. One of the most charming refinishers I ever had the pleasure to meet—a seventy-two-year-old great-grandmother—brushes a dark brew of hot tea over many of her refinishing projects. I even stumbled into a workshop one day where a young man was brushing red paint on one side of a new, unfinished cupboard while his partner was on the other side furiously scrubbing it off. The resulting red tint made the new pine look amazingly old. I didn't ask what their plans were for the piece, but their sheepish looks made me awfully suspicious.

Here, then, is a brief summary of the four most common means available for altering the color of wood:

PAINT—Although you might think of paint as covering wood, it can also be thinned with turpentine or water (depending on whether it is oil-base or latex paint), brushed on, and wiped off. This created a ''pickled'' effect on oak in the fifties and is now used to re-create the look of worn paint on unfinished reproduction furniture. (See Chapter 10 for techniques.) The problems with using diluted paint as a stain, though, are serious ones: not enough control and way too much mess.

PIGMENTED WIPING STAIN—By far the most popular type of stain used by weekend refinishers, most brands consist of an oil-base liquid containing added dyes and colored pigments. When brushed on the wood, left to stand anywhere from a few seconds to five minutes, and then wiped off, pigmented wiping stains leave in the wood microscopic remains of the pigments and the dyes, which, in their turn, affect the color of the wood.

DYES—Any natural or synthetic material that dissolves in either water, denatured alcohol, or turpentine can be used as a dye. Home-brewed tea has been a popular dye for centuries. The range of dyes is limitless, but you should experiment before using any on furniture. While professional refinishers agree that dyes penetrate deeper into the wood and are less likely to obscure the grain of the wood than pigmented wiping stains, dyes are often unpredictable and time-consuming. Most refinishers, myself included, prefer the convenience of pigmented wiping stains whenever possible.

CHEMICAL ACTION—Cabinetmakers have known for centuries that certain chemicals will actually alter the color of the wood without imparting any dyes or leaving any pigments on the surface to cloud the grain. Ammonia fumes, for instance, react with the tannin in oak, turning it a pleasant tannish-brown and giving it the look of a board that is nearly a hundred years old. If the chemicals needed in the wood for a reaction to take place are no longer present in sufficient quantities, as often happens in older furniture, the chemical change may not take place.

◀ Pigmented Wiping Stains

Without a doubt the most widely advertised and widely used furniture stain on the market, the pigmented wiping stain makes applying a stain about as easy as it could possibly be. But like everything else, its convenience has its price. In the case of pigmented wiping stains, the cost is not just measured in terms of dollars and cents. As a well-known professional woodworker explains, "the difference between dyeing and staining is like the difference between getting a deep suntan and using makeup to imitate one."

A pigmented wiping stain consists of a colored powder that has been suspended in a liquid carrier, such as mineral spirits or lacquer thinner. Some brands, such as Deft and Minwax, contain a sealer that hardens as it dries, preventing the stain from later bleeding into the finish. Pigments alone do not actually change the color of the wood, but lodge in the fibers and pores, giving the impression of having changed the color. Most manufacturers have begun including additional chemicals for deeper penetration and more durable colors. While they may not offer the variety of colors found in powdered dyes, they are easy to use, leave no lap marks, show good resistance to sunlight, and can be effective, if chosen wisely and used properly.

Not long ago I received a letter from a woman in Ohio in which she asked, "Am I allowed to use a Golden Oak stain on my butternut dresser? I couldn't find a stain called Butternut, though I did find several brands of Fruitwood. Would that be better than Golden Oak on butternut? P.S.—What color is Provincial?"

Indeed, what color is Provincial? Or Special Walnut? Fruitwood? Or Colonial?

In their rush to fill the shelves with dozens of cans of stains, manufacturers have created meaningless names for numerous stains which, in truth, don't look all that much different from many of the others around them. Rather than offering you one can of stain labeled Light Brown, another called Medium Brown, and a third marked Dark Brown, and encouraging you to mix the three together to create any variations you might need, you have to sort through not only Walnut and American Walnut, but Danish Walnut, and a whole bunch of other walnuts that you won't find at the local nursery. My particular favorite name in the stain world, though, is Deep Swedish. Does that mean that somewhere there is a Shallow Swede stain?

The first rule for selecting a pigmented wiping stain is simple: Don't put too much faith in the name on the label.

There is nothing in any can of wiping stain that precludes it from being used to tint any type of wood. Extra Dark Walnut can be used on oak, pine, or persimmon; Medium Maple can be applied to walnut, mahogany, or teak; Deep Swedish can even be brushed on Philippine mahogany without a United Nations resolution. The names on the labels simply give you something to remember them by—and all without giving you any sense of how to use them.

Rule No. 2: Consult a wood sample chart before selecting a stain.

A brown mahogany stain may look beautiful on the color chart and just as beautiful on a sample piece of mahogany, but if you are staining a maple desk, then you had better be able to see what brown mahogany looks like on maple before you invest $6.48 in a quart of it. Quality paint and hardware stores will have extensive sample boards demonstrating what each stain looks like on several different types of wood: oak, mahogany, walnut, pine, and maple. Use that—and not the name on the label—to judge how that particular stain might appear on your piece of furniture.

Rule No. 3: Stains react differently to refinished wood than they do to unfinished wood—including unfinished wood samples.

In most cases, wood that has been previously stained or finished will not achieve the same darkness as a fresh, unsealed board. While the store sample may demonstrate what Salem Maple looks like on unfinished maple, what it doesn't show you is what it looks like on a piece of maple that has been stripped. Too many variables enter the picture for anyone to predict accurately how any stain will react on a refinished board: the type of previous finish, the depth of any previous stain, the method of stripping, the amount of sanding or bleaching—these all affect the process. Pigmented wiping stains rely on open pores for deep penetration, and if those pores are sealed with a previous finish or stain, they may not bring about the color you were looking at in the store.

The only way you can be certain that the particular stain you buy will give you the color you want is by taking a representative board—a drawer front, say, or a table leaf—to the paint store and asking the clerk to demonstrate what the stain will look like on your piece. It takes a big, helpless smile and a friendly clerk to get this kind of service, but if you select a time of day when they are not busy, you might just get the help you need.

Rule No. 4: Each can of stain contains more than one color.

Pigmented wiping stains are as much a mixture as they are a solution. The heavier pigments settle to the bottom of the can, leaving a light, semitransparent stain at the top, a medium stain in the middle, and a dark, murky stain on the bottom. To achieve the color represented on the sample board, you must thoroughly stir the stain, distributing the heavier pigments throughout the liquid.

If you are staining a large piece, you will want to stir the can of stain thoroughly before you begin and once every fifteen minutes thereafter to maintain a constant color. But if you are attempting to blend a repaired section with the rest of a piece, it would be smarter first to try the liquid at the top of the unstirred can. If it proves to be too light, stir the can only slightly, bringing a few of the heavier pigments to the top. If an additional test proves that it is still too light, you can then continue stirring until you discover the proper mixture. This way, each can of stain can actually offer several different shades of each basic color. Rather than buying all twelve different varieties of walnut stain, you might only need to buy one or two for your workshop.

Rule No. 5a: Do not mix different brands of stain.
Rule No. 5b: Do mix different varieties of the same brand of stain.

Manufacturers guard their secret formulas so closely that even an experienced chemist cannot always determine the precise ingredients by reading the label. Combining two different brands of stain might produce a mixture that simply won't work. On the other hand, most professional refinishers don't hesitate to mix different colors of the same brand of stain to produce new stains. When they do, they make it a point to measure each ingredient carefully and to note it for future reference on the side of the mixing jar. You would hate to discover the perfect stain for duplicating one-hundred-year-old walnut only to realize that you had forgotten the right combination of ingredients.

Rule No. 6: Buy small and buy often.

A gallon of dark walnut stain goes a long way—like from the top of your workbench all the way across the floor to the washing machine. Even if the savings are substantial (which they generally aren't), large cans of stain are difficult to store and easy to spill. Small cans, while costing a few cents more per ounce, offer a wide range of colors and the potential for creating endless variations. It would take a trained mathematician to compute the number of different stains that could be produced using just these five basic stain colors:

Ebony (black)   Walnut (brown)   Mahogany (red)
Golden Oak (yellow) Maple (tan)

So for a little more than ten dollars you can buy either a one-gallon can of any color you want—or five basic stain colors, and start mixing your own variations.

Staining ▶
Techniques
Pigmented wiping stains can be applied with either a rag, a brush, or both. Whichever way you choose, though, it's messy work. The stain penetrates the pores of your skin just as quickly as it soaks into the pores of the wood and leaves your hands looking more stained than your furniture. And what's worse, it does not wash off, so unless you are prepared to get the cold shoulder from

your spouse that night or feel like a leper at work Monday morning, think about your hands before you pop the lid off a can of red mahogany stain.

The best preventive measure you can take is to wear rubber gloves while you are staining. The thin plastic won't inhibit your movements, but it will prevent the stain from permanently altering the color of your cuticles. Sold in boxes of one hundred at drug and medical supply stores, disposable surgical gloves enable you to touch up a missed spot, brush on a quick coat of sealer, or rub out a dried finish—and walk fearlessly into the finest restaurant in town a few minutes later.

However, if you find yourself out of gloves with no time to get them, coat your hands liberally with hand cleaner, cold cream, or even liquid soap before diving into your can of stain. Any of these will help seal the pores of your skin and make cleanup a lot easier.

As with nearly every aspect of furniture work, it is imperative that you first test any stain on an inconspicuous spot. Had I first tried my walnut stain on an underside of my maple bookcase, I wouldn't have gone any further, and today I would have a beautiful honey-maple bookcase rather than a dark, muddy-looking box. The inside of a leg, the underside of a table leaf, or an interior of a drawer (provided the wood is of the same type) will give you a good idea how your wood is going to react to the stain you have chosen. Pay close attention to how the stain looks when it first goes on, for that is a fair indication of how it will look after a finish has been applied. After a while the stained area is going to dry, turn dull, and tempt you into putting on another coat. Don't—or the wood will end up darker than what you want.

Since all of the stain you apply is going to be wiped off the surface of the wood, it doesn't matter how much you brush or wipe on. If the wood has large, open pores, you may need to work against the grain to force it into the pores. Wiping it off in the same manner will insure that no spots have been missed, but to be safe, give each section a final wiping in the same direction as the grain to eliminate the possibility of any cross-grain marks.

Soft rags seem to work better than a brush on flat surfaces, both for applying and for wiping off the stain. Brushes tend to splatter on anything less than eight feet away. A rag will offer you far more control, but beware—your hands will come into intimate contact with the stain. Brushes have the edge in staining carvings, corners, and trim. Often, you'll have to load the bristles with stain in order to reach the far recesses of the carvings. Be prepared to wipe the stain out immediately, however, for exposed pores on carvings and turnings tend to absorb stain faster and deeper than flat boards. Cotton swabs and inexpensive foam brushes can serve as sponges to draw excess stain out of carvings before they turn too dark.

Once you are satisfied with how your test spot looks, start at the top of the piece and begin by applying your stain to only one section, such as the top headrest on a chair or the splashboard on a buffet. One of the crucial factors that is going to determine how dark a pigmented wiping stain will turn the wood is how long it is left undisturbed on the wood. The longer you wait to wipe it off, the deeper it penetrates and the darker the wood will become. The sooner you wipe it off, the lighter it stays. Attempting to stain the entire piece before wiping off even the first section is going to mean that certain boards are going to be exposed longer than others. As a result, parts of your furniture are going to be lighter or darker than others. Instead, stain one section, test it, time it, and, when it has reached the color you want, wipe it off. Then proceed to the next.

If for some inexplicable or unavoidable reason one particular board turns darker than you expected, pour a liberal amount of turpentine over a rag and start scrubbing. The turpentine will dilute the stain, take some of the pigments further down into the wood and allow the rag to pull others up off the wood. Speed is critical, though, for every second the stain is on the wood, the more difficult it becomes to remove.

Once the entire piece has been stained, it is best to let it dry overnight in a warm room. Many finishes will react to a fresh stain, either by pulling the stain out of the wood and into the finish, or by not drying properly. Once that happens, your only solution will be to strip it and start over.

Special ▶
Staining
Problems

End Grain

Imagine, if you will, a bundle of long, hollow straws. The sides are relatively nonporous and will not readily absorb any liquid. The ends, however, are a different matter. Here the straws are open and anxious to absorb any liquid they come in contact with.

A board is rather like that bundle of straws. The end grains of boards on a tabletop or along the edge of a chair seat absorb more stain and finish than the sides simply because these are the pores that formerly carried moisture through the living tree. In fact, some woods, such as oak or ash, are so porous that you can actually breathe through a section one inch wide.

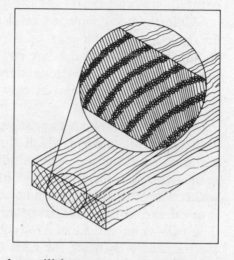

If you aren't prepared for what will happen as you stain your piece, you may be caught off guard when the end grain suddenly turns much darker than the rest of the piece. Once that happens, it is nearly impossible to reverse. The best thing you can do is to offer the end grain a sacrifice. Or, if you prefer, call it an appetizer. If you first give your end grains a light coat of tung oil, mineral oil, or even very thin shellac, the open pores will consume it instantly, thereby preventing them from absorbing as much of the stain that is going to follow a few minutes later. There will still be room for your stain, but the final color will come closer to matching that on the top of the board if you have first lightly sealed the end grain.

Sapwood

Sometimes you may encounter the opposite problem. If the original cabinetmaker used a piece of light-colored sapwood in the furniture, it generally won't turn as dark as the rest of the wood. Sapwood is a term used to represent the newest growth of a tree, that nearest the bark. Unlike the older heartwood at the center of the trunk or limb, sapwood will not have yet acquired the color found in a mature board. Conscientious cabinetmakers generally cut off any sapwood found in a board before they use it, but once furniture manufacturers discovered that they could disguise sapwood under a heavy stain, they began to use it more and more frequently. Many times you won't even realize it until after you have stripped the piece and found that between your darker walnut or cherry boards you have streaks of lighter sapwood to deal with.

Unfortunately, sapwood refuses to absorb as much stain as heartwood; thus, you may find that even after staining, lighter streaks still remain. If they are not obnoxious, you can leave them and continue to the finishing step, but if they detract from the beauty of the piece, then you may want to try adding some additional color to them.

One of the worst cases of sapwood I ever encountered was in a small walnut table in which three boards had been glued together to form the top. The middle board was no more than six inches wide, but the outside two inches on either side were nearly white. The heartwood needed no stain whatsoever; to have stained it any darker would only have blurred the beautiful walnut grain. The two white streaks of sapwood running the entire length of the top, however, made the table look ludicrous.

I began by carefully brushing on a thin coat of shellac over the heartwood to prevent the stain from darkening it. After it had dried, I applied strips of masking tape along its edges to protect it further. I then sanded the sapwood lightly before I began experimenting with various stains, hoping to find one that would match the adjacent heartwood. After trying a pigmented wiping stain, which proved ineffective, I turned to powdered stains. After a good deal more experimentation, I discovered a combination of powders I could mix in thinned shellac and brush onto the wood. I began tinting and applying thin coats to just the sapwood. Each coat took approximately twenty minutes to dry, and after about five thin coats, the lighter area began turning as dark as the heartwood. After a couple of more coats I removed the masking tape, sanded the whole top lightly, and applied the final finish.

Chemical ▶ Staining

Technically speaking, chemical staining isn't staining, because you actually change the color of the wood rather than simply add color to it. But since we can't always speak technically, we are still going to occasionally refer to it as staining. As you might have learned in your old high school laboratory, when you bring certain chemicals together, drastic changes occur. Chemical staining is similar, for when certain chemicals or their fumes are brought in contact with wood and the chemicals present in it, the color can change tremendously.

Woodworkers have experimented with chemical staining for centuries for one very good reason: unlike pigmented stains, chemical staining leaves nothing on the surface of the wood to distort the beauty of the grain. The result is a depth and clarity manufacturers have been unable to duplicate through any other means.

Since it is difficult to work with, however, chemical staining does not play a major role in the weekend refinisher's workshop. But in the event that a piece has lost its authentic color while being stripped and sanded, or if, as in the case of a new, unfinished reproduction, it never had the desired color to begin with, chemical staining may be a viable alternative for us.

One side effect of liquid chemical stains is grain raising, requiring a light sanding afterward. Chemical stains do not work on wood dough or wood putty; thus, these spots will have to be touched up afterward. They do affect metal hardware, however, so be sure to remove all pulls, hinges, and latches before applying any chemical stain.

Two important drawbacks to chemical staining occur in the application process. First, many of the required chemicals are difficult to obtain. Second, a number of them are dangerous to use. You need commercial-strength (26 percent) ammonia, for instance, to get the highly prized look of aged oak, but ammonia that strength is dangerous and must be handled wearing rubber gloves, protective glasses, and appropriate clothing in an extremely well-ventilated area.

One final warning: Do not use any chemical stain over wood that has been subjected to a chlorine bleach. Under some circumstances the chemical reaction could produce a poisonous chlorine gas—and that might just ruin your day.

Ammonia Fuming

One of the oldest chemical stains that has an application in woodworking and refinishing is that which occurs when the tannic acid in woods such as oak and ash comes in contact with ammonia. As Gustav Stickley described in his writings in 1909, the discovery may have first been made in horse stables, where the ammonia present "would darken white oak naturally, giving it the appearance which ordinarily would result from age and use." One anonymous and very crafty antiques counterfeiter claimed one of the keys to his success was covering new oak lumber with horse manure until it achieved the look of two-hundred-year-old wood.

While most chemical stains start with dry chemicals dissolved in water and applied with either a sponge or a brush to the wood, one of the most common, ammonia, is generally employed as a vapor in a process called "fuming." In order for the fumes to reach the level of concentration necessary to darken oak, chestnut, walnut, or mahogany (all woods with a naturally high tannin content), the piece must be placed in an airtight container. Large pieces, such as library tables or settles, may require the construction of a plastic tent; small parts, such as replacement pegs for a Morris chair or a new runner for a rocker, can be fumed in a three-pound coffee can, trash can, or even a plastic garbage bag. Each piece must be strategically positioned to give the fumes access to all sides; if necessary, you can suspend small pieces on cords strung from a framework, but don't use wire. Most metals will react adversely to the ammonia and may leave an unwanted stain on the wood.

Once the container and the piece to be fumed have been prepared, the liquid ammonia is carefully poured into shallow glass bowls placed around the piece. The container or tent should then be totally sealed and left undisturbed. The wood should be checked every six to eight hours, taking care not to breathe the dangerous fumes. The time required to achieve the desired color will depend on a variety of factors: the density of ammonia fumes, the temperature of the room, the amount of tannin in the wood, and the amount of finish left on the wood. The chemical reaction between the ammonia and the tannic acid will continue for a short while even after the container has been opened and the pans removed, so it is advisable to stop the process as soon as the desired color begins to appear. Use household fans to help disperse the fumes before entering the tent. Wearing a respirator would be wise.

Ammonia fumes can penetrate some thin finishes, but the process will take longer. A Mission Oak rocking chair, for instance, that has sat on a porch for years and lost much of its original color, can be refumed without necessarily removing the existing finish. It may require three or four days in the fuming tent, but if the ammonia fumes can penetrate the old shellac finish and rejuvenate the color, then the results will be well worth the wait.

When it becomes necessary to darken a small damaged area

on a piece that has been fumed, the ammonia can be applied directly from the bottle. Make sure, however, that you have a fan positioned behind you to blow the fumes away from your face. For accuracy and safety, use a small brush to apply the ammonia to the lighter area. Several applications may be necessary, however, to achieve the desired color, for the ammonia will evaporate quickly. Wrapping the area with a clear plastic bag will slow the evaporation process.

Other Chemical Stains

Another popular, but safer means of altering the color of oak was utilized by another Arts and Crafts firm whose furniture is much sought after today. Elbert Hubbard's colony of artisans, known as the Roycrofters, kept ''a barrel of soupy water left standing, apparently for years on end, full of rusting nails and other pieces of scrap metal. . . . '' After the wood had been sanded, this iron solution was brushed on the bare wood, then allowed to dry. Like the ammonia, an iron solution causes a chemical reaction with the tannic acids in the wood, turning it a light brown or, with repeated applications, a darker gray or even ebony.

A slight adjustment in their formula can speed the process for you. To a quart of vinegar add a couple of handfuls of rusty iron: nails, screws, hinges, and so forth. Let the solution stand for two weeks, then strain it through a cheesecloth, bottle it, and store it in a closed cabinet. Naturally, the longer the iron is permitted to rust in the liquid, the stronger the stain will be. When you are ready to use it, brush the solution on the oak and let it dry overnight. The next day either repeat the process or, if the color is correct, sand lightly and proceed to the finishing step.

Woods naturally low in tannin, such as pine, birch, maple, or poplar, or any whose tannin content has been depleted, can be treated with a solution consisting of one ounce of tannic acid dissolved in one quart of warm water. If tannic acid is unavailable, a strong brew of tea can be brushed directly on the wood. In either case, let the liquid remain on the wood overnight before subjecting to either ammonia or an iron solution.

Here, then, are some of the more common chemical stains. Presume, unless assured otherwise, that all chemicals are poisonous, should be kept out of the reach of pets and children, and should only be used wearing proper safety equipment in a well-ventilated room.

Wood: Oak

Color: Ebony—Soak rusty iron scraps in half gallon of vinegar until solution turns gray. Strain. Brush on, let dry; repeat until dark gray color appears; will further darken under finish.

Color: Brown—Brush ammonia on surface, let dry. Repeat until desired color is achieved.

Color: Gray—Brush on weak solution of iron sulfite, let dry. Repeat for darker gray.

Wood: Walnut

Color: Ebony—Same as for oak.

Color: Brown—Same as for oak.

Color: Gray—Dissolve one teaspoon of copper sulfate crystals in one cup of warm, distilled water. Brush on, let dry. Repeat for darker color. Rinse with water.

Wood: Mahogany

Color: Brown—Same as for oak.

Color: Reddish Brown—Mix a saturated solution of bichromate of potash in distilled water. Cap, label, and store. Dilute with equal quantity of distilled water before brushing on. Let dry, rinse with water. Neutralize with vinegar, repeat water rinse.

Wood: Pine, Maple, Birch (low tannin content)

Color: Brown—Brush on strong brew of warm tea; let dry. Follow with application of ammonia, let dry.

Color: Gray—Brush on strong brew of warm tea. Let dry. Follow with application of iron-vinegar solution (see Oak). Let dry, repeat until desired shade appears.

Dyes ▶ Aniline dyes are not widely used by weekend refinishers, but are favored by restorers and conservationists intent on saving valued antiques. Their greatest advantage is also their greatest disadvantage: they must be dissolved in a liquid (such as lacquer thinner, water, or denatured alcohol) before they can be applied. My experience has shown that they are better suited for finish repairs than for staining an entire piece of furniture. I must not be alone in my thinking, for it is nearly impossible to find a store that stocks powdered aniline dyes. If you want to experiment with aniline dyes for touch-ups, mail-order restoration supply firms offer kits equipped with nearly two dozen various powders and solvents (see Sources, Chapter 12).

One traditional nonaniline dye that remains a favorite with those who work with reproduction antique furniture is tea. A strong brew of tea brushed on and left to dry will turn many new woods a soft, golden hue reminiscent of a fine eighteenth-century antique.

Of our four major means of changing the color of wood, then, namely paint, pigmented wiping stains, chemical stains, and dyes, pigmented wiping stains remain the most popular, for they are easy to find, buy, and use. Most pigmented wiping stains are ineffective on small areas that have been damaged, such as edges that have been nicked, feet that have suffered water damage, or chips that have been filled. Even when carefully applied, they tend to either look like dried mud or wipe off with the first pass with a rag.

◀ **Touch-Up Staining**

Fortunately, alternatives do exist that make touch-ups easy:

Acrylic Paints

Artist and craft supply stores carry a wide range of acrylic paints in small, inexpensive tubes. The pigments can be thinned with water and applied with a fine brush. Since they are inexpensive and can be easily mixed, acrylic paints are ideal for blending repairs with the surrounding wood. Not only that, they can be removed with water if it appears that the touch-up does not match. This distinguishes them from oil paints, which are also inexpensive and easily mixed, but which are more difficult to remove once they have dried. If oil paints must be used, first seal the area with shellac so that you can wipe them off later without affecting the wood.

While more than two dozen different colors are available, you need only start with these six:

        burnt umber = dark brown
        raw umber   = light brown
        burnt sienna = reddish brown
        raw sienna   = yellow brown
        zinc white   = white
        lamp black   = black

With these basic tints, you can duplicate nearly every color found on the most common furniture woods. Shallow tuna cans and pet food cans are ideal containers for mixing the paints. Remove the lid and any metal burrs, then give to your cat to clean out. After a quick soap and hot water wash, it will be ready for your workshop.

Additional colors can be added to your collection for a wider range of touch-ups. With each trip to the store you might want to bring back one of these:

> Vandyke = grayish dark brown
> Venetian = deep red
> vermillion = bright red
> French ochre = light yellow
> chromium oxide = green
> ultramarine = dark blue

While experimentation is the key to a perfect match, you can use these formulas to help you get started in the right direction:

Golden oak:	3 parts raw sienna
	1 part burnt umber
Dark oak:	3 parts burnt umber
	2 parts burnt sienna
	1 part raw sienna
Light maple:	3 parts raw sienna
	1 part burnt sienna
Cherry:	3 parts burnt sienna
	1 part raw sienna
Red mahogany:	2 parts burnt sienna
	1 part Venetian red
Brown mahogany:	2 parts burnt umber
	1 part burnt sienna
Dark walnut:	Vandyke brown
	or burnt umber
Light walnut:	2 parts raw umber
	1 part burnt sienna

Zinc white and lamp black can be added in small quantities to lighten or darken any formula slightly, but too much of either will drastically change the color of the stain. It is better to increase the principal ingredient in the formula than it is to simply add black tint to any mixture that appears too light.

Finally, keep a special notebook near your mixing area to record the formulas you develop. Knowing precisely which colors you used on your cherry bookcase, for instance, will help make later repairs and touch-ups fast and easy.

Powdered Stains

Although rarely available in paint, hardware, or even craft stores, powdered stains have remained popular among professional restorers. Specialty supply firms offer dry powders that can be dissolved in water, denatured alcohol, or lacquer thinner (see Sources, Chapter 12). They are available in a wide variety of colors and can either be mixed in small quantities for touch-ups using a fine brush or can be used as a regular stain or to tint coats of shellac or lacquer. Powdered stains come in the same colors found in acrylic and oil paints.

◄ Paste Filler

Anyone who has had a bad experience with paste filler—and that includes nearly every professional refinisher—cringes at the mention of paste filling. For those who have been spared the experience, paste filling is the step that insures a glass-smooth finish on wood with open pores, such as oak, walnut, and mahogany. The process involves thinning a thick paste, tinting it the necessary color, forcing it into the pores of the wood, and then, at just the right moment, wiping off 98 percent of it before it hardens. When it works, the results are truly amazing; when it doesn't, well, ask anyone who has had a bad experience with it.

Most bad experiences with paste filler, though, are avoidable. If someone had warned me how difficult it is to sand dried paste filler out of carvings, I would have taken an entirely different approach to a fancy oak wardrobe I refinished early in my career.

Having grown up in a square, sturdy, two-story Victorian home, I was deprived of excess closet space. I suspect that's why I have always been attracted to wardrobes, those "white elephants" of the antiques business. I can recall still my amazement at having won a monstrous oak wardrobe with a bid of only forty dollars at an Illinois country auction years ago, oblivious to the wry smiles of the veteran dealers in attendance. It wasn't until I discovered that my 7½-foot monster wouldn't come apart, let alone fit in a station wagon, go through a normal doorway, or make the turn on a stairway that I understood why they had been so reluctant to bid on it. As I stood in the deserted farmyard with my 7½-foot date, I considered knocking it apart with an axe just for the wood. Instead I convinced a friend with a pickup truck to come to my rescue.

As it turned out, that particular wardrobe never made it into my house, but went directly to my friend's garage, where I had another first experience—this one with paste filler. After investing several quarts of paint and varnish remover and nearly a sleeve of sandpaper (I had a lot to learn back then), I painted it with paste filler. While I dawdled about, it quickly dried, turning a color and consistency near to that of concrete. I immediately panicked and attacked the hardened shell with rags, burlap bags, even sandpaper when it became apparent that I had waited too long. But even no. 100 grit sandpaper wasn't going to get all of the paste filler out of the fancy carvings across the top—at least not in one refinisher's lifetime.

Dejected and discouraged, I left that day never intending to return, but since my friend insisted on having his garage back, I did, this time armed with a gallon of turpentine and a wad of steel wool. I eventually removed all of the paste filler, but that took longer than it did to strip the old finish. The wardrobe looked wonderful when it was finished, but it had lost its appeal to me. My friend and I moved it one last time—from his garage into his house.

Looking back, I doubt if the oak wardrobe actually had to be stripped, but that was the way it was done those days. Today we place more value on a restored original finish than we do on a new finish, which, in addition to making life easier for us, eliminates the paste-filling process altogether.

There are ways you can avoid having to resort to paste filler. First, don't strip a piece unless it is absolutely necessary. Paint and varnish remover softens both the natural filler in the pores of the wood and the man-made filler rubbed in the open pores by the original craftsman. Cleaning and restoring an original finish insures that the filler beneath it will remain intact.

Second, if stripping is required, try to avoid using any type of stiff bristle brush or coarse steel wool. Once the filler is softened, the bristles and fibers can easily scoop it out of the pores, but if you carefully use a putty knife, medium steel wool, and rags, you can removed the old finish without automatically destroying the original filler as well.

Third, avoid harsh stripping techniques. Excessive scrubbing, tank dipping, and high-pressure water remove the softened filler; many professionals—myself included—use air pressure to clean the stripper sludge out of corners and carvings, but too much pressure will also blow out the softened filler.

It is important to know how to properly paste-fill wood, however, since you will sometimes encounter those pieces of furniture which either have been or will have to be stripped and which may lose their natural filler in the process. Leaving the pores on an oak library table or a mahogany buffet unfilled is as much an indication that a piece has been refinished as a sign proclaiming, "This table has been stripped."

You first need to know which types of wood are candidates for paste filling. Many varieties of "closed-pore" wood do not require the paste-filling step. Their pores are so small that the finish you apply will also fill the pores, creating a level surface when you are done. Some of the more frequently encountered closed-pore woods are pine, poplar, birch, maple, and cherry.

Oak, ash, walnut, and mahogany, on the other hand, have large, open pores which, if not filled, reflect light and give the wood a textured, porous look. Scandinavian Modern furniture made of either walnut or teak was purposely left unfilled and simply oiled to highlight the texture of the open-grain wood, but most of the furniture made before that particular style became popular was intended to be filled. The ultimate paste-filled effect appears in grand pianos, where the pores are completely filled and several glassy layers of finish applied over them.

Contrary to what most of us would like to believe, a finish alone is not sufficient to fill the open pores in either a new piece of oak, walnut, or mahogany, or one that has been harshly stripped. While it looks as if the pores are filling as you brush on your varnish, shellac, or lacquer, once the liquid carriers evaporate, it becomes evident that the thin layer of finish was unable to completely fill the pores. Additional coats will help, but by the time the pores have been completely filled, the rest of the wood has a thick, opaque look that distorts the natural beauty of the wood.

What you need to do is to apply a coat of paste filler to the wood AFTER it has been stained and sealed, but BEFORE it is finished.

The process involves seven steps.

Step One: Preparing the Wood

If you look closely at the pores in a piece of old oak, walnut, or mahogany, you will notice that they are often nearly black. Most paste filler comes in what is called a "natural" shade, meaning it has virtually no color. You must add color to the paste filler, and that same pigment will also stain the wood darker than what you want—UNLESS you take these two steps to prevent it:

1. Stain the wood, if necessary, to achieve the color you want.
2. Then seal the wood with a thin coat of finish to lock in the desired color.

These two steps will guarantee that the paste-filling process will not affect the color of any part of the wood except the open pores.

Step Two: Buying Paste Filler

For years the only paste filler available was "natural." The refinisher was responsible for selecting and adding color to the paste filler, for without any color, the natural filler would dry nearly white.

Recently a few companies have started selling tinted paste filler. This represents a major advancement for the weekend refinisher, for it eliminates the problem you often have with paste filler not accepting the color you add to it. The only remaining problem is finding tinted paste filler. I have yet to find a retail store that stocks it, and that means you have to anticipate and order it from one of the major refinishing supply companies (see Sources, Chapter 12).

Given the choice between ordering tinted paste filler and adding color to natural paste filler, I'll order every time. But if you don't have the time to wait for your order to arrive, read on.

Step Three: Thinning the Paste Filler

Unless the directions indicate differently, the paste filler will need to be thinned with mineral spirits to the consistency of pancake batter. I have found it best to scoop out a portion of paste filler with a wooden mixing spoon, drop it in a clean peanut butter jar, added a little mineral spirits, and begin stirring. Add more mineral spirits or paste filler and continue stirring until you reach the proper consistency. If you do not plan to use the filler immediately, close tightly and label.

Step Four: Tinting the Paste Filler

If you purchased tinted paste filler, skip to Step Five.

Your thinned paste filler will have the texture and the color of pancake batter, but if you study the pores in most antiques closely, you will notice that they are almost always dark brown or black. Your next step will be to tint your paste filler to match.

Take it on faith: Pigmented wiping stains are not strong enough to thoroughly tint natural paste filler.

Since both the stain and the paste filler are oil-based products, the paste filler will appear to take the color of the stain when the two are added, but what you won't realize is that the solid matter does not completely accept it. You mix it, you brush it on, you let it begin to harden, and you remove it—and the next day you discover white, tan, and gray pores throughout the piece, evidence that portions of the natural paste filler didn't accept the stain you added.

Instead, purchase a small tube of universal tinting colors in black, burnt umber, or whatever color is appropriate for the piece. Slowly add a few drops of color to the thinned paste filler, stirring it until the two are thoroughly combined. Continue adding drops of color until you reach the right combination of paste filler and tint.

Step Five: Applying the Paste Filler

Paste filler can be applied with either a rag or a brush, though personal experience has found that an inexpensive brush with all

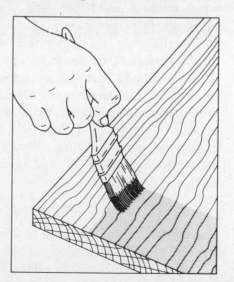

but one inch of the bristles removed works very well. Longer bristles tend to splatter the paste filler about, but the short bristles can be used like a flexible putty knife to force the particles down into the pores.

This is one of the few occasions in the refinishing process that your brush strokes should be against the grain. This way, the particles will lodge in the pores. Stir the mixture occasionally to prevent the heavier particles from settling to the bottom of the jar. Force the particles into the pores of the wood, covering all areas completely. Do not work too far ahead; complete one section, then set your brush and paste filler aside and prepare for the next step.

Step Six: Removing the Paste Filler

The most crucial aspect of the paste-filling process is judging when the paste filler has dried, but not yet hardened. Wipe it off too soon and you will pull it out of the pores. Wait too long and it won't wipe off at all.

Traditionally, refinishers have used burlap bags to remove the dry filler from the surface of the wood, but I recently watched a professional refinisher brush on a heavy coat of paste filler, wait a few minutes, and then, instead of reaching for the traditional burlap bag, take a small piece of Plexiglas (a windshield ice scraper works just as well) and, pulling it across the grain, carefully remove the majority of the paste filler. He had discovered that the plastic scraper forced the filler into the pores—unlike the burlap, which tends to pull it out. Afterward, he waited until the remaining paste filler had dried a little more and then, working first against the grain and then with it, wiped the remaining paste filler off the surface of the wood with a rag.

I have found that removing the dried paste filler in two steps, rather than one, works best. Once the paste has started to dry, I like to remove the excess, using either a plastic scraper or burlap bag across the grain. I then let it dry further before using a soft cloth to wipe off the remainder with the grain. The second drying time gives the paste filler in the pores a chance to harden and resist the final wiping.

Step Seven: Cleanup

Since I hate to do any more sanding than is absolutely necessary, I prefer to wipe off the excess paste filler. Before leaving my project, I moisten a rag with mineral spirits and *lightly* wipe off the surface. I emphasize "lightly" because the mineral spirits can soften the paste filler in the pores if you are not careful. I look for deposits in places that are difficult to sand: corners, carvings, and trim. I also watch for spots where the paste filler was pulled out of the pores and, using my fingertip, transfer excess paste filler from my earlier rag to pores that remain unfilled.

With careful attention to timing and a little practice, you can become an expert paste filler—and your projects will reflect the difference. If you need a clear comparison of the difference paste filler can make, drop by a large antiques shop that specializes in oak furniture and compare a buffet or tabletop still in its original finish with one that has been refinished, but not paste-filled. You'll notice the difference right away, because the original finish will be smooth to the touch and won't look like it was meant to match a Scandinavian Modern dining room set.

One final note: If your first application of paste filler dries and leaves some of the pores still empty, you can repeat the process the next day. It really is worth it.

Shopping List

— pigmented wiping stains   — clean rags
— turpentine   — rubber gloves
— acrylic paints   — hand cleaner
— paste filler   — screwdriver
— tints   — plastic scraper
— brushes   — burlap bags

CHAPTER 8
The Finishing Touch

When I was twenty years old and about to get married, my grand-mother pulled me aside one day and asked what for others would be a rather delicate question.

"Have you got a bed yet?"

A bit shaken, I shook my head.

"Come out to my house tomorrow," she said, "and wear some old clothes."

For my grandmother, tomorrow didn't just mean tomorrow; it meant tomorrow at seven o'clock in the morning. I arrived a half hour late and she had already started pulling bed rails out of the basement and laying them out on her lawn. I caught up with her on her next trip down and together we hauled out the foot-board and the headboard to a wonderful hard maple cannonball bed.

"Grandma, it's beautiful."

"Not yet, it's not, but it's going to be. I want you to start by scrubbing off all those fly specks. I've got banana bread in the oven, so I'll be back in a little while."

I found the turpentine and a coarse rag she had laid out for me and started scrubbing. As years of dirt and grime and a couple of hundred fly specks began disappearing, the delicate, wavy grain of the hard rock maple began to shine. Encouraged, I renewed my efforts until all of the turnings and each of the maple cannon-balls atop the four posts were clean. The bed still had its original finish, but it was worn through in places. As the turpentine evap-orated, I watched it grow dull and lifeless.

"It's clean," I announced, "but I think we'll have to strip it."

My grandmother looked up from the jar of yellow liquid she had been stirring. "Take that brush over there," she pointed, "and brush this on."

"What is it?"

"Shellac."

I groaned. "Grandma, nobody uses shellac anymore. I've got some polyurethane at home. Why don't I just run and get that?"

She shook her head. "This is just as good. My mother used it fifty years ago on all her furniture and I've been using it ever since on mine. Here, try it."

I did, but reluctantly. It brushed on easily, it dried quickly, and when I last looked in on it—seventeen years later—that shellac finish was still looking as good as the day I brushed it on.

Since that time I have probably used as much polyurethane varnish as I have shellac, but I've also used gallons of lacquer, tung oil, regular varnish, and a few other finishes as well. Each had its strengths and weaknesses, and none, so far as I could tell, was perfect.

For centuries furniture makers, refinishers, and cabinetmakers have been experimenting, trying to unlock the secret to the perfect finish. No one has yet succeeded, at least as far as we know. Many of the formulas from the seventeenth and eighteenth centuries went to the grave with their inventors—and with them may have gone the formula for the perfect furniture finish. The contest continues today, but the participants have changed. Instead of Chippendale, Sheraton, and Roubo, we now watch Formby, Watco, Deft, and Sherwin-Williams compete for the multimillion-dollar prize.

The formula for the perfect finish remains elusive, however, and for five very good reasons. In order for one particular finish to stand atop all the rest, it will have to prove that it can meet the following strict criteria:

- It must be easy to apply and maintain.
- It must enhance, not distort, the natural beauty of the wood.
- It must protect the wood indefinitely against normal wear, water, heat, insects, and the ultraviolet rays of the sun.
- It must slow the absorption and evaporation rate of moisture in the wood.
- It must not discolor, chip, crack, or peel with age.

With these goals in mind, the race continues—and the field is wide open to all entrants. Find the proper ingredients and you can become as rich and as famous as Colonel Sanders did with his secret blend of herbs and spices.

Types of ▶
Finishes

While I can appreciate and respect the museum conservationists and chemists who continue to research and experiment with early, obscure formulas calling for a pinch of sandarac, a little litharge, some gum elemi, oil of aspic, and a few drops of dragon's blood—as well as a few things I can't spell, let alone pronounce or find in the grocery store—I enjoy the convenience offered by twentieth-century finishes, imperfect though they may be.

There are approximately seven basic types of modern finishes. Since none can be considered the perfect furniture finish, you may well be using different finishes for different pieces of furniture. Once you recognize the strengths and weaknesses of each finish, you can also consider combining some of them to create one that is even stronger. In the end, it is simply a matter of deciding which type of finish is best suited to your particular project.

Paste Wax ▶
Finish

While many people think of paste wax simply as a furniture dressing, like lemon oil or Endust, it really is a finish in its own right. During the seventies, paste wax finishes were nearly trampled in the stampede for polyurethane varnishes and polymerizing oils, but now that serious questions have come up regarding many of these modern finishes, the paste wax finish is enjoying renewed popularity. French and Scandinavian country furniture, once painted, but now stripped and waxed, has helped promote paste wax as a finish again, for its natural, no-gloss beauty is a perfect compliment to the furniture's grain lines.

Paste wax should not be confused with any of the liquid waxes, which, while easy to apply, don't provide the protection offered by paste wax. Nor do shoe polishes, which, believe it or not, some people actually swear by as furniture finishes. Shoe polishes have enough trouble holding up on shoes, let alone on a table or dresser top. If you need proof, don't try it on your pine cupboard—just take a look at your shoes.

A former customer of mine once had the idea of trying car wax on a piece of furniture. It made sense: If car wax can withstand rain, high winds, rocks, and hailstorms while maintaining a high-gloss shine, then why wouldn't it do the same on his table? In theory, he was right, but he forgot that car wax, unlike furniture wax, turns white when it dries. When he had finished buffing, it looked great, but just as soon as the wax dried in the joints, cracks, and pores, it turned white, leaving him—and me—with a table that looked as if it had once been painted white.

One turpentine bath—and a fair amount of teasing—later, his table was ready for a quality furniture paste wax.

Beeswax remains the basic ingredient of most commercial paste waxes, but beeswax alone does not have the durability required of a modern furniture finish. To strengthen it, some manufacturers add carnauba wax, from a Brazilian palm tree by the same name, which, after being refined, is the hardest known furniture wax available. The higher the percentage of carnauba, the higher the quality of the wax, though 100 percent carnauba wax has proven to be too difficult to buff by hand. If the list of ingredients on the can includes either silicone additives or paraffin wax, watch out. Silicones are harmful to the wood, and paraffin wax, unlike carnauba, is a soft, inferior wax that holds down nothing but the cost.

A paste wax finish is best suited for vertical surfaces that will not receive a great deal of wear, such as mirrors, picture frames, chair and table legs, drawers, and the fronts and sides of case pieces. Tight-grained woods—such as maple, birch, cherry, or poplar—respond well to a paste wax finish. One of the most popular furniture styles today is stripped pine that is simply sanded and waxed. If you are considering using it on table, buffet, or dresser tops, however, remember that additional coats will be required every few months. Every few years, the accumulation of wax should be washed off with turpentine before you wax again.

Application

You can apply paste wax directly to raw or stained wood, but a sealer coat of one part shellac and two parts denatured alcohol will speed the job up. The shellac base will prevent the wood from absorbing the first two coats of wax and will save you from having to apply a few extra coats. The sealer should dry in less than fifteen minutes, and it will lock in the color of the wood while giving the wax a foundation upon which to build.

Paste wax can be applied with either a short-bristled brush, a soft cloth, or a pad of no. 0000 steel wool. I prefer using a pad of steel wool for the first coat, for in addition to smoothing out any remaining roughness in the wood and removing any dust particles dried in the sealer, the heat resulting from the friction between the steel wool and the wood makes the paste wax flow easier, spread more evenly, and dry faster. For that reason, it is important to work only on one section at a time, at least until you have determined how long it will take on that particular day for the wax to harden. On soggy days it may take fifteen to thirty minutes; on dry days, though, paste wax can start to harden in less than five. Unlike car wax, which starts to turn hazy as it dries, paste wax needs to be tested with a sensitive scientific instrument, like the tip of your index finger. If the wax is still fluid, wait; if it starts to shine under your fingertip, it's ready. Timing is important, for if you buff it too soon, you simply wipe off most of the soft wax; if you leave it on too long, your buffing marks will be enshrined in the hardened wax—until, like my friend with the car wax finish, you scrub it off with turpentine and start all over again.

Steps	*Materials*
1. Remove and label all hardware.	screwdriver
2. Remove all dust from the wood.	vacuum and/or tack rag
3. Protect the floor, nearby furniture, and upholstery	drop cloth newspapers masking tape
4. (optional) Seal the surface of the wood. Let dry.	one part shellac two parts denatured alcohol brush jar or can
5. Dip the applicator into the paste wax.	no. 0000 steel wool, stiff brush, or rag paste wax
6. Apply the wax liberally in small, swirling motions, forcing it into the pores.	
7. Wait 5–10 minutes.	
8. Buff lightly in small, circular motions, removing and redistributing the excess wax.	clean cloth
9. Wait 15–20 minutes or until the wax is nearly hardened.	

Steps	*Materials*
10. Buff a second time, but only in the direction of the grain, until all swirling marks disappear.	clean cloth
11. Wait 2–6 hours until the wax is completely hardened, then buff to desired sheen.	clean cloth
12. Repeat steps 5–11.	

Since thin coats dry faster and harder than thick ones, I generally plan on three thin, tough coats of wax. The second and third coats I apply with a soft cloth rather than steel wool, but use the same buffing technique. It is important that each coat be completely dry before applying the next one, for if a soft layer is trapped beneath the top one, it will never harden. Before applying the second and third coats, buff the previous coat one additional time. If it is dry, the rag will run smoothly and effortlessly across the top; if it doesn't, the wax needs more time to harden.

Maintenance

One of the things I like best about a wax finish is that it is easy to repair. If the side of your cupboard picks up a scratch, you may only need to apply another coat of paste wax to the damaged area to make it disappear. If it has to be sanded, though, remove the paste wax with a rag dipped in turpentine first—or you'll waste several expensive sheets of sandpaper trying to get through it. Afterward, simply repeat the wax application process.

◄ Oil Finishes

For those steeped in tradition, an oil finish is often considered the true "antique" finish. At one time or another most veteran refinishers and learned museum curators have presumed that the time-honored tradition of rubbing coat after coat of raw or boiled linseed oil into the wood gave the best possible furniture finish. They reverently obeyed the age-old adage:

> Once an hour for a day;
> once a day for a week;
> once a week for a year;
> once a year—forever.

Nowadays, the truth is that while linseed oil finishes are easy to find, easy to apply, and easy to repair, they are not perfect. In fact, some researchers are now warning that they can actually cause irreversible damage to the wood. In addition to darkening certain woods to the point of obscurity, raw linseed oil never completely dries; it remains tacky, attracting dust and dirt, and is impossible to remove entirely—especially when it has been applied according to the old adage.

Boiled linseed oil still remains a favorite with a few older cabinetmakers and traditional refinishers, but the complex refinement process used to turn raw linseed oil into boiled linseed oil, while helping to reduce the drying time, doesn't eliminate the more serious drawbacks of linseed oil. Many formulas and refinishers still call for boiled linseed oil, and I have always questioned its merits, especially since we now have better, more improved furniture oils at our disposal.

Theoretically, almost any natural oil can be used as a finishing oil—mineral oil, soybean oil, sunflower oil, walnut oil, cedar oil, olive oil, or vegetable oil—although their weaknesses can range from a flimsy moisture barrier to a lingering rancid odor. Of the list of natural oils, mineral oil, the main ingredient in baby oil and lemon oil, is considered the best all-purpose lightweight oil. While it is not strong enough for tables, chairs, and footstools, it is the best of its class for cutting boards, salad bowls, and any other wooden utensils that will come in contact with your food. If, after a fast handwashing, any wooden utensils appear dry and lifeless, coat liberally with mineral oil, let sit for thirty minutes, and then wipe off the excess. And unlike vegetable or olive oil, mineral oil won't turn rancid.

Manufacturers have produced and promoted two types of oil furniture finishes that have proven themselves to be stronger, more durable, and more practical than either raw or boiled linseed oil or any of the natural oils. They are the tung oils and the penetrating oils, more commonly known as Danish oils.

Tung Oil ▶
Finish

Tung oil is really China nut oil, extracted from the nuts of the tung tree. Although the tung tree is now grown in the South, it first was discovered in the Orient, where the oil was reportedly used to help preserve the Great Wall of China. Tung oil has been an important ingredient in varnishes for years, but it is only recently that it has been widely promoted as a finish in its own right.

Tung oil is available in at least two forms: pure tung oil and thinned tung oil. A minority of professional woodworkers prefer pure tung oil, but then, they generally prefer any product that is "pure," that costs more, and is harder to apply. Seriously, pure tung oil is unthinned, and it costs more than the regular tung oil. Moreover, it is more difficult to apply and is becoming harder to find. If you are a purist, go for it. If you're not, then you will want to know about regular tung oil, which has been thinned, has had drying agents added to it, is easier to use, and costs a little less.

The bottom line is this: It may take a couple of more coats, but a regular tung oil finish looks and wears just as well as a pure tung oil finish.

It's hard to find anything wrong with tung oil. Properly applied, it is a tough, durable, water- and wear-resistant finish. It enhances the natural color and grain of the wood, it is easy to apply, and its cost is comparable to that of quality varnishes, shellacs, and lacquers. As it dries, it hardens, thus permitting each coat to build upon the previous one. At the same time, though, it retains a great deal of flexibility, bending and absorbing blows before it breaks or chips.

Most of the negative reaction to tung oil has come from people who did not realize that the flexibility and fast drying associated with tung oil come with a price: namely, that it needs several coats. As one woodworker remarked to me, "Tung oil may have replaced linseed oil, but the formula is the same: Once a day for a week, once a week for a year."

I'm not so sure I'd go that far, but I do know that two coats of tung oil are just a start on open-grained woods such as oak, ash, mahogany, and walnut. The more porous the wood, the more oil it will absorb.

When weather conditions are perfect, you can apply three coats of tung oil a day: one first thing in the morning, the second at noon, and the third at the end of the day. In two days time your project can have six smooth, tough coats of finish. And if that's not enough for you or your wood, then there's nothing stopping you from continuing. The finest hand-crafted walnut grandfather clock I have ever seen had a near perfect satin sheen finish—the result of fourteen coats of hand-rubbed tung oil.

Although it is absorbed by the wood and builds on the surface, tung oil does not offer the hard protection that both varnish and lacquer do. For that reason, I don't use regular tung oil on tabletops that will get a great deal of use, such as dining room or coffee tables. (For those who insist on using tung oil on tabletops, see Combinations later in this chapter.) On chairs, vertical case pieces, frames, and accessories, however, especially those made from cherry, maple, birch, or pine, tung oil will provide a fine finish.

Application

Homer Formby made his millions not so much by his version of tung oil as by his technique. He was the first to go on national television and demonstrate how we could achieve a beautiful and lasting finish on our antiques and fine furniture—*without* using a brush. Formby's tung oil isn't that much different from the other tung oils on the market, but he recognized one human foible that Freud overlooked: most people hate brushes.

Paintbrushes, scrub brushes, varnish brushes, wire brushes, even toothbrushes: they are all associated with either pain or unpleasant tasks. When Homer Formby went before millions of viewers to stick his fingers in a puddle of tung oil, he found an eager audience excited about the prospect of never having to ruin another seven-dollar varnish brush again. As a result, more people today are using tung oil than ever before.

Steps	*Materials*
1. Remove and label all hardware.	screwdriver
2. Remove all dust from the wood.	vacuum and/or tack rag
3. Protect the floor, nearby furniture, and upholstery.	drop cloth newspapers masking tape
4. Place the section to be finished in a horizontal position.	workbench or sawhorses
5. Apply a liberal coating of oil to the wood.	tung oil soft rag, brush, or fingers
6. Allow to be absorbed 10–15 minutes or until oil becomes tacky.	
7. Wipe off excess.	clean cloth

Steps   *Materials*

8. Let dry a minimum of 1–3 hours.

9. Repeat process. (Option: if   no. 0000 steel wool
   surface feels rough, buff dried
   coat lightly.)

Tung oil, like all oil finishes, goes on faster, farther, and deeper (and dries more quickly, too) if it is first warmed in a double boiler. If you don't want to go to that much trouble, fill the sink or a pan with hot tap water and set your bottle or can of tung oil in that for a few minutes. It's optional during the summer months, but mandatory if it has been in a cold car or unheated garage for more than a few hours in the winter.

If the phone rings and, upon your return, you find that your liberal coating of oil has become too tacky to wipe off, don't panic. Simply pour more oil on top of the sticky mess and wait. In a few minutes you'll be able to wipe off all the excess oil.

One of the advantages of tung oil has also proved to be a disadvantage for most of us. I estimate that I have had to throw away nearly one fourth of all the tung oil I have ever purchased simply because it dried in the container. Tung oil is conditioned to begin hardening when it comes in contact with oxygen, but it has not been trained to distinguish between the air in the container and that around your furniture. As the volume of air in the container increases and the volume of tung oil decreases, the process starts—and may not finish until the remainder of the tung oil has hardened. The solution is simple, although the manufacturers don't always tell you that on the backs of the cans. You can either transfer what is left to a smaller, yet well-marked container, or you can do as one refinisher suggested and drop in clean marbles until the oil rises, forcing all of the air out of the can. Either way, if you eliminate the air, you can save the rest of your tung oil— and about four dollars.

Maintenance

Shallow surface scratches in a tung oil finish can often be removed using a pad of no. 0000 steel wool dipped in the oil. Buff the entire section lightly, keeping the pad well moistened. You can apply extra pressure to the damaged area, but be careful not to buff through to the wood. Wipe off the excess oil and steel wool slivers, then follow the steps outlined above for a final application of tung oil.

Unlike varnish or lacquer, furniture finished with tung oil may require semiannual applications in order to maintain the protection it requires. Before following the recommended steps, wipe off any polishes, waxes, or excess oils with a rag dipped in turpentine. Simply adding another coat of oil to the piece you refinished six months earlier may be all it needs to regain that missing glow.

Penetrating ▶ Oil Finishes

Several companies have developed a penetrating oil finish that hardens in the wood. While these finishes may contain some tung oil or boiled linseed oil (manufacturers are reluctant to reveal their formulas), they deserve a category of their own. Among them are Watco Danish Oil, Minwax Antique Oil, and Deft's Danish Oil Finish. They are somewhat unique in that they are available both clear or with added coloring pigments. Each also appears to contain drying agents as well as a variety of other ingredients that, while remaining secret, have certainly helped these penetrating oils to be an improvement over the early raw and boiled linseed oil finishes.

These oil finishes are easy to apply with either a brush or a rag, dry hard in a matter of minutes, and offer protection similar to that of standard tung oil. While the pigmented oil can be used as a shortcut in the refinishing process, it does offer a time-saving solution to refinishing projects that have suffered from a slight loss of color due to overuse, water damage, or the bleaching effects of the sun.

I once was called to a retirement village to pick up a teak dining room table which the owner, an elderly woman who loved to bathe her plants with sunshine, was convinced needed to be refinished. The table had been made in the fifties and purchased while she and her husband, a building contractor, had been traveling in Sweden. While she had obviously taken good care of the table, as soon as the leaves were set in, it became evident that the sun had bleached away much of the color.

She had asked two other refinishers to make estimates on refinishing the table, which they had, and I was tempted to do the same. I realized, though, that there wasn't any need to; the problem wasn't with the finish, but the lack of one. I pulled from my touch-up kit a can of walnut-tinted Minwax Antique Oil and tested it on an inconspicuous spot on the apron. It matched the leaves perfectly. The next afternoon I returned with a drop cloth, a pint of oil, and some clean rags—and forty-five minutes later I was on my way out the door again.

Although they do dry and harden, none of the penetrating oil finishes offers the most durable surface protection. Like tung oil, they are best suited for furniture that will not experience hard wear or constant contact with lamps, ashtrays, dinnerware, and small toys. Clocks, vertical case pieces, chairs, rockers, and accessories are excellent candidates for a penetrating oil finish. Don't get me wrong, they can be used on tabletops, but you have to realize that a seventy-year-old lady is apt to be a bit less hard on her table than a pair of seven-year-old boys.

Application

Since the oils made by the various firms have different amounts of driers added to them—driers that respond according to humidity and air temperature—watch your first application carefully to judge when it becomes tacky. For that reason, it is advisable to work in sections and not attempt to cover the entire piece all at once.

Steps	*Materials*
1. Remove and label all hardware.	screwdriver
2. Remove all dust from the wood.	vacuum and/or tack rag
3. Protect the floor, nearby furniture, and upholstery	drop cloth newspapers masking tape
4. Place the section to be finished in a horizontal position.	workbench or sawhorses
5. Apply a liberal coating of oil to the wood	oil soft rag, brush, or fingers (optional: no. 320 wet-dry sandpaper)

Steps	*Materials*

6. Allow to be absorbed 10–15 minutes
   or until oil becomes tacky.

7. Wipe off excess　　　　　　　　　　clean cloth

8. Let dry overnight.

9. Repeat process. (Option: if surface　　no. 0000 steel wool
   feels rough, buff dried coat lightly.)

The number of coats required will depend on how much the wood absorbs. Leaving excess oil on the surface won't contribute toward any sort of a surface buildup, but it might become a sticky mess. Penetrating oil finishes rely on their hardening ability once they have been absorbed into the wood. When the wood has taken in all the oil that it is capable of consuming, you should wipe off the remainder completely.

Maintenance

As you can imagine, wood finished with oil is susceptible to scratches, but fortunately, most shallow ones can be removed simply by applying another coat of oil with either a pad of no. 0000 steel wool or, for deeper scratches, no. 320 sandpaper. Semiannual applications may be necessary to replenish lost oils.

Shellac Finish ▶ Remember the museum conservationists who, when they realized their antiques were turning dark and sticky, decided to find another finish to use in place of linseed oil? They now have a new slogan: "Back to Shellac."

My grandmother wouldn't be surprised.

Historically speaking, shellac may well have been the first surface finish to be developed. Shellac reigned as the most popular furniture finish through the eighteenth and nineteenth centuries, but its fall from favor was due not so much to its weaknesses—which it has—but to the technique with which it was often applied. "French polishing" involved carefully prepared cotton pads, called "rubbers," which were dipped in a thin shellac solution before they were wisked across the surface of the wood in a variety of patterns. The objective was to apply just enough pressure to the rubber to deposit additional shellac on the surface with each pass. It is a tricky process: too much pressure meant that the rubber would be removing the shellac previously deposited; too little allowed the shellac to harden on the rubber instead of the wood.

While a dwindling band of disciples still uses the technique, French polishing requires the sensitivity of a surgeon and the patience of an elementary school teacher. The resulting finish has been described as ''phenomenally lustrous and durable,'' but it can take up to sixty days of French polishing to achieve a piano finish. When asked, I'm sure all of the famous eighteenth- and nineteenth-century cabinetmakers claimed to be using it, but after trying it a few times myself, I wonder how many of those guys really went to all that trouble.

If the tedious nature of French polishing wasn't enough to make them search high and low for a better finish, I don't know what would be. Toward the end of the nineteenth century, additional forms of lacquer and varnish were being developed, and shellac, both as a brushing and a padding finish, began to drop in popularity. In time it was considered weak, ineffective, and old-fashioned. Eventually it was removed from the shelves of most stores.

Now that polyurethane varnishes are under attack and museum curators are questioning the long-term effects of penetrating and even tung oils on fine antiques, shellac is getting a second look—and it's looking better than expected.

Like salt and pepper or bread and butter, shellac and denatured alcohol are a team. You don't buy one without buying the other. If you are a purist, you can order shellac flakes from one of the specialty supply firms list in Chapter 12 and dissolve them in denatured alcohol to create your own particular ''cut'' of shellac. If you aren't, then you can buy liquid shellac right off the shelf, all ready to use. Be sure to read the lid, though, for shellac has a shelf life of approximately one year, and either the date of manufacture or the expiration date should be clearly stamped on the top. Old shellac does not dry properly; in fact, it sometimes doesn't dry at all, which means you have to wash it off with denatured alcohol and go screaming back into the store where you bought it—unless you've held on to it for more than a year.

Shellac is not an iron man finish. It can be scratched, it is rather thin, and it is more likely to react unfavorably to heat, water, and alcohol. So why bother with it? Because shellac is easy to apply, it dries in a matter of minutes, it's easy to repair, and it comes the closest of any of the surface finishes to looking the most natural on wood. Museum curators prefer it for their fine antiques over all of the other finishes primarily because, if they ever need to, they can simply wash the shellac off with a denatured alcohol bath without posing any risk to the wood or its patina. In their jargon, it is "reversible,"—another term that is destined to become as popular at cocktail parties as "patina."

Personally, after having been spoiled by expensive lacquer spray equipment and troubled by varnish's unpredictable drying times, I have found shellac to be an acceptable compromise for my garage workshop. Although it does not have the strength of varnish, it does offer the speed of lacquer. And what it lacks in strength it makes up for in flexibility. Unlike the new plastic finishes, shellac will bend extensively before it chips and peels.

Not all that long ago I was refinishing two pieces simultaneously—not that that is unusual, it is just that both of these were oak tables. One was a new, unfinished oak table that was going in a breakfast nook; the other was a 150-year-old library table. The new oak table was going to be subjected to gallons of hot coffee, milk, and maple syrup, not to mention all their accomplices; I used polyurethane varnish on it. The antique library table had originally been finished with shellac, which had been stripped by a previous owner. That was going into a study, where it would be subjected to only the occasional cup of coffee or sandwich plate. I refinished it with shellac. A year later the shellac on the library table was holding up well; it had a few scratches here and there, but nothing that another coat of shellac wouldn't fix. The polyurethane finish, however, was beginning to chip around the edges, and I could detect air pockets in places under the finish. I estimated it would last perhaps another two years before it would have to be stripped and refinished.

I'm not going to tell you that the shellac wouldn't have looked just as bad as the varnish on the breakfast table. But we may have presumed too quickly that polyurethane varnish was going to replace it entirely. I continue to use shellac on fine antiques, especially clock cases, tall vertical pieces, chairs, and small tables. I like it on tabletops, but I like standard varnish on tabletops, too. But more on that later.

Application

Since it is susceptible to moisture, shellac should not be applied in the middle of a thunderstorm or on one of those days when both the temperature and the humidity are hovering around ninety. It has been known to turn hazy or white on those days, but if you avoid them, you'll find that shellac dries in a matter of minutes, enabling you to apply your finish and display your piece in less than a day.

If you are inclined to play with your finish, brace yourself to resist the temptation. Shellac does not react well to excessive brushing. It dries too quickly for that. Load your brush up with shellac, get it on the wood, and spread it out over a small area quickly. Unlike varnish, I don't try to apply it across the grain first and then straighten out all of my brush marks with a final "tipping-off." On an ideal day shellac will start drying in seconds and tug at your brush. Don't be tempted to go back and touch up a spot you missed or straighten out a cross-grain brush mark. Chances are you didn't miss that spot. Rather, it has already dried.

Steps	*Materials*
1. Remove and label all hardware.	screwdriver
2. Remove all dust from the wood.	vacuum and/or tack rag
3. Protect the floor, nearby furniture, and upholstery.	drop cloth newspapers masking tape
4. Place the section to be finished in a horizontal position.	workbench or sawhorses
5. Thin first coat of liquid shellac with equal part denatured alcohol.	shellac denatured alcohol jar with lid
6. Brush on first coat.	brush
7. After it dries, sand lightly.	no. 220 sandpaper or no. 000 steel wool
8. Remove all dust and dirt particles.	tack rag and/or vacuum
9. Brush on second coat without thinning.	
10. After it dries, sand lightly.	
11. Repeat until suitable finish is built on surface.	

It's tough to know when you've built up a suitable finish, but you will soon learn. Each coat of shellac bonds with the one beneath it, giving it additional strength and flexibility with each pass of your brush. Each coat also dries thinner than it goes on, for as the denatured alcohol evaporates, it leaves the shellac alone on the wood. In the old French polishing technique, the craftsman might apply a dozen or more coats to build up one tough, durable film of finish. Although you will be using a brush instead of a polishing wad, you will still be applying thinner coats than you might use with varnish. Experience has shown me that while three or four coats of shellac are sufficient on vertical surfaces, any parts that might someday have to protect the wood against water, alcohol, or a hot plate should have at least five or six coats.

Maintenance

Unlike the oil finishes, shellac will not require additional coats every six months to replenish the lost finish. Since each coat of shellac dissolves and bonds with the previous one, an additional coat will make any minor scratches disappear. You should sand and touch up deeper scratches before adding another coat of finish.

Shellac, like all surface finishes, can be strengthened with a coat of paste wax (see Combinations a little later in this chapter), but you should first remove any waxes or polishes with turpentine before applying another coat of shellac.

Lacquer ▶ Finishes

Lacquer is the uncontested king of the furniture finishing world. In sheer numbers, more pieces of furniture are now finished with lacquer than all of the other furniture finishes combined. Furniture factories, full-time cabinetmakers, and professional refinishers have all switched to lacquer because it dries as fast as shellac, but with the toughness and durability of varnish. And if that weren't enough, lacquer can easily be tinted with special stains, doctored to produce satin finishes, or rubbed out to a high-gloss piano finish.

So why isn't this the "perfect finish"?

Because lacquer, with one exception, has to be sprayed using expensive equipment in a tightly controlled environment. It requires an air compressor, air hoses, a high-quality spray gun with sensitive adjustments for both the flow of lacquer and the injection of air, a dust-free spray booth, and a high-powered, explosion-proof ventilation system. A modest estimate of the capital required for a small spraying operation would be three thousand dollars—a hefty sum for a weekend hobby.

And it won't fit in your kitchen.

After using professional spray equipment for nearly a decade, I decided to sell mine when I moved from Iowa to North Carolina. One of the first decisions I had to make as I was planning my garage workshop was whether or not I was going to invest in an air compressor and spray equipment. For weeks I wavered, but once I grew accustomed to having a brush in my hand again—not to mention the extra three thousand dollars to spend on Gustav Stickley furniture—I never (well, hardly ever) regretted the decision. Granted, I miss the speed, the ease, and the evenness of a lacquer finish, especially on chairs, but once I reverted from being a full-time pro to a weekend refinisher, I never could justify the expense.

For those who want to pursue the notion of buying and using spray equipment, I would recommend that you scan back issues of *Fine Woodworking* magazine for articles written by experienced woodworkers who spray lacquer daily. They are willing to share their individual experiences and solutions for spraying problems, and offer suggestions on such matters as building a spray booth.

And though you and I have decided not to invest in spray equipment, that does not mean that we cannot make use of lacquer, because it is still available to us in two forms: brushing lacquer and aerosol lacquer.

Aerosol Spraying

Aerosol cans of lacquer were never intended for finishing medium-sized to large projects. Not long ago, though, I found myself trying to get excited about varnishing a child's chair I had stained the previous day. It was a Saturday morning and I wanted to go to the Raleigh flea market, so I took what I thought was a chance—I popped the lid off an aerosol can of lacquer and started spraying. In less than three minutes the first coat was on, and five minutes later it was dry. I picked up the can and gave it a second coat, taking care to hit those places I had missed the first time and not to get any runs. Once I did, but a quick swipe with my finger and a follow-up pass with the can, and all traces of it were gone. After a light smoothing with a pad of no. 000

steel wool, I gave the small chair a third coat—and less than thirty minutes after I had started, I was on my way to the flea market.

Now, don't get me wrong. I am not about to finish a dining room table with eight cans of aerosol lacquer. While the manufacturers have improved the spray patterns, they are still too narrow, too unpredictable to use on large, flat surfaces. It might be fast, but it certainly wouldn't be inexpensive.

I am a real believer, though, in partial refinishing. If you find a table that has sat in a damp basement and has lost the finish around its feet, you don't have to refinish the entire piece. With a little light sanding, a touch of stain to replenish the color, and a series of careful mistings with a can of aerosol lacquer, you can refinish the damaged areas without having to resort to a brush, let alone a gallon of stripper.

Aerosol cans, though, come with a few problems that you can deal with if you do the following:

First, *shake the can*. Like other types of finish, the heavier ingredients settle to the bottom. Since you cannot see when they have been thoroughly mixed, shake the can for twice as long as the directions indicate and repeat this periodically as you work.

Second, *always spray for a few seconds on a piece of scrap wood* or cardboard before turning to your project. This will enable you to blow out any particles around the tip or any unmixed finish in the tube without affecting your project.

Third, *keep your distance*. The secret to a run-free, even application is to hold the can the manufacturer's recommended distance from the project and to move your entire arm and not just the can as you travel the length of the board. There should be no flexibility from your elbow down to the tip of the can. Your wrist should remain locked. Start spraying a few inches beyond your project so that your can is already in motion when the spray first hits the wood. Continue moving at a steady pace, but do not release the button until you have passed beyond the wood and are actually spraying into the air again.

Fourth, *alternate spraying across the grain on one application and then spraying with the grain on the next*. This will insure even coverage. Overlap each pass slightly to eliminate bare sections. Avoid spot spraying. If you missed one section, make a pass the entire length of the board. Don't risk a motionless blast from close range.

Fifth, *plan on several light applications* rather than one or two heavy passes. Too much finish will result in a run or sag that you will have to let dry and sand off before you can continue.

Finally, to insure that your can of lacquer will operate when you next reach for it, regardless of whether that is five minutes or five weeks later, step outside, *turn the can upside down, and spray until all of the lacquer has been discharged from the feeder tube and the tip.* If you don't, it may harden and will prevent you from ever using the rest of the finish you have already paid for.

Brushing Lacquer

If you have ever stepped into a refinishing shop or antiques mall and smelled something that took you back to your high school wood shop days, it was probably Deft. Industrial arts instructors love Deft; it is a lacquer that can be brushed on like varnish, but unlike varnish, it dries in minutes, not hours. The development of Deft and other brushing lacquers kept those wood shop drying rooms from becoming as crowded—or as sticky—as a pep bus in August.

Brushing lacquers have been specially formulated to extend their drying time from seconds to minutes. This allows you to brush them on much as you would varnish. Like all lacquers, brushing lacquers dry even thinner than they go on, requiring several coats to build a tough, protective layer over the wood. For that reason and the fact that it requires a quick stroke to brush it out before it begins to set up, many refinishers have stuck with varnish, despite the knowledge that they would probably appreciate the faster-drying lacquer.

Steps	*Materials*	
1. Remove and label all hardware.	screwdriver	◀ **Brushing Lacquer Finish**
2. Remove all dust from the wood.	vacuum and/or tack rag	
3. Protect the floor, nearby furniture, and upholstery	drop cloth newspapers masking tape	
4. Place the section to be finished in a horizontal position.	workbench or sawhorses	

Steps	Materials
5. Thin first coat of lacquer with an equal part of thinner.	brushing lacquer lacquer thinner jar with lid
6. Brush on first coat.	brush
7. After it dries, sand lightly.	no. 220 sandpaper or no. 000 steel wool
8. Remove all dust and dirt particles.	tack rag and/or vacuum
9. Brush on second coat without thinning.	
10. After it dries, sand lightly.	
11. Repeat until suitable finish is built on surface.	

Brushing lacquers are available in either satin or high-gloss finish; the high gloss is slightly tougher than the satin, which has had flattening agents added to it. Refinishers who want a satin finish often use a high-gloss for all but the final coat, switching only then to a satin lacquer. Others prefer to stick with the high-gloss throughout the finishing process, after which they rub out—and off—the glossiness.

Maintenance

Since lacquer thinner can dissolve hardened lacquer, it follows that a coat of lacquer thinned with lacquer thinner and applied over a scratched and worn finish will act as a reviver. Small scratches can be rubbed out using dry no. 0000 steel wool followed with an additional coat. Once a lacquer finish has hardened, all that is necessary to maintain it is an occasional dusting and, like all finishes, care to minimize contact with standing water, alcohol, excessive heat, and sunlight.

Varnish Finish ▶ I enjoyed the time when varnish was easy to understand. You went to the store and, depending on whether you were varnishing your front door or a footstool, you picked out either interior or exterior varnish. Now there are nearly as many varnishes as there used to be finishes: alkyd resin varnish, ester gum alkyd varnish, phenolic resin varnish, polyurethane varnish, and even latex varnish. That some are also available in aerosol cans makes it all even more confusing.

Despite the fact that the names can be as intimidating to read as a prescription, each major type of varnish has a specific use. Loosely translated, they look something like this:

Type	*Common Name*	*Use*
alkyd resin varnish	interior	furniture
phenolic varnish	spar or marine	exterior wood
polyurethane varnish	plastic	table and bar tops

Interior varnish is the most popular and easiest of the various types of varnishes to work with. It also comes as close as any to being the perfect finish. It brushes on well, is resistant to wear, water, heat, and alcohol, and helps stabilize the moisture in the wood. While it does not offer the resistance to scratching and moisture of its cousin, polyurethane, it has proven itself to be more flexible under stress, easier to repair, and easier to rub out.

Spar varnish, also called marine or exterior varnish, is designed never to completely harden. This curious characteristic makes it useful on boats, outdoor furniture, and exterior doors, which have to endure both abuse and the daily expansion and contraction of the wood. A brittle finish would wear off faster and would be more apt to chip or crack under stress than the softer spar varnish. As a result, spar varnish does not rub out well, nor does it have the look and the feel you want for your interior furniture.

Polyurethane varnish is a complex mixture of ingredients that might best be described as liquid plastic. Originally intended for bar tops, it is currently being used on everything from unfinished furniture to hardwood floors to fine antiques. Polyurethane varnish is unsurpassed as a protective finish, but like the home run hitter who also leads the league in strikeouts, it also has the dubious distinction of being the least natural appearing of all of the major finishes.

Its greatest strength is also its greatest weakness: polyurethane varnish is so good at repelling other liquids that it can even repel itself. It has a hard time adhering to any surface and accepting additional coats of finish. As the directions indicate, specially designed sealers should be used before polyurethane varnish can be safely applied. In addition, the timing of second and third coats is critical: wait too long and the two may not bond; too soon and the first coat may never harden. Read the manufacturer's directions carefully and stick to them—or your polyurethane varnish may not stick to your tabletop.

Brushes

Interior varnish has lost some of its longtime supporters to tung oil and the penetrating oils simply because they don't require a brush. As I said before, most of us don't like brushes: we don't enjoy paying seven dollars for a good varnish brush, we don't know what to do with a brush between coats, we don't enjoy cleaning it when we are finished, and we especially don't enjoy finding a stiff brush each time we start a new project.

Before you decide to forget all varnishes and return to the tung oil section, remember that none of the oils can give you the protection of any of the varnishes. So what if you have to use a brush? All you need are a few tips on buying and taking care of a brush— even not taking care of a brush—to get over that hurdle.

First, if you don't want to ever clean a brush again, you don't have to. You can buy a handful of inexpensive, disposable foam brushes for less than seventy-five cents each, use them once, and throw them away. No cleaning, no mess, no jar of turpentine, no guilt. Personally, I love foam brushes. They come in a variety of sizes, hold up pretty well, carry a nice load of varnish to the wood, don't splatter, don't shed bristles, and don't make me feel like I have to clean them when I'm done.

Unfortunately, foam brushes begin to dissolve when they come in contact with denatured alcohol or lacquer thinner, so they're not a good tool to use with either shellac or brushing lacquer. They do work well for varnish, though, and offer better control than a cheap bristle brush.

If you are the type who enjoys buying a good brush and taking care of it, much as you would any good-quality tool, then you may want to invest in the seven-dollar varnish brush. Either synthetic or natural bristles are suitable for brushing on varnish, although veteran refinishers will generally insist on natural-bristle brushes. A blend of ox hair and china hog bristle makes a fine all-purpose varnish brush that will last as long as you continue to keep it clean.

In choosing either type of brush, synthetic or natural bristle, look for the following characteristics:

- a gentle taper of the bristles from the handle to the tip
- good spring in the bristles
- bristles at least 50 percent longer than their width
- no excessive shedding
- a comfortable handle—preferably long, round, and unpainted

Many years ago I took the advice of a famous author of refinishing books and began buying new, inexpensive or moderately priced brushes for each project. His theory was that it is better to start each project with a new, inexpensive brush and then, after a quick cleaning, delegate it to stripping and staining afterward. The problem I found with his theory was that inexpensive and moderately priced brushes shed worse than my cat. I was spending more time picking bristles out of my finish than I was varnishing. I have come to the conclusion that, as far as I am concerned, there are only two types of varnish brushes: foam throwaways and expensive clean-it-and-keep-it bristle brushes.

The secret to maintaining a good brush isn't in how you use it, but how you clean and store it. Begin by selecting the proper solvent. For varnish, that is turpentine, also called mineral spirits, paint thinner, or turpentine substitute. Pour enough in a jar or can to cover one half the length of the bristles, then work the bristles around in it. Make sure the turpentine has a chance to penetrate to the interior bristles, where varnish will remain, especially if you have been working with your brush upside down. It is better to work the brush around in the turpentine, using your fingers if necessary for good penetration, than let it soak and allow the bristles to curl.

After the turpentine has had an opportunity to dissolve all of the varnish, wash the bristles with soap and hot water, then rinse thoroughly. This is the step most people leave out; and those are the same people who can't understand why their varnish brush is stiff the next day. What happens is that the turpentine evaporates, leaving a deposit of varnish around the bristles. The soap and warm water remove the varnish after the turpentine has dissolved it, before it has a chance to reharden.

After the brush has been rinsed, mold the bristles into shape with your fingers. I like to wrap the brush in a paper towel held on with a rubber band around the handle, not the bristles. To insure that the bristles will dry and that they will dry as you molded them, hang your brush from a nail, clothespin, or spring clip. I generally drill a small hole in the end of the handle of my good brush so that I can hang it on the same nail each time. I leave it wrapped in the paper towel just to keep dust from settling on the bristles.

What about between coats? What do I do with my brush for six, twelve, or twenty-four hours? Naturally, you can clean it, and perhaps you should, but I have been known to resort to a few tricks of the trade to save myself some time and trouble. In more than one instance I have simply wrapped my brush tightly in aluminum foil or wax paper and popped it in the freezer. The finish won't harden in the cold, so you can pull it out and brush on your next coat. Other times I have rinsed out the majority of the varnish with turpentine and then wrapped the bristles in either foil, wax paper, or a freezer bag. The important thing is to keep the air away from the bristles. If the turpentine can't evaporate, the varnish won't harden.

Finally, there is the matter of what to do when you find your brush is no longer usable, or at least not suitable for varnish. First, if you can still flex the bristles, then you might toss it in the coffee can you use for your stripping. There is no sense in buying a brush just for splashing on stripper when you already have one that's no good for anything else. If we recycle our cans and bottles, why not do the same with our brushes?

If your treasured seven-dollar varnish brush has been improperly cleaned, then I would recommend buying a small can of commercial "brush saver." One of the best I have ever used is Zip-Kleen's Brush and Roller Cleaner, which can be strained and reused so long as it has not been mixed with water. It is a combination of solvents, including methylene chloride and acetone alcohol, that can help you to save your good brush rather than have to replace it. As with all specialty products, read and follow all recommended directions carefully.

Dust

One other problem that refinishers associate with varnish more than any other finish is dust. Part of the problem you can blame on the varnish itself, which stays wet long enough to permit dust to settle and dry in it. If the dust doesn't come in the varnish, then it has to come from somewhere—even if it's out of thin air.

If you have a problem with dust in your finish, you should be able to pinpoint it just by checking the following:

The **AIR**—Tiny particles of dust seem to be constantly floating through the air, but you may be aggravating the situation if you are varnishing near an active furnace or air-conditioning duct. Working in an old basement can also be a problem, especially if the foot traffic above you is shaking dust off the floor joists and into your varnish. If your workshop area is doomed to be dusty, consider finding another spot for your varnishing. Otherwise, make sure that the air around your project is going to be as dust-free as possible—and will remain that way while the varnish dries.

The **FLOOR**—I can remember a time when I stopped on the way back from making a delivery to watch a man varnish an oak dresser in his garage. He used a tack rag to get all of the dust off the wood, opened a new brush, and even cleaned off his work-bench. His floor, however, was covered with dust, dirt, and shavings, and from where I sat in my van across the street I could see that every time he moved around the dresser to varnish another section, he stirred up a small cloud of dust that landed and stuck to the wet varnish.

The first time I watched Vern and Don at Classic Auto Coach-works prepare to paint a Mercedes, they hosed down the walls, floor, even the ceiling, in their spray booth just to wash away any dust that might have been there. If you are working on a dusty cement floor, consider taking a few minutes just to hose it off before you start varnishing. Believe me when I tell you it's faster and easier than sanding off dust that has dried in your finish.

The **BRUSH**—Just because a brush is new, that doesn't mean it's clean. Once you dip a dusty brush in a new can of varnish, you have contaminated the varnish and increased the chances of getting dust on your furniture. The solution is simple: Dip your brush into some clean turpentine first, then shake and brush it out on a piece of clean scrap wood. The little turpentine remaining in the brush isn't going to hurt the varnish, but the dust that had been there before certainly would have.

The **WOOD**—Since wood is the major source of dust, it should receive the majority of your attention. Unfortunately, most refinishers get in such a hurry to see what the varnish is going to look like on their wood that they don't bother to clean all of the dust out of the pores, joints, and cracks. But if you don't, your varnish will.

Dry rags and workbench brushes may actually create more of a dust problem than they solve. They don't remove any dust, but simply push it someplace else: another spot on the furniture, on the floor, in the air, or on your clothes. Regardless of where it goes, chances are much of it is going to settle back down on the wood—right after you finish laying on a wet, sticky coat of varnish.

The best way to remove dust from a piece of furniture is with a vacuum cleaner. The old canister type with the flexible hose and bristle brush attachment is ideal for your work area. Instead of just pushing the dust around, you can remove it entirely—from corners, drawers, joints, cracks, repairs, and pores. In seconds it's gone forever. If there isn't one in your closet, start checking the yard sales, community auctions, thrift shops, and appliance repair centers. People don't seem to like them anymore, and that just makes it easier for you to find one for your workshop.

The alternative—or perhaps the companion—to the vacuum cleaner is the tack rag. You can either make them or buy them, depending on your frame of mind. I prefer to make my own, and generally I make several at a time. Take a package of cheesecloth and cut it up into two-foot squares. Dampen each with turpentine, working it into all parts of the cloth and then wringing out the excess. I then wad the wet cheesecloth up into a loose ball and begin adding varnish to it a tablespoon at a time. After each spoonful, I work the varnish into the cheesecloth vigorously, spreading it throughout the fabric. I only add enough varnish to make the entire cloth sticky. Once it (and my hands) are thoroughly tacky, I fold the cloth into a six-inch square and insert it into a self-sealing freezer bag. I then force out all of the air, seal the bag, and set it next to my can of varnish.

When it comes time to remove any remaining dust particles from the wood, I remove one of the tack rags from its bag and begin wiping off the wood. When the rag becomes dirty, I lay it out to dry and later discard it. If the rag dries out before it wears out, however, I just add a little turpentine and a little varnish to rejuvenate it.

Varnish Finish

Steps	*Materials*
1. Remove and label all hardware.	screwdriver
2. Remove all dust from the wood.	vacuum and/or tack rag
3. Protect the floor nearby furniture, and upholstery.	drop cloth newspapers masking tape
4. Place the section to be finished in a horizontal position.	workbench or sawhorses
5. Brush on a sanding sealer.	commercial sanding sealer or 50 percent varnish and 50 percent turpentine mixture brush
6. Let dry.	
7. Sand lightly, then remove dust.	no. 220 sandpaper tack rag
8. Brush on a coat of unthinned varnish.	varnish
9. Remove brush strokes by "tipping-off," i.e., running tips of bristles the length of the board with the grain.	brush
10. Let dry.	
11. Repeat steps 7–10.	

Since varnish builds on the surface of the wood faster than any of the other finishes, fewer coats are generally necessary. Vertical surfaces may only require two coats, but table, dresser, and buffet tops should receive a third coat.

Maintenance

Varnish is tough. While it may not be as easy to apply as an oil finish, and while it may not dry as fast as shellac, once it has been applied, it will take more abuse and require less maintenance than any other finish. And though it is never a good idea to subject any finish to extended exposure to dirt, water, heat, and sunlight, varnish is the most forgiving of the furniture finishes and won't demand that you do much more than occasionally wipe it down with a rag moistened with lemon oil. Unlike shellac, lacquer, and oil, however, when varnish is scratched it cannot be repaired simply by applying another coat of finish. Minor scratches can be rubbed out with no. 0000 steel wool and oil or be wet-sanded (see Chapter 6). Deeper scratches, though, can only be disguised (see Chapter 2) until the time comes to refinish the section again.

Finish ▶
Combinations
Like peanut butter and chocolate, combining two well-known finishes can oftentimes produce a third. The number of possibilities with just a half dozen major finishes is beyond my arithmetic, but I want to introduce you to the three most important just to give you an idea what you can discover when you start experimenting.

Paste Wax over Shellac

What do you get when you combine two historical finishes, each with a major weakness?

One strong historical finish.

I happen to be one of those people who like the finish on my antiques to look appropriate to the piece. Now, I'll use spar varnish on my outside pine doors, polyurethane varnish on my new, unfinished oak table, and professionally sprayed lacquer on my cherry kitchen cabinets, but when I'm refinishing a hundred-year-old rocking chair, I like to use a finish that looks like it might actually constitute the original finish.

For many pieces that finish is shellac, but shellac doesn't have the resistance against water that I always need. What I have started doing isn't original and I'm not going to take credit for it. But after you have brushed on three or four coats of shellac, rub the last coat out with paste wax. Dip a pad of no. 000 steel wool in a can of Minwax or Briwax paste wax and, working according to the steps outlined earlier, rub on and then buff up a satin paste wax shine. It's a tough team to beat. The shellac protects the wood and the paste wax protects the shellac. When you are finished you've got the best of both worlds: an authentic antique finish with good resistance to everyday life.

Varnish over Shellac

While shellac may not be cut out to stand on its own against heavy use and abuse, it still has two distinct advantages over every other finish: first, it adheres to just about every surface; second, it dries in less than fifteen minutes. What that means for you, especially when pressed for time, is that instead of using a slow-drying varnish sanding sealer, you can brush on two or three coats of shellac according to the steps outlined earlier and top that off with one final coat of varnish. The shellac will seal the pores of the wood and will provide a firm, smooth foundation for the varnish. And strange as that may seem, varnish actually adheres better to a shellac sealer than it does to an earlier coat of varnish. Bringing the two together will give you a quick yet durable finish.

Tung Oil and Varnish

Back when I had time to do everyone's refinishing but my own, I got a call to meet the assistant city manager in the council chambers the following morning. After checking to make sure I had paid all the parking tickets my assistants had collected in the delivery van, I arrived to find her standing next to a twelve-foot-long teak conference table. That's when I realized she didn't want to talk parking tickets.

"We're having the room redecorated, and while the workers are in here, we would like to have you refinish the conference table," she announced. "But there's a problem."

Isn't there always? I thought.

"The table is teak and it matches the chairs, but the council doesn't want the chairs refinished."

"But they want the table to still match the chairs."

"Right, and they don't want it to look refinished."

"What would they like it to look like?"

"Just like it does now—natural—but they don't want it to water-stain."

Now, if there was ever a case of wanting to have your cake and eat it, too, it is having a table with a new finish that doesn't look refinished. Actually, what they wanted wasn't that unreasonable; it was just that it ruled out shellac, lacquer, and varnish. I was afraid that an oil finish alone wouldn't hold up under the kind of use this conference table was going to get—especially when I saw the ashtrays scattered about it. This table would have to withstand coffee cups, felt-tipped pens, clipboards, soda cans, and an occasional dropped cigarette—and still look "natural."

Despite the fact that I wasn't sure yet what that finish was going to be, we took the table (plus one chair to serve as a match) back to the shop, where we scrubbed off the accumulation of oils, waxes, and dirt. We also repaired a few cigarette burns and filled more than one dent left by a councilman trying to make a point.

Meanwhile I had been on the phone and in the library, trying to find a solution to the problem. It came in the form of what was then a relatively new product called tung oil varnish. Actually, tung oil has been an ingredient in quality varnishes for decades, but it wasn't until woodworkers and refinishers started using pure tung oil as a finish that someone decided to reverse the formula. Instead of adding a little tung oil to the varnish, he decided to add a little varnish to the tung oil.

What he and subsequent wood finishers discovered was that the combination of varnish and oil produced a finish that soaked into the wood and yet hardened on the surface. The beauty of the combination is that you can adjust it to suit your needs as well as that of the wood you are finishing. If you want the look of an oil finish with only a little of the protection of varnish, you can start with a mixture of 75 percent tung oil and 25 percent varnish. If you want the opposite, combine 25 percent tung oil with 75 percent varnish. And if an equal balance is what you want, then combine equal parts of both.

On this particular table we used a commercial blend of tung oil and varnish produced by Hope's. After warming it slightly to encourage penetration, we poured the first puddle on the table and began working it over and into the wood with rags. The oil brought the grain of the teak to life, but did not change the color significantly. What little excess there was we wiped off after ten minutes and left the table to dry. At the end of the day I returned, buffed the surfaces lightly with a dry pad of no. 000 steel wool, and repeated the process. In the course of the next three days we applied six coats of tung oil varnish, stopping before the varnish on the surface detracted from the "natural" look of the wood.

I must admit, the table looked beautiful, but I expected that. Teak is a beautiful wood, and it would be difficult to ruin it with any oil finish. I was more concerned with how the table was going to look after a couple of stormy council sessions. Before leaving, I gave the head of maintenance a fresh can of Hope's tung oil varnish and told her to use it whenever the table began to show any wear or dull spots. Six months later I stopped in to pay another handful of parking tickets and peeked in at the table. It had a few new scratches and it looked like the same councilman was still trying to make his point, but all things considered, the table still looked good—and it looked natural.

While some woodworkers use boiled linseed oil in place of tung oil, and at least one swears by tung oil and polyurethane varnish, I have found that the best combination, for both appearance and durability, came from refined tung oil and standard interior varnish. Feel free to experiment, though, with any combination and any of a number of different types of oils—natural or synthetic—and any of a number of different types of varnish.

But the last I heard, no one had found the perfect finish—yet.

Steps	*Materials*
1. Remove and label all hardware.	screwdriver
2. Remove all dust from the wood.	vacuum and/or tack rag
3. Protect the floor, nearby furniture, and upholstery.	drop cloth newspapers masking tape
4. Place the section to be finished in a horizontal position.	workbench or sawhorses
5. Pour a warmed mixture of tung oil and varnish on the wood.	tung oil varnish
6. Work the finish into the wood.	clean rags
7. After 10–15 minutes or just as the finish becomes tacky, wipe off the excess in the direction of the grain.	clean rags
8. Let dry (approximately 6–12 hours)	
9. Buff lightly.	no. 0000 steel wool
10. Repeat steps 2–9	

You can stop whenever you feel you've provided enough protection for your piece of furniture. As with the council conference table, whenever the wood begins to show any wear or reveal any dry or dull spots, wipe it off with a rag dipped in turpentine and apply another coat of finish.

Summary ▶ Just as you wouldn't even consider using one set of clothing for every occasion, you shouldn't expect one type of finish to fulfill the needs of every piece of furniture you refinish. Each finish has its strengths and weaknesses that determine whether it's right for your project. Consider each one carefully, follow the recommended directions for application, take good care of it, and you may never have to refinish that piece of furniture again.

Shopping List

— paste wax
— shellac
— denatured alcohol
— turpentine
— tung oil
— penetrating oil
— brushing lacquer
— aerosol lacquer
— lacquer thinner
— varnish

— no. 000 steel wool
— no. 0000 steel wool
— no. 220 sandpaper
— assorted brushes
— tack rags
— rags
— drop cloth
— newspapers
— masking tape
— cans and jars
— stirring sticks

CHAPTER 9
Ah, There's the Rub

To my list of criteria for the perfect furniture finish I should have added one more:

> It should not have to be rubbed out.

I have always been amazed at how often a refinisher—professional or hobbyist—will spend hours stripping, sanding, repairing, staining, and finishing a piece of furniture, only to forget or ignore the last and most obvious step—that of rubbing out the final coat of finish. At one time it might have been understandable, when pumice and rottenstone were both hard to find and messy to use, but now that refinishers have easier ways of giving the final coat a sleek, satin smoothness, there's no reason why someone should run a hand across the table you refinished last month and wonder why it feels so rough.

You might even wonder yourself.

If you had a fast-drying finish, an absolutely dust-free finishing room, and a piece of furniture that also was completely free of any dust particles, raised fibers, or uneven surfaces, then you might never have to rub out a piece of furniture. Some people do, of course—Henredon Furniture or Baker or Ethan Allen—but they spend hundreds of thousands of dollars researching and testing spray equipment, exhaust systems, lacquer finishes, and special additives to enable their finish both to flow out and dry quickly before any foreign particles have a chance to land on their furniture.

But then, Mr. Henredon doesn't have to store his lawnmower in his finish room.

I do, along with a half dozen rakes and hoes, a broken bicycle, a pile of oak lumber, a screen door I have been intending to patch for a year, and the rear seat out of my Dodge Caravan. For me, rubbing out a finish isn't a chore—especially when my other option is cleaning out the garage every time I want to finish a piece of furniture.

There is a difference, however, between removing a few fine dust particles and chiseling out bolders. Even though I know I am going to rub out a piece when it is dry, I still make it a point to vacuum the wood thoroughly, to let the dust in the air settle, to not stir up any additional dust, to clean my brush, and to change shirts if necessary to keep dust away from my wet varnish. I also try to make sure that I am not knocking particles of dried varnish off the rim of my can into the varnish, later to be spread to my tabletop. I may not be able to have a dust-free finish room, but at least I don't feel like I'm varnishing in the middle of the Sahara Desert.

The efficiency experts at major furniture factories don't like to see their employees rubbing out finishes if it can be avoided. Almost all of the new furniture being mass-produced today is finished with lacquer, and for one very good reason. In addition to being tough and durable, lacquer dries quickly—so quickly, in fact, that the little dust in the air can seldom have time to land before the lacquer has dried. Even though it needs additional time to harden completely, lacquer can dry dust-free in less than a minute. Any dust that lands on it after that can simply be wiped off. When all goes as planned, most of the new furniture being sprayed with lacquer today is never rubbed out.

If you are spraying lacquer with professional equipment at home or in a workshop, you may be able to flow on such a smooth coat of lacquer that you won't have to rub it out. But if you're like me and your spraying is limited to aerosol cans of lacquer on small projects, then you can be sure that you will have some dust and 'overspray'—fine particles of dried finish that land in the wet lacquer—to rub out afterward. Deft and other brushing lacquers do dry more quickly than varnish, and they trap less dust, but they dry so quickly that they often capture brush marks instead—and those have to be rubbed out as well.

Varnish requires a minimum of thirty minutes on a near perfect day to dry dust-free. On a cool, humid day it can remain tacky for as long as four hours or more. I once had a chair that I varnished in an April shower that you still couldn't sit on in May. As long as it is tacky, anything that lands on it sticks to it—dust, cat hairs, leaves, or the seat of your pants. Even under near ideal conditions, you are still going to have some dust trapped in your varnish finish.

Oil finishes fall somewhere between lacquer and varnish; since you wipe off the excess before it hardens, the dust doesn't actually have much to stick to in the brief time that the thin film of oil remains tacky. It dries slower than lacquer, but faster than varnish, and under the same conditions you won't have nearly as much dust to be rubbed out afterward as you would if you varnished the piece. To achieve a satin-smooth oil finish, though, you'll still need to give it a light buffing.

While I am sure that there are several unique and individual techniques for rubbing out finishes, I have found that most fall into one of three categories: powder, sandpaper, or steel wool.

◄ **Rubbing Materials**

PUMICE AND ROTTENSTONE—Though they sound like an old vaudeville comedy team, pumice and rottenstone are probably the two oldest and most commonly used abrasive powders. Traditional furniture makers relied on them for centuries, but in the last twenty years they have practically disappeared from the shelves. The fault is not entirely their own; the development of fine sandpapers, steel wool, and other abrasives have simply made rubbing out easier than the old method.

For those who enjoy doing things "the old-fashioned way," pumice and rottenstone are still highly recommended. Pumice, a light-colored powder, is used to obtain a semigloss finish; rottenstone, an even finer, darker-colored powder, is used after pumice to buff up a high-gloss shine. Bondex, one company that still offers pumice and rottenstone, sells each in a twelve-ounce container resembling a milk carton for a little more than two dollars.

Before starting, you will want to assemble a few tools and materials. A shallow bowl, plate, or pan is ideal for holding the lubricant—mineral oil for shellac and either mineral oil or water for lacquer, varnish, or paint. If you have a second one available, use it to hold your pumice; if not, you can shake it directly onto the finish. You will also need a block of wood similiar to your sanding block, but instead of wrapping it with sandpaper, you will substitute a piece of felt or soft, clean cloth. Once you are ready, you can start the procedure:

Pumice or Rottenstone

Steps   *Materials*

1. Wait until the finish has thoroughly hardened.

2. Position the piece so that the section to be rubbed out is horizontal.

Steps	*Materials*
3. Dip a rag in the lubricant and moisten the finish.	mineral oil or water clean cloth
4. Dip the felt block in the pan of lubricant.	shallow pan felt block mineral oil
5. Either press the felt block in the powder or sprinkle powder over the finish.	pumice or rottenstone
6. Begin rubbing the block over the finish in straight strokes with the grain. Apply light to moderate pressure.	
7. Check the finish often, adding more oil or powder as necessary. Keep the surface wet at all times.	
8. When desired sheen and smoothness are obtained, wipe clean with a sponge or rag.	sponge or rag
9. Remove film with rag dipped in turpentine.	turpentine clean cloth
10. Polish with dry cloth.	

Although pumice is a fine abrasive, you can still rub through the finish if you apply too much pressure and too little oil. The idea is to remove only the imperfections in the top of the finish and not the layer of finish itself. Check your progress often to make sure that you are not sanding through to the wood.

You will not save yourself any time by skipping the pumice and going directly to rottenstone for a high-gloss finish. Rottenstone is designed to polish the finish after the pumice treatment has removed the imperfections. Omitting the pumice will simply mean that you will have to use more rottenstone and still may not achieve a perfectly smooth finish.

SANDPAPER—Pumice and rottenstone remained starting players for all woodworkers and refinishers until researchers developed a waterproof sandpaper in extremely fine grits. As silicon carbide sandpaper in grits above no. 400 became readily available, pumice and rottenstone began spending more time on the shelf and less on the furniture.

In some respects, rubbing out with sandpaper is similiar to rubbing out with pumice and rottenstone. You will still need a lubricant, such as mineral oil, but the effect achieved by the powder and felt has been made more convenient by attaching the abrasive to a waterproof backing. My experience has shown that to achieve a semigloss finish you will need no. 400 sandpaper; high-gloss finishes will require no. 600 or finer.

Sandpaper

Steps	*Materials*
1. Wait until the finish has thoroughly hardened.	
2. Position the piece so that the section to be rubbed out is horizontal.	
3. Dip a rag in the lubricant and moisten the finish.	mineral oil or water
4. Dip sandpaper in the lubricant and begin sanding with light to moderate pressure in straight strokes with the grain.	no. 400–600 sandpaper
5. Check the finish often to insure that you are not sanding through to the wood.	
6. Rinse the sandpaper often in the lubricant. Keep the finish wet at all times.	
7. When desired sheen and smoothness are obtained, wipe clean with a sponge or rag.	sponge or rag
8. Remove film with rag dipped in turpentine.	turpentine rag
9. Polish with dry cloth.	

Just as pumice and rottenstone have the disadvantage of being messy and inconvenient, sandpaper is not perfect. If you choose to wrap your sandpaper around a block of wood, you run the risk of sanding through the finish on high spots and leaving the finish in low areas untouched. While a woodworker might think that the solution is more sanding until the surface is completely flat, an antiques lover will know that high and low areas are the result of either the aging process of the wood or of hand planing—both signs of antiquity that should be preserved. A more practical solution is to wet-sand with your fingers rather than a block of wood, but you may have problems around carvings and trim. Don't worry, though, you still have another alternative.

STEEL WOOL—Whenever I talk to a group of refinishers I always bring along my display board of the seven most common grades of steel wool. When I first mention steel wool, most of them think of the steel wool they have used when stripping furniture—steel wool so coarse that it looks exactly like what it is, a ball of wire. What they are surprised to see and feel is the finest grade of steel wool—no. 0000—which is so soft you can rub it against your cheek without any discomfort.

What I have discovered is that no. 0000 steel wool is (1) easier to use than pumice and rottenstone and (2) more effective than sandpaper when rubbing out irregular surfaces. It assumes the shape of the wood beneath it without applying excessive pressure to the high areas. And you can bend, tear, and shape it to fit inside carvings and along moldings.

What it has in common with the other two, however, is that it needs a lubricant. Once again, you don't want to remove a layer of finish; you simply want to burnish off the dust and particles that have dried in the top layer. Too much pressure or too little lubricant and your steel wool will cut right through your finish. Another advantage I find to using steel wool is that I can use it to rub out and wax a piece of furniture simultaneously. Instead of dipping it in oil, I load the steel fibers generously with a high-quality paste wax and begin buffing the finish in the direction of the grain. The friction between the fibers and the finish removes the dust particles and creates enough heat to make the wax flow onto the surface. When the wax has nearly dried, I buff it to the sheen I like, giving me a smooth and durable finish.

Steel Wool and Oil

Steps	*Materials*
1. Wait until the finish has thoroughly hardened.	
2. Position the piece so that the section to be rubbed out is horizontal.	
3. Dip a rag in the oil and lubricate the surface.	mineral oil rag
4. Dip the steel wool in the oil and begin buffing with light to moderate pressure in straight strokes with the grain.	no. 0000 steel wool
5. Check the finish often to insure that you are not buffing through to the wood. Keep the finish and the steel wool wet at all times.	
6. When desired sheen and smoothness are obtained, wipe clean with a sponge or rag.	sponge or rag
7. Remove film with rag dipped in turpentine.	turpentine rag
9. Polish with dry cloth.	

In case you are not aware, lemon oil is basically mineral oil with approximately 1 percent synthetic lemon oil added for fragrance. While it is more expensive than generic mineral oil, years ago called paraffin oil, lemon oil can be used with no. 0000 steel wool for the final rubbing out.

Steel Wool and Paste Wax

Steps	*Materials*
1. Wait until the finish has thoroughly hardened.	

Steps	Materials
2. Dip the steel wool in the paste wax and begin buffing with light to moderate pressure in straight strokes with the grain.	no. 0000 steel wool paste wax
3. Check the finish often to insure that you are not buffing through to the wood. Keep the steel wool fibers loaded with wax.	
4. Before the wax begins to harden, buff lightly in circular strokes with a soft rag to remove excess wax.	rag
5. As soon as wax begins to set (5–10 minutes after application), buff in straight strokes with the grain.	
6. Return an hour later for a final buffing to remove any rag marks.	

If you are accustomed to your paste wax taking nearly fifteen to twenty minutes to harden when applied with a rag, readjust your time schedule to allow for the heat produced by your steel wool. The wax will dry faster, and if you aren't prepared, you may discover that your steel wool or rag marks are visible in the dried wax. If a vigorous rubbing does not erase them, wipe the wax off with a rag dipped in turpentine and start over.

Type of Finish	Rubbing Method	Lubricant
Shellac	Pumice and Rottenstone	Mineral Oil
	no. 400–600 Sandpaper	Mineral Oil
	no. 0000 Steel Wool	Mineral Oil or Wax
Varnish	Pumice and Rottenstone	Mineral Oil or Water
	no. 400–600 Sandpaper	Mineral Oil
	no. 0000 Steel Wool	Mineral Oil or Wax

Type of Finish	Rubbing Method	Lubricant
Lacquer	Pumice and Rottenstone	Mineral Oil or Water
	no. 400–600 Sandpaper	Mineral Oil
	no. 0000 Steel Wool	Mineral Oil or Water
Paint	Pumice and Rottenstone	Mineral Oil or Water
	no. 400–600 Sandpaper	Mineral Oil
	no. 0000 Steel Wool	Mineral Oil or Wax
Oil	no. 0000 Steel Wool	Mineral Oil or Wax

◄ The Ultimate High-Gloss Finish

I wasn't in the refinishing business too long when I came to the conclusion that whenever anybody runs into a problem they can't solve, they call a professional refinisher. It might be a broken spring on a swivel office chair, a rolltop desk that was locked and the key lost, a burn in a Formica top, or a piano that won't hold a tune.

Then, of course, there's always the pickled oak imitation Oriental buffet.

It sounded crazy to me, too, but when I went out and saw the buffet, I thought it might work. The couple had inherited one of the low buffets made during the fifties and finished in a "pickled" oak. The workmanship was excellent and the piece showed little wear, but there was no way around the fact that it was *ugly*. That may sound a little extreme, but whoever got the idea of rubbing white paint into the open pores of oak and then covering that with a tinted varnish was looking for a novel way to use oak. Once you recognize that it is unattractive, your opinions are limited: you can't sand it out, you can't strip it out, and you can't throw it out. The only thing you can do is paint it.

I'm generally not a big advocate of painting pieces that weren't originally painted, let alone turning a piece from one era into that of another, but when they showed me what the pickled buffet would look like with Oriental hardware and a gloss black finish, I became a believer. Once you got past the pickled look, the piece did have a low, sleek Oriental feel. I just had to make it gloss black to match their imported table and chairs.

We started by sanding the piece and filling the pores with paste filler. I was fortunate that my shop was located next to an automotive paint shop, for they were able to help me pick out a General Motors gloss black lacquer-based paint that was going to flow on smoother and wear better than any interior household paint on the market. After a coat of sealer and the first four coats of black lacquer, I could see that the fifties buffet was going to make a successful—if strange—transformation back a century or so. What I could also see was that General Motors gloss black wasn't going to be glossy enough.

After a light sanding and an additional four coats of paint for depth, it was time to turn a gloss black into a high-gloss black. I started with the traditional pumice and oil, then switched to rottenstone and oil, but the shine just wasn't there. As I stood looking at it, Vern from the automotive shop next door stopped in to check my progress.

"Still not glossy enough?"

I shook my head.

"Be right back." I didn't know what he had in mind, but I was hoping for a miracle. In a few minutes he was back with a fresh rag and a plastic jug.

"What's that?" I asked as he poured a puddle of brown liquid on the top of the buffet and started spreading it out with his rag.

"Rubbing compound."

As I watched, the brown film began to dry and turn hazy on the top of the buffet. As it did, Vern began buffing, and in a matter of seconds I could see the jet-black gloss begin to appear. I grabbed a clean rag and started buffing beside him, and in less than five minutes we had buffed up a deep, glossy shine that matched the chairs and table perfectly. We stood back and admired our work.

"Why didn't you tell me about this stuff before?"

Vern shrugged. "Figured you knew about it."

I didn't then, but I've kept a bottle of rubbing compound on the shelf next to the paste wax ever since. Hardware stores don't stock it, but automotive paint and supply stores carry two or three different grades, rather like the gradations of pumice and rottenstone. You may not want to buy it before you actually need it, but when the day comes that you want a high-gloss shine, you know now how to get it.

Shopping List

___ pumice
___ rottenstone
___ mineral oil
___ clean rags
___ felt block
___ turpentine

___ no. 400 sandpaper
___ no. 600 sandpaper
___ mineral oil
___ clean rags

___ no. 0000 steel
    wool
___ paste wax, or
___ mineral oil
___ clean rags

CHAPTER 10
As Good As Old

One day a woman burst into my shop brandishing a small pine wash bench.

"I finally found it," she declared as she banged it down on a workbench full of tools.

"Hope you didn't spend too much time looking for it," I commented as I came over to inspect the piece. "I think my mother still uses one of these to ripen her tomatoes on."

"Not as good as this one, I'll bet," she countered. "It's pine, it's sturdy, and it's just the right size."

"It's just not very old."

She shrugged. "I don't care. It's just what I need to use as a coffee table in front of my new couch."

I looked at the wash bench skeptically. It wasn't more than thirty or forty years old and was obviously homemade. As wash benches go, it was okay, but a *coffee table*?

"Are you sure?" I asked.

"Look," she began explaining as she pulled a paint chart out of her enormous black purse. "See this? Colonial Cream. That's the color I want you to paint my bench."

"Mildred, you know I don't paint antiques."

"Who said anything about painting an antique? You said yourself it wasn't very old. I just want you to make it look older."

"How much older?"

"About two hundred years, that's all."

The idea was so ridiculous, it almost made sense. The bench wasn't going to last more than a few years in the condition it was in now, but I still didn't like the idea of turning it into a fake antique. If we did it the way she wanted, and did it right, what was to keep someone fifty or a hundred years from now from thinking Thomas Jefferson had used it to ripen his tomatoes on? Nothing—except maybe this year's date carved across the bottom of it in numbers three inches high.

"Okay, Mildred. Two hundred years—at a dollar a year. A deal?"

Mildred laughed as she bounced out of the room. "Call me when it's done, boys."

I had seen enough legitimate Early American antiques to know that Mildred's bench, as shaky as it was, didn't have enough wear to look two hundred years old, so we started by taking a sheet of no. 120 sandpaper and rounding all the edges. Mildred's wash bench had already spent some time standing in water, no doubt in someone's basement, but its feet still looked too new, so we set each pair of legs in a pan of water for a couple of days, then started drying them with a heat gun. In a matter of minutes the wood was steaming and swelling and quickly developed some fine "old" cracks. I purposely snapped off a couple of large splinters on the legs, just as you would expect to find on a bench that had been dragged across a rough floor a few thousand times. A legitimate bench wouldn't sit level any longer, but I refrained from cutting one leg shorter than the others. Somehow I didn't think Mildred would want her table to be *that* authentic.

Mildred kept in touch, making it clear that she wanted to see not only the grain of the wood, but the remainder of the paint it had been "originally" finished with. What little finish her bench may have ever had—if any—had long since disappeared, and I was afraid that if I simply painted her bench, it might look too new for Jefferson to have lent it to Franklin to support his gout-swollen foot.

After we had sanded two hundred years of wear into the bench, I brushed on a coat of thin shellac to act as a sealer. It only took a few minutes to dry, then I sanded it lightly with no. 220 sandpaper to remove the gloss and any brush marks I might have left. The shellac sealer was my insurance policy. I knew that if Mildred didn't like the look of Colonial Cream, I could strip off the paint without leaving any traces in the pores and cracks. I also knew that it would allow me to wipe the paint off of those areas that got the most use over the course of those tough two hundred years.

I stirred the paint thoroughly and began coating one of the end boards. I had studied enough legitimate antiques to know that most of the paint should come off the feet, while most of the paint would still be intact under the recess of the overhanging top. I waited for the paint to begin to dry before I started carefully wiping it off with a rag. I scrubbed the feet hard, but as I worked my way up the leg, I left more paint on the wood. I continued on around the inside of the leg and then painted and wiped down the opposite leg. All that was left was the top. Mildred and I had discussed it at length, so I knew exactly what she wanted: traces of paint in the cracks and pores, but bare wood on the edges, corners, and across the top. I brushed on the paint, but barely let it begin to set up before I began scrubbing, first across the grain to force the paint in the cracks, and then with the grain. In some places I dabbed on a little more paint; in others I simply wiped it all off. When I was done the bench looked as if it had originally been painted—about two hundred years ago.

After the paint dried, I aged it with a pad of medium steel wool, taking off the gloss and making the finish look more than a day old. In the spots that would have received the most use, namely the corners and side edges, I purposely buffed through the shellac sealer, exposing the bare wood. I was having a great time, but the real fun was yet to come. The finish on Mildred's bench was starting to look antique, but the wood still looked less than thirty years old. Her wash bench needed to be abused.

Distress marks on reproductions—and there was no other word to adequately describe Mildred's bench—generally fall into two categories: those done to the wood before the finish is applied and those that were done with the wrong tools. Both are totally inappropriate. First, no eighteenth-century woodworker in his right mind would have purposely beat on his proud new wash bench with a two-foot length of chain and then painted it. The abuse that his bench would have taken would come after, not before, the finish. Likewise, when you make your reproduction antique, you need to lay down the first coats of finish so that they can be abused along with the rest of the pieces. Dents and scratches should be on top of the paint and not under it.

Second, the signs of age and abuse must be appropriate to the piece. I remember seeing a table in a new furniture store that someone had used a small Phillips screwdriver on to imitate wormholes; one glance and you could see by the impression it made that the holes not only were recent, but were made by a tool that didn't exist when the table was supposedly built. I could never imagine anyone beating a bench with a chain, yet so-called 'experts' still advise people to use a chain to imitate age marks.

A bench is a bench; a desk is a desk. One is going to have ink stains, sealing wax, and small rings left by cups and glasses. The other is going to have large rings and dents caused by buckets full of water being slung up on it. Down in the basement I found an old metal bucket, the type you would expect to find sitting on top of a pine wash bench. After leaving a few well-placed dents, I was ready for my next weapon—a young boy's pocketknife. Two games of mumblety-peg later and we were on to the next—a baseball bat—and the next. . . . Pretty soon everyone in the shop was involved, and I quickly had to restrain them before they turned Mildred's bench into a pile of kindling. But it was fun re-creating some of the events that would have left permanent marks on top of a two-hundred-year-old pine wash bench.

When I judged that we had left enough marks on Mildred's bench to last for the next two hundred years, I went over them with a piece of no. 220 sandpaper, smoothing any rough edges that might have revealed their true age. When I was satisfied with the look of the piece, I gave the bench the final finish—a coat of paste wax. The wax served two purposes. First, it protected the wood and the paint against the use to which Mildred and her guests were going to put it; second, it added still more 'age.' The wax wedged in the holes left by the knife and in the cracks that had developed naturally. When it dried, I buffed it, building up a satin sheen on the worn areas and leaving it rather dull in the recesses. Without it, Mildred's wash bench would have still had the look of a reproduction.

I saw Mildred's bench a year later. It had picked up a few scuff marks from shoes (we never thought about them) and a few new scratches, but it still looked far older than it actually was—and far better than it did the day she brought it in.

◄ Reproduction—or Fake?

Turning new or recent furniture into furniture looking several decades, if not centuries, older is nothing new. Fakes and reproductions have been plaguing antiques collectors since the day after antiques started becoming desirable. The trend has never diminished, but simply changes to meet the current need. When Chippendale is hot, Chippendale reproductions start cropping up; when round oak tables and oak iceboxes captured everyone's attention in the late seventies, a flood of reproductions eventually drove down the prices and killed the market. When the "country look" stepped in to take its place, the counterfeiters simply started making pine benches, tables, and cupboards. It has even been reported that Mission Oak reproductions are filtering into the market and may threaten that revival as well.

To Mildred's defense, and my own as her accomplice, I need to distinguish between a reproduction and a forgery. Mildred was not in the wrong, ethically or legally, when she decided that she wanted a pine bench that looked as if it were two hundred years old. She could have spent years looking for an authentic one, only to discover that it would cost not one dollar a year, but ten. And if she had found an authentic Early American wash bench, could she have felt comfortable placing it where people might prop their feet? Or worse yet, let their cigarettes fall on it?

So long as Mildred is content to use her wash bench in her home, there's nothing wrong. But if she should decide to hold a yard sale and somehow advertise the piece as being older than what she knows it to be, she would be perpetrating a fraud. Wary counterfeiters—people who make a portion of their living turning recent furniture into more valuable ''antiques''—get around this by playing dumb; a counterfeiter won't claim that his cupboard is 175 years old, but he won't admit that it isn't either. He'll just let you think that you have discovered a real gem buried under a half dozen feed sacks in the back of his barn, knowing full well that you're not going to come running out shouting about the early Pennsylvania cupboard you just found—which he is asking a very modest nine hundred dollars for.

"Yep," he'll say, "she's a beaut."

"How old do you think it is?"

Long pause.

"Well, son. That's mighty hard to say. I got it from a peddler, but my grandma, God bless her soul, why, she had one looked just like it, and this here feller from up New York way, why, he come plumb down here, took one look at it, and up and offered her four thousand dollars for it. Four thousand dollars, mind ya. That was more than my grandpappy made his best year walking a plow behind those two old mules of his. 'Roger' and 'Dodger,' he called 'em. Those two mules was the stubbornest things you ever see'd, but you know what? My grandpappy, he declared they could smell a rattler 'fore they ever stepped on it. Why, one day he was plowing down by Widow's Creek—"

"I'll take it."

"Smart lad. But I can't take no checks. My wife, she don't allow it."

No claim, no crime.

No paper, no proof.

In other words, there is nothing illegal in making or owning a reproduction. It's just when you go to sell it that you might get yourself in trouble.

Although I did comply with Mildred's request to turn an old bench into one that looked much older, I don't generally recommend taking even a piece that is only twenty or thirty years old and modifying it. I have done it and imagine that I'll do it again in the future, but it actually is much easier and faster just to purchase a new, unfinished piece of furniture and work with that. Theoretically, Mildred's bench would someday be an actual antique—hard as that may be to believe—so it should have been left as it was. Theoretically.

◄ **Unfinished Furniture**

For example, I make no apologies for liking Arts and Crafts-style furniture, but I have to agree with my wife that many antique dressers and chests of drawers simply do not work well. The few that do have smooth-running drawers are hard to find—and very expensive. I like the look of authentic antiques, but I don't like a dresser with drawers that don't slide properly either. So we compromised. I sold our stubborn antique dressers and bought new, unfinished oak dressers, then stained and finished them to match our other Mission Oak furniture. We now have the Arts and Crafts look with the benefit of modern drawer runners and guides. Besides, I reasoned, I would rather spend my money on Stickley furniture for our living room than put it in the bedroom, where no one else would ever see it.

Our bedroom furniture situation illustrates another problem those of us who enjoy living with antiques often encounter. I have been collecting Arts and Crafts furniture since 1980, but it wasn't until 1986 that I even had my first opportunity to buy a high-quality Mission Oak dresser, and not until 1987 that I found an Arts and Crafts–style bed that I could afford. You might have the same problem looking for a cherry corner cupboard, a Windsor chair, or a matched set of eight pressed-back oak chairs. When it comes to antiques, "wanting" and "finding" are two distinctly different things. Only when you find the piece of your dreams do you have to worry about "buying."

Once we had decided that we were going to buy a pair of unfinished oak dressers and refinish them to match our other Arts and Crafts furniture, it took less than an hour to pick them out, pay for them, and take them home. Two days and ten dollars worth of stain and varnish later, they were ready to go in the house. If I were looking for a pair of Stickley dressers that I could afford, I would still be looking.

Ten years ago unfinished furniture stores were most often associated with low-quality pine furniture—you know, the type with staples instead of dovetail joints, and eighth-inch particleboard backing. Today unfinished furniture stores stock well-constructed furniture made from quality pine, oak, cherry, maple, and mahogany. While they may not rival furniture from custom-made furniture shops or high-quality furniture stores, they have improved their former image. They also offer a wide variety of styles, from simple dorm room furniture to Victorian, Shaker, Golden Oak, Country, and Early American. And with one or two simple modifications, you can create a few more of your own.

When buying unfinished furniture, be sure you look past the obvious. Once you have located the type of wood and the style you want, such as an unfinished maple corner cupboard you plan to turn into an early-nineteenth-century reproduction, you will want to see how well it is constructed. Pull out the drawers, open the doors, and slide the piece away from the wall; then ask yourself—or the salesperson:

Are the drawer joints dovetailed or are they simply nailed together? Nailed joints soon work loose and will require a regluing in a few years. Ideally, a drawer will be dovetailed in the back joints as well as the front.

How sturdy is the drawer bottom? Is it simply an eighth-inch piece of mahogany plywood that you can almost push out with the force of your hand, or does it feel as if it can withstand the weight of two phone books and a J. C. Penney's catalog?

How sturdy is the backing on the piece? It will be a piece of plywood, but is it only an eighth of an inch thick, or worse yet, is it wall paneling?

Does the interior framework have a substantial number of glue blocks reinforcing the joints? Could you pick it up by the top without pulling the top off the framework?

Does the interior framework that supports the drawers look as if it could withstand several thousand openings and closings?

Are the shelves solid wood, plywood, or particleboard? Plywood is now considered acceptable and is less apt to warp or buckle than wide solid boards, but the edges of the plywood should be covered with a strip of wood to disguise the layered edge grain. Particleboards are common, but realize that if and when they do break or chip, they are virtually irreparable.

When veneer is used in construction, how thick is it? Check the edges of the boards carefully to determine (1) if it is actual wood and (2) how thick the veneer is.

How many rungs are there between the legs of the chairs? Two or three are ideal; one will mean a yearly regluing. How is the back attached to the seat? Arms give a chair additional support; side chairs need to have two internal dowels attaching the seat to the back posts. Sit in the chair, just like you do at home: leaning back on the rear legs.

◀ **Modifications**

The good thing about working with unfinished furniture is that many of the preceding problems can be corrected. The furniture company may have cut costs by using particleboard for the shelves in the maple cupboard you want, but if they are loose, adjustable shelves, you can take them out and replace them with solid maple or birch shelves. Drawer bottoms generally slide in and out of grooves cut in the drawer sides; all that you need to do is change a drawer bottom from cheap and inappropriate mahogany to birch, maple, or even an authentic old drawer bottom you salvaged from a wrecked piece. Remove two or three small nails holding the bottom in place and slide it out.

And once you get started, there's no stopping you. If you aren't satisfied with the number of glue blocks holding the top to the sides, cut and glue in a few more. If you want a thicker and stronger back, remove the brads or staples holding the thin backing on and replace it with one cut to the same dimensions. If the manufacturer used plastic shelf tabs, replace them with steel or brass ones that look far more authentic.

What aren't as easy to change, however, are the drawer joints. You can't make a silk purse out of a sow's ear, and you can't turn a nailed butt joint into a dovetail joint. If you are satisfied with everything else, including the price, you might do well to buy the piece, knowing full well that someday you will have to reglue those drawers. If you want to go that extra step, you can turn a butt joint into a very strong joint by pulling out each nail holding the two boards together and, one at a time, drilling out the hole left by the nail with an eighth- or quarter-inch bit, squeezing in some glue, and tapping in a precut length of dowel. It isn't as difficult as it may sound at first and will leave you with a strong, attractive joint similiar to a type used in the Victorian era (see illustration).

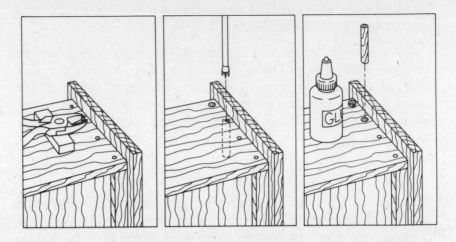

Before you buy a piece, though, be sure to add the cost of the modifications you plan to make to the showroom price. If they end up being more than you expected, check out a few more shops—antique and unfinished—before you write out that check.

Here are a number of other simple, inexpensive modifications you can make to a piece of unfinished furniture that will help give it the appearance of a quality antique:

BACKS—Furniture built more than a hundred years ago will have backs consisting of several narrow, vertical boards. They will be finished on the inside only; rough saw cuts will be evident on the exposed back side. The Late Victorian era saw the introduction of paneled backs, an early form of plywood. If your piece of unfinished furniture has come with a particleboard backing, you can improve its appearance and its strength by removing it and attaching a piece of either birch, maple, or oak quarter-inch plywood purchased from a cabinet shop. If you want your piece to look two hundred years old, replace the plywood backing with individual boards.

DRAWER BOTTOMS—One of the cheapest plywoods available is mahogany, and manufacturers often use it for drawer bottoms in unfinished furniture. On furniture other than mahogany, they look inappropriate, but you can easily replace them with quarter-inch plywood made of the same wood as the rest of the piece. Simply turn the drawer over, remove the nails attaching the mahogany bottom to the back of the drawer, and slide it out. Lay the mahogany bottom on the replacement plywood panel, trace around it, and cut it out using a hobby knife. Afterward, slide your new panel in the drawer slots and nail it in place.

SCREWS—Manufacturers of unfinished furniture tend to use Phillips screws for their hinges and hardware, but since cabinet-makers one hundred years ago never had Phillips screws, they are an obvious sign of a reproduction. It is both simple and inexpensive to remove the modern screws and to replace them with standard single-slot screws. Brass screws are a little more expensive, but they look more authentic. New screws can be aged by heating the heads with a small flame, then submerging them in water. Use a pair of vise grips to keep from aging your fingertips as well. The same applies to square-headed nails, which can either be used in place of modern nails or screws or added in appropriate places. Flea markets and refinishing shops are excellent sources of authentic nails, but they can also be ordered from restoration supply firms (see Sources, Chapter 12).

PEGS—At different times in furniture-making history, it was considered a sign of quality if the major joints were strengthened by ''pegging.'' In addition to being glued together, important joints were pinned together with a peg approximately one-quarter to three-eighths inch in diameter that was glued in place and then sanded flush with the surface. If you find photographs indicating that antiques of the style your unfinished reproduction is attempting to imitate used pegs, then consider drilling the proper-sized hole *in*, but not *through*, major joints. Tap in a maple, walnut, or oak dowel (purchased or whittled) and sand flush.

Installing either irregular or machine-turned dowels in a joint is not difficult, but it does require some attention to detail. First, study a similiar, but authentic antique closely, noting exactly which joints are pegged and which are not. Second, note the precise location of the pegs. How far is each one from the edge of the board? Third, what is the diameter of the pegs? On some older pieces the pegs may only be an eighth inch in diameter, while on later pieces they may be as large as seven-sixteenths of an inch. Fourth, do the pegs protrude slightly or are they flush with the surface? Fifth, do the pegs go completely through the joint, showing on both sides of the board?

Once you have determined and marked the location of the pegs, you need a sharp spur drill bit. Unlike standard twist bits, spur bits have a vertical cutting blade that trims off the outside edge of the circle (see illustration). This spur prevents the wood around the edge of the hole from splintering or chipping, as often happens with even a sharp twist drill bit. Wrap a piece of masking tape on the shaft to indicate the depth the bit should travel into the wood. If your peg is a false peg, you don't need to drill any deeper than three-eighths of an inch into the wood. If your peg is actually going to strengthen the joint by passing through both boards, then you need to determine how far your bit can travel without breaking through the back of the board.

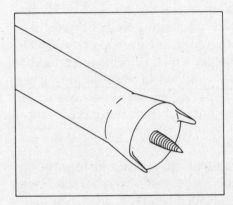

Once you've drilled your hole, then you cut your dowel. I prefer to cut mine slightly shorter than the length of the hole so that I can tap it all the way in, leaving the end flush with the surface. The extra space in the hole is necessary to hold excess glue and compressed air in front of the peg. If you don't compensate for both, you won't be able to drive your peg completely into the wood. If you want your peg to be flush with the surface, sand it before you tap it; if you plan to let it protrude slightly, then wait and sand it after the glue dries.

Here are two tips: You may discover that a three-eighths-inch dowel is actually a little smaller than the hole left by your three-eighths-inch drill bit. Regardless of whether your bit wobbled or the dowel had shrunk, the result is the same—a loose fit. My solution is simple. As soon as the dowel is tapped in place, I put a few drops of water directly on it. The open pores absorb the water immediately. As the dowel swells, it pushes against the wall of the hole. There it contacts the glue as it dries, locking it in place.

Speaking of glue, it does not take much to hold a peg in place. Rather than coating the peg with glue, most of which you will have to wash off afterward, use a toothpick or splinter to spread a drop or two of glue around the inside of the hole. The excess glue will then be pushed to the bottom of the hole by the peg rather than squeezed out on top of your board. The small amount of glue also dries quickly, so you can come back a few minutes later to finish sanding it.

HARDWARE—Modern furniture manufacturers will often order thousands of pulls of the same traditional "antique" design and place them on dozens of different styles of furniture. A typical Chippendale-style pull can show up on Victorian, Federal, or Art Deco–style furniture. Even when the hardware does match the furniture, it is often cheap and always too shiny.

Hundreds of different styles and designs of pulls, knobs, hinges, key plates, locks, and castors are available in wood, steel, porcelain, and brass from nearly two dozen national reproduction hardware firms (see Sources, Chapter 12). Many antiques dealers and restoration shops have replacement hardware on hand, or at the least catalogs from these companies. Once again, you should consult antiques shops, museums, and reference books to determine which style of hardware is appropriate for your particular style of furniture (more later in this chapter).

◄ Look Before You Beat

One snowy December I was helping a friend pick out a Christmas gift for his father. We had traveled to nearly a dozen antiques shops looking for a particular style of rocking chair he felt would suit him, but without any luck. Finally we found one that he really liked, and the saleslady scurried over to help us. "That's a wonderful rocker," she commented, "and it's in original condition. It's never been touched."

I wasn't so sure, but my friend was beginning to like the rocker, so I didn't say a thing. I thought the price was a little steep, but if it really was original, it would probably be a good investment. Something about it bothered me, though, so I continued to look it over. Finally I pushed the rocker backward so that I could look underneath it. "Are you sure this rocker has never had anything done to it?" I asked.

"Positive," came the reply.

"Well, I don't want to sound like Sherlock Holmes, but the runner on the right is worn nearly flat and the one on the left doesn't show any wear at all. In fact, I'd say it was a replacement."

Needless to say, the dealer wasn't happy to hear that, even

though she did agree with me. Seems that whoever sold her the rocker forgot to mention that little detail. We left without the rocker.

One other time, though, I knew a dealer was lying to me. I was looking at a set of six pressed-back chairs that he was claiming he had brought from his home directly to the shop. "We've been using these chairs for years and they've never had to have anything done to them. They haven't even been reglued."

I thanked him and left. I knew someone had reglued the chairs recently because two of the rungs were worn on the wrong side. While the tops of the other rungs were worn almost flat, two of the rungs were worn on the bottom side. I wouldn't have cared if they had been reglued, even if someone did put two of the rungs back in upside down. But as soon as I realized that the dealer either wasn't telling me the whole truth or didn't know the chairs as well as he thought he did, I knew I couldn't trust anything he did—or didn't—say.

The point I want to make is this: Stand back and look at your piece and ask yourself, "Where would you expect to find wear on this piece of furniture two hundred years from now?"

Few antiques survive a hundred years of use without some sign of wear, but fewer still would have ever been beaten with a two-foot length of chain, dunked in a pond, or peppered with birdshot, despite these questionable recommendations from well-known refinishers.

Distressing—the act of duplicating age marks on a replacement piece of wood or an entire piece—is not a means of taking out your frustrations on a helpless piece of furniture.

The two most valuable tools to a distresser are a sheet of sandpaper and a fine metal file. Chains are simply too indiscriminate in their damage. While some marks on an authentic antique may seem puzzling, the majority make perfectly good sense when you consider how the piece was used. Study antiques of the same type and vintage of the one you are attempting to age. You need to look for obvious signs of wear, such as on:

Chairs: Front rungs may be worn flat on the top side from heels of shoes and boots being hooked over them. Outside corners on front legs will be marred from banging into dining room table legs; inside corners should be relatively crisp. Tops of arms will have been grasped by many hands, and so will be worn smooth. Tops of back posts will also be worn. Early tavern chairs will show evidence of moisture damage from dirt floors on their feet; all chair feet will be rounded, even chipped or splintered from being dragged across the floor. The seat may be worn at the front, but not close to the spindles.

Tables and Desks: Front edges will be worn smooth; outside of front legs will show evidence of contact with chairs. Bottom of apron should be worn smooth by many knees, but will have few of the gouges, scratches, or stains normally found on the top. Corners will be rounded. Footrests, rungs, and cross members will be worn from shoes. The end grain edges may be chipped. Feet may show water marks.

Drawers: Front edges will be rounded; back piece may still be crisp. Wood around the pulls will show wear. Front corners will be rounded and chipped from contact with framework. Bottoms of runners will be worn, especially from the middle up to the front. Veneer chips will be evident along the edges.

Cupboards: Front edges and corners will be rounded. Doors will be worn on the bottom edge; corresponding wear will be found on the inside of the framework. Base should show wear from contact with brooms, mops, and vacuum sweepers. Less wear will appear on tops over five feet high. Shelves will be worn in middle of front edge, and less toward sides. Plate grooves will be worn, especially toward the middle of the shelf.

Dressers and Chest of Drawers: Top edges of drawers will be rounded, as will be the corners and runners. Front edge of top will be worn, with less wear evident on the sides; rear corners and edges will be relatively crisp. Wear will be evident around pulls; minor chips will be found on edges of drawers.

You need to begin the distressing process as you are fine-sanding your piece of furniture. In standard furniture factories, the piece travels very little from the time it is constructed to when a finish is applied, but unfinished furniture is crated, shipped, stored, shipped again, stored again, loaded, and unloaded a dozen times before it is finally unpacked in your home. The wood may look ready to finish, but on close examination, will reveal smudges, bruised pores, and other packing marks. While you might like to think these are simply the first stage of your distressing process,

◀ **Distressing: Sanding**

if they don't occur where they would be expected historically, then you need to remove them.

As you sand first with no. 180 sandpaper and then no. 220, you can begin to duplicate the wear your research has indicated an authentic antique would have experienced. Corners can be rounded, rungs flattened, and edges smoothed. Small ridges left by planers and jointers need to be sanded off the tops of boards, as well as circular saw marks on the ends and sides. A metal file (don't use a wood rasp!) can round sharp corners and edges that might otherwise tear your sandpaper, but all file marks must be removed with fine sandpaper. The wear you are duplicating occurred slowly and naturally, from hands, sleeves, soles of shoes, and dusting cloths—none of which would leave sanding scratches.

Distressing: ▶
Staining

Not long ago my friend George and I flew up to New York to attend an important auction. Among the most impressive pieces on display was a large oak conference table with low stretchers between the four legs. The table was attracting a good deal of attention, but George wasn't impressed.

"The refinisher didn't know much about antiques," he complained. "Look at those stretchers. You can see that they're worn down from everybody putting their feet on them, but the refinisher stained them the same color as the rest of the table. If you ask me, they just don't look right."

And he was right. You come to expect worn areas to be lighter than the rest of the antique. The older the piece, the more marked the contrast between the original finish (which continues to darken with age) and the wood that has had both the finish and the original stain worn away. When it all looks the same, something's not right. Antiques and reproductions are meant to show wear, and a refinisher's job is not to disguise that wear. If that particular refinisher had thought about what the stretchers on the conference table would have looked like before it was stripped, he could have duplicated the original color and finish rather than ending up with an old table with an obviously new finish. The table did well at the auction, but could have done even better had the refinisher used more common sense and less dark walnut stain on the worn areas.

If you study the type of piece you are attempting to duplicate, you will see that the exposed sections, which receive a good deal of use, are lighter in color than the recesses, which have been sheltered from both sunlight and hard use. Your staining should reflect that exposure, so when you come to the arms on the Windsor chair you are staining, either switch to a lighter color tone or wipe the stain off before it has a chance to penetrate deeply into the wood. If you discover that you left a section too dark, dip a rag in turpentine and rub the stained area briskly. Oftentimes that will remove enough stain to duplicate the wear the wood would have received over the course of a hundred years. Naturally, if you let it dry and the turpentine has no affect, you can lighten it using a piece of sandpaper.

After the stain has dried, I recommend brushing or spraying on a light coat of sealer, either shellac, lacquer, very thin varnish, or oil, depending on what your final finish is going to be. The sealer will lock in the color of the stain and will permit you to begin the actual distressing without risking any damage to the color of the wood.

◄ **Scratches and Dents**

If you closely examine a six-inch square on the top of an authentic antique desk, table, or bookcase, you may well be astonished by all of the minor scratches, dents, and gouges—even holes and paint splatters—that you will find. From across the room, few are visible, but together they combine to give a piece of furniture that look often referred to as patina.

While they may appear to have no particular pattern, most can be predicted—and duplicated. The top of a desk or library table, for instance, is going to have hundreds of tiny cross-grain scratches left by everything from paper clips to letter openers to magazines to typewriters, but the apron or the sides that have been protected by the overhanging top will show few of these same marks. Every time the telephone receiver was dropped, a cup knocked over, or a box slid across a dusty top, they left small dents or scratches in the wood or finish.

You can begin to duplicate these marks after your sealer has dried, for in doing so you will not disturb the stain itself. Your tools need to be no more specialized than those which left the marks originally: a knife, a hammer, a heavy metal pan, or any blunt object. It is going to feel strange at first, intentionally scratching, gouging, and marring beautiful wood, but it is necessary in order to transform a new piece of furniture into one that is going to look more than a hundred years old. Plan each mark thoughtfully, though, simulating how it would have actually occurred. A dropped ashtray, a knife cutting through a sandwich, a rolling pin banged several times against the edge of the table, a chair knocked over, a bench used to change a light bulb, a dresser top catching each day's loose change, a can dropped on a table, a box slid across a buffet, a rocking chair tipped over backward—each action would have left its own particular mark.

You must be careful, though, not to become obsessed with your new ability to destroy a piece. Consider each mark, carefully taking the time to change objects often. Distressing is far more serious than simply taking a hammer, wrapping a sock around it, and banging on the top as if you were driving nails. Iron skillets left more marks on tabletops than claw hammers; coffee cups and ashtrays have done more distressing than two-foot lengths of chain. If you can use the same type of object that would have left the original mark, then your reproduction is going to come even closer to looking real.

Distressing: ▶
Special Marks

I can recall being totally puzzled one day in my shop when I turned a table over to discover dozens of half-inch circles impressed in the wood along each end. I could not imagine what had left those perfect circles until a flashback on the tiny screen in my mind revived a childhood memory. There I was, standing on a kitchen chair, turning the handle on a food grinder my mother had attached to the edge of the table. I wasn't allowed to push the stalks of celery or boned chicken into the shiny jaws until I was much older, but I remember climbing down when we were finished to loosen the thumbscrew that held the grinder in place on the underside of the table. I know now that each time we used that food grinder, we left another mark under the table.

Granted, only a perfectionist may go to a flea market, buy a food grinder, and attach it to the edge of her reproduction table 143 times to duplicate authentic food grinder marks, but it serves to make a point: Some pieces of furniture will have special wear that you need to consider. You may choose to omit some of those special marks, such as cigarette burns on an end table or oil can rings on the top of a rolltop desk that was used in a filling station, but you must first recognize them before you make that decision.

I have worked on antique sewing tables whose tops looked like road maps, library tables with permanent impressions left by typewriters, rocking chairs with runners worn nearly flat from use. My father's rolltop desk has had a pencil sharpener screwed to the top of it for as long as I can remember—and I still smile when I see those telltale screw holes in similar desks in antiques shops.

I once was asked to strip a painted drop-leaf table for a customer; then I discovered why it had been painted. Right in the middle of the top I found a perfect outline of an old iron burned into the wood. I dreaded the phone call to my customer, but she was ecstatic about the burn. "I can remember the day it happened," she explained. "My father was furious. My mother had been using the table to iron clothes, and somehow the iron was knocked over. By the time she realized it, the damage had been done. We lived with it for a while, but eventually my father painted the table to hide it."

Needless to say, she wanted the burn left undisturbed, so we carefully refinished the table—preserving the outline of the iron in the middle.

While you may not wish to purposely duplicate burns or other household disasters in your furniture, you may discover that wormholes left by powder-post beetles commonly occurred in antiques of the same era. Wormholes, however, are difficult to duplicate accurately, for close study reveals that they are neither perfectly round nor do they go straight into the wood. Poorly duplicated wormholes, such as those often found in new furniture, are worse than no wormholes at all.

Veteran antiques dealers enjoy laughing about setting a reproduction up in the backyard, standing back thirty yards, and firing a load of birdshot into it, but anyone who has ever seen what shotgun pellets do to wood knows that the holes they leave don't look anything like those left by powder-post beetles. Wormholes don't appear haphazardly, but are almost always grouped closely together. While a shotgun might do the job quickly, it won't do it accurately.

A nail of the appropriate diameter can be used to duplicate wormholes. The point can be flattened into an oval rather than a perfect circle, and the shaft can even be bent slightly to duplicate the angular tunnels of the insect. Nails, however, can split wood, especially near the end of a board; and unlike the beetles, nails don't remove wood, they simply push it aside.

For these last two reasons, many refinishers use an electric drill with a carefully selected bit to duplicate wormholes. Held at various angles to the wood, the flexible drill bit can reproduce the exit and entrance holes left by the beetles. As with all distress marks, however, too many is worse than not enough. Seven to ten closely arranged holes of the proper size and angle will go further toward duplicating age marks in an antique than fifty or sixty scattered throughout the piece. As always, study authentic antiques to determine where the beetles would be most apt to be found in your particular reproduction.

When I was first learning to buy antiques on the Saturday farm auction circuit, I overheard a veteran antiques dealer say to his young apprentice, "If a desk doesn't have an ink stain, be suspicious. It may be a fake."

I had the opportunity again recently to test his theory at a preview for a large auction in which there were seven fall-front desks and five library tables on display. Of the seven desks, every one had at least one significant ink stain on the writing surface. Two had experienced major spills. Three of the five library tables had ink stains in the drawers. So when I am aging a desk, I always have some ink on hand. While cabinetmakers may call it desecration, I call a desk without an ink stain a reproduction.

Duplicating ink stains is very simple. Office supply stores still carry black India ink similar to that used a hundred years ago. But rather than knocking over a bottle or squirting it out of the end of an antique fountain pen, I have found that a disposable syringe takes all of the mess out of the project and gives you control over where and how much ink you are going to "spill." As you might expect, a little ink goes a long way and since different woods under different finishes have different absorption rates, be sure to experiment with a small spot before going any further.

Antique furniture that at one time sat on dirt floors, such as tavern tables, early Windsor chairs, or rough benches, and those that may have suffered water damage, such as oak iceboxes and tables relegated to the basement, will show a distinctly different type of wear around their feet. When wood absorbs moisture, it swells; consequently, when it dries out, it shrinks. This causes wood fibers and glue joints to begin to separate, and the moisture itself will break down stains and finishes. The result is a foot that shows excessive wear, including chips, rounded corners, lost color, and shrinkage.

The most authentic way to duplicate moisture damage on the foot of a reproduction tavern table, for instance, is to set each foot in a cat food can containing a mixture of dirt and water. Leave the mud pack around the lower inch of the wood for twenty-four hours, then remove and wipe off the excess. Using a hair dryer or electric heat gun, remove the moisture from each swelled foot. As the fibers dry, they will shrink, leaving small cracks in their trail. Once again, the type of wood and finish will affect how rapidly the fibers respond to both the moisture and the heat. Repeated applications may be necessary, depending on how worn you want the feet to appear.

One of the best reproduction desks I have ever seen was constructed by a New Hampshire cabinetmaker for a museum curator. The curator insisted that the desk be an exact duplication of a rare model the museum had in its collection, right down to the number of wormholes. The desk was over two hundred years old and had been damaged and repaired several times. In order to carry the duplication to its completion, the cabinetmaker went so far as to cut out a section of wood in one corner of the reproduction and to patch it with a wood of a similar, though not identical, grain pattern. Structurally, the repair was entirely unnecessary, but since the original had been damaged and patched, the reproduction had to be as well. The finished product came so close to duplicating the original desk that most of the curator's guests never questioned its authenticity. Some had to be shown the modern cabinetmaker's signature and date on the side of one drawer to be convinced that it was, indeed, a reproduction.

Distress marks can be carried to an almost absurd extreme, including water rings from flower pots, holes left by nails, screws, or even mice, cabinetmaker's scribe marks along dovetail joints, or old repairs—just so long as they actually appeared on the authentic antique. Before I add even the first mark, I study similar authentic antiques closely, then lightly mark with a pencil the areas on my new piece I want to distress with a particular stain. If it is a desk or library table top, I'm apt to add one or two small ink stains, remembering that I don't want to make them large enough to detract from the beauty or value of the piece. I've seen authentic library tables with enormous ink stains, but that doesn't mean that I want mine to look like that. A few small, well-positioned stains, including one or two inside the drawer, where the ink or a fountain pen would have been kept, will convey the feeling of age without ruining the piece.

Desks, tables, and the shelves of cupboards often end up with one or two black rings left from when a wet glass was allowed to sit long enough for the water to penetrate the finish. Sometimes the rings will be complete circles; other times they will only be partial circles or arcs. The easiest way I have found to duplicate either is to set a small can, such as an empty soup can, on a sheet of newspaper, spray the lip lightly with black spray paint, and then immediately press the painted end of the can down onto the wood. I would recommend that you first practice a few times on a piece of scrap wood to get the feel of it; I would also advise you to wipe the lip clean with a rag or paper towel between sprayings to prevent excess paint from building up on the inside of the can and running down on your wood. You can obtain similar results by coating the lip of the can with ebony or dark walnut wood stain rather than black paint. One or two rings or partial rings will be enough to give your top or shelf the proper aged look.

Before you begin, then, think about how your piece would have been used, and some of the marks that you might make to suggest that use, such as:

Bookcases—a water mark on the top where a plant had been set; hundreds of fine cross-grain scratches indicating where books had been pulled out and slid back; nicks around the legs from vacuum sweepers, brooms, and mops; wear around the pulls; small scratches on the top from picture frames, pottery, and glassware.

Nightstands—water rings; dye from candle wax; perhaps a spot of ink from a midnight writer.

Dressers and Chests of Drawers—wear around the pulls; hundreds of fine cross-grain scratches on the top from loose change, picture frames, jewelry boxes, and so forth; nicks around the base from vacuums and brooms; sides relatively unblemished; wear along top edges of drawers.

Beds—few marks except for wear around the tops of posts and the top of the foot rail.

Chairs—scratches in the seat; chips at the front corners where they would have come in contact with desks and tables; scratches and wear on the tops of rungs, arms, and head rail; finish worn on back interior, but no scratches.

Dining Tables—scratches on top from plates, silverware, hot plates, vases, and so forth; a few water spots and/or black rings; apron worn on bottom edge, but relatively scratch-free; legs show dents where they come in contact with chair seats, but only on outside; interior of legs clean; outside edges show dents, worn smooth.

Desks—scratches on top, especially in middle; ink stains, water marks; wear around pulls; dents where contact made with desk chair; footrest worn down to bare wood; nicks on feet from vacuums and brooms; sides in very good condition.

The list could go on indefinitely, but once you get the idea, you can judge what type of wear your piece would have received and what objects you can use to duplicate it. I once had to make a new set of shelves for a cupboard, so after I added a couple of black rings and a coat of satin finish, I put the shelves in the cupboard, loaded them with cups, stacks of plates, platters, and pottery, and began sliding all of them in and out, in and out, changing their locations and repeating the process, in and out, in and out. It took about thirty minutes for me to duplicate about a hundred years of moderate use.

And I never once had to use a two-foot length of chain.

The same also applies even if you are just duplicating the wear on a replacement part, such as an arm, spindle, or, as I did not long ago, a runner on a rocking chair. Holidays are tough on furniture, but nothing compares to the abuse furniture takes on Super Bowl Sunday. If it was a lopsided game, our business at the restoration shop the next day wouldn't show a sudden increase, but when the game was close and the referee made a disputable call near the end of the game, you can literally hear the furniture breaking. In a single moment all across the country, rungs snap, arms come loose, rockers break in half—and refinishers smile, for they know the next day most of those broken chairs are going to be sitting in their shop.

One of my last was a sixty-year-old rocking chair, certainly not old by antique standards, but one that had still begun to accumulate its share of nicks, scratches, and dents. Late in the fourth quarter the guilty party had leaned too far back and the runner snapped where they most often do—at the point where the back post joins it. The break was clean and permanent. I could push the two pieces of the runner back together well enough to trace a pattern on a new piece of wood, but experience had shown me that an internal dowel couldn't withstand the stress a runner has to be able to take. In a few minutes I had a new runner cut and sanded, and by the end of the day the stain and first coat of finish were dry. But my runner looked obviously new. I laid it on the workbench alongside the broken runner, and starting at one end, I systematically duplicated every nick, scratch, chip, splinter, dent, and worn spot I found on the original. When I was done—and it only took ten or fifteen minutes—the replacement runner looked just as old and just as worn as the broken one.

Distressing: ▶
The Finish

A reproduction can only look as authentic as its finish. Even though most true antiques have been refinished at some point, the most treasured are those that come the closest to having—or appearing to have—an original finish. And duplicating an authentic finish doesn't take any longer than duplicating the signs of wear in the wood.

The first step in duplicating an original finish is to identify what the appropriate finish was for the antiques of that era. In nearly every instance, you can count out polyurethane varnish, lacquer, and even standard varnish. What you have to select from, then, are oil, shellac, and paint.

Oil Finishes ▶

Oil finishes are perhaps the easiest to duplicate, since the majority of the oil is absorbed into the wood. The most obvious characteristics of an authentic oil finish, though, are the smell and, unfortunately, the stickiness often associated with raw and boiled linseed oil. Experience and research have taught us that linseed oil is no longer the best finish for true antiques, since it tends to darken wood and becomes nearly impossible to remove after it has dried.

Since you are working with a reproduction, however, and not an authentic antique, you may choose to use a mixture of two parts boiled linseed oil and one part turpentine, applied, according to the time-honored formula, once a day for a week, once a week for a month, once a month for a year, and once a year for life. The oil mixture should be applied generously and rubbed into the surface of the wood for ten to twenty minutes. As soon as it begins to harden, remove the excess with a clean cloth, then immediately begin buffing up a luster with yet another clean cloth. Allow the oil in the wood to harden completely before repeating the process, otherwise the previous coat will never harden, leaving the finish soft and sticky.

If you want to take advantage of modern technology, which has discovered a means of achieving an oil finish without the stickiness associated with linseed oil, you can get the same look, feel, and smell of a boiled linseed oil finish without the adverse side effects. Modern oil finishes, such as tung oil or Danish oil (see Chapter 8), should be applied as directed on the container, since the ingredients may vary from brand to brand. To achieve the "antique" smell of a boiled linseed oil finish, wait until the final application of finish has dried thoroughly, then thin one part boiled linseed oil with four parts turpentine, dip a pad of no. 0000 steel wool in the mixture, and rub out the piece lightly. Follow immediately with a rapid buffing with a soft cloth to remove any excess oil. The result will be a modern oil finish with the look and smell of a traditional linseed oil finish.

Shellac was a favorite of cabinetmakers for centuries, and while modern furniture firms have switched to lacquer for the most part, shellac is still a better choice for an antique surface finish.   ◀ **Shellac Finish**

To achieve an authentic antique finish using shellac, thin the shellac as it comes from the can with three parts denatured alcohol. Brush on a minimum of four coats, letting each coat harden before buffing it with dry no. 000 steel wool. After the last coat has dried, dip a pad of no. 000 steel wool into a can of paste wax and rub the finish to a satin waxed smoothness. As soon as the wax begins to harden, buff with a soft, clean cloth. Fifteen minutes later return to buff the remaining wax one additional time.

The story has often been told of the old counterfeiter in New Hampshire who used to make a piece or two of Early American furniture every now and then when his cash supply was beginning to dwindle, brush on a coat or two of shellac, rub it out, and then put it in his chicken house for a few weeks for his hens to roost on. After it had ''aged,'' he would drag it out, wipe some of the accumulation of dust and dung off, and set it up on his front porch, just so you could catch a glimpse of it as you were driving by. During the tourist season he had trouble keeping it there for more than two or three days before someone would turn around, come back, and, after about thirty minutes of pleading, talk him into taking their money for it.

It's a good idea, but I refuse to keep chickens in my workshop.

Early American painted furniture is finally receiving the recognition it deserves, but not before thousands of valuable painted antiques had been dipped, stripped, and belt-sanded into naked submission. Those that survived the dipping tanks of the sixties and seventies have skyrocketed in value, bringing tens of thousands of dollars at major auctions across the country.   ◀ **Painted Finish**

Unless you woke up this morning to hear your lottery number being read on the radio, you probably can't afford or would prefer not to invest your savings in a rare painted piece of authentic Early

American furniture. Fortunately, you are in a situation similar to that of the very same cabinetmakers who made that highly desirable painted furniture: you can't find or afford the highly exotic and expensive hardwoods and you don't enjoy the bland grain of the common and less expensive softwoods.

So why not do the same thing they did?

Paint it.

Locate a new reproduction maple, birch, or pine piece of furniture that fills your needs, such as a corner cupboard, a Shaker-style table, or a Windsor chair, select the color you want (hopefully choosing one that, according to the reference books, is historically accurate), and prepare to give it a coat of antique paint. Even though the paint will cover the wood, you still need to sand the wood as smooth as possible and to round the edges, corners, and tops that would have received the most wear.

Our early cabinetmakers were experimenters, both in the types of paint they used and in the pigments they added to them. I urge you to be just as bold, trying any of a number of different routes. Like Mildred, the woman with the "two-hundred-year-old" wash bench, you can simply pick out a premixed latex or oil-base interior paint with a flat or dull sheen from a color chart. Either can be used directly from the can or diluted with the proper solvent (turpentine for oil-base paints, water for latex) for a thinner, almost translucent effect and can be rubbed out afterward with steel wool to either increase the sheen (no. 0000) or to reduce it (no. 0).

Several companies now offer milk paints, similar to the formulas used by those early self-sufficient craftsmen (see Sources, Chapter 12). The advantage to these paints is that the manufacturers have already researched the proper colors and have reduced the gloss by adding flattening agents to give the paint that antique look. If you want to make your own milk paint, it isn't difficult. You simply mix enough hot water with instant nonfat dry milk to make, as one furniture maker describes it, "a thick, smooth syrup." The amount of milk base you mix will be determined by the size of your project, but since the ingredients are not expensive, you certainly can afford to experiment.

Once you have achieved the quantity and consistency you want, you can then experiment with various pigments. Any natural or synthetic dyes can be added to the base, but I must admit to taking the easy way out. I prefer using small tubes of acrylic paints in universal colors as tints for the milk base. If I want a particular red paint, I have a half dozen shades of red to choose from; if I need a special green, yellow, or blue, it is simply a matter of finding or blending the proper paints and adding them to my milk base.

Even though it is not mandatory, I often seal the wood with a thin coat of shellac first; it enables me to wipe the paint off easily in those spots I want to highlight, yet it won't interfere with the adhesion of the paint to the furniture. Like all finishes, the milk paint goes on easier if it is applied while it is still warm. I wouldn't sacrifice experimentation just for the sake of a warm finish, however; practice brushing or wiping your milk paint on a piece of scrap wood, letting it dry to determine what the finished color will look like. If your milk paint cools, you can rewarm it or try working with it at room temperature.

As with Mildred's wash bench, you can determine how much use and abuse your "new antique" received simply by how much paint you wipe off. Before you even start, I would strongly suggest that you find photographs or, better yet, actual pieces which you can use to judge how much use yours would have received, and where, had it been an actual antique, for if your "wear" is not consistent with the type of furniture, then people are going to realize immediately that not only is your piece a reproduction, but you didn't take the time to research it very thoroughly. If you are using a milk paint, wring out a wet rag to wipe the paint off those areas that would have received the most use. Sides and fronts of cabinets and cupboards may remain a solid color, while around drawer and door pulls, latches, feet, and tops the paint may be worn through to the wood.

After the piece dries, you can duplicate additional wear using a pad of no. 000 steel wool. You might also want to add a few appropriate distress marks, after which you can buff the entire piece with no. 0000 steel wool to remove any gloss, dust, or wood fibers that remain. Afterward I recommend waxing the entire piece, both to help "age" the distress marks and to seal and protect the milk paint.

Along with thin drawer bottoms and flimsy backs, the other weakness in unfinished furniture is the hardware. It's not unusual to see several different styles of furniture—Victorian, Shaker, or Early American—all with the same Chippendale-influenced brass hardware. Historical accuracy is sacrificed in the name of econ-

◀ **Hardware**

omy, for rather than order smaller quantities of several different types of hardware, most companies tend to order several thousand of one style at a discount and slap them on every piece they produce.

What you can do, though, is to change that hardware. Ideally, you would like to replace the gaudy hardware with actual antique hardware. Flea markets, antiques shops, and refinishers often have hardware salvaged from damaged furniture. Check with them first, especially if you only need a pair of pulls or a cupboard latch. Authentic sets of six or more are difficult to find, but there are several companies that manufacture reproduction hardware for every style from Pilgrim to Oriental, Hepplewhite to Art Deco (see Sources, Chapter 12). They range from brass pulls to cherry knobs to porcelain teardrops. All it takes to switch from factory hardware to more appropriate hardware is a screwdriver and about fifteen minutes. Many larger refinishing shops and antiques stores will also stock a line of reproduction hardware for the do-it-yourselfer.

If the hardware that either came with your piece of furniture or that has come from a reproduction furniture company arrives too bright and shiny to fool anyone into thinking that it is any more than a year or so old, you can speed up the tarnishing process using a mild acid labeled and sold as a ''Brass Antiquing Solution'' (see Sources, Chapter 12). Several companies that sell reproduction hardware offer small, inexpensive bottles of an antiquing solution, which you simply pour into a container and dip the hardware into. The longer you leave the hardware in, the darker it turns. Afterward you can use a pad of no. 000 steel wool to duplicate the wear you would expect to find on an old, authentic pull.

One of my first experiences with reproduction antique furniture came in a refinishing class I was teaching for the local community college. One of my students wanted to turn a new, unfinished drop-front desk into one that looked more like it was built around the turn of the century. Each night that she worked on it the desk looked older and older, as she rounded corners, added a few distress marks and a couple of ink stains, rubbed on a light oak stain, and finished it with satin varnish and paste wax. After she had assembled it, three or four of us stood there, looking it over. But something was not quite right. It took a few minutes to determine what it was, but once someone pointed it out, it was obvious to everyone: the screws in the hinges were Phillips-head screws. Right offhand, I'm not sure what year Phillips-head screws were patented, but I know they weren't used in furniture before 1920. As soon as she found the appropriate-sized flat-head screws in my box of old screws and made the switch, her desk looked real.

If you don't have an assortment of old screws to choose from, you can still improve on the Phillips-head screws that come in most unfinished furniture. If you can find them, brass screws look more authentic than new zinc or steel screws, but all three share the same problem: they look too new. Like nearly all problems, though, you do have a solution. Grasp the tail of the screw in a pair of pliers and hold the head in a small flame, such as a cigarette lighter or the flame on your gas stove. Keep it there from one to two minutes or until the protective coating has burned off, then remove the screw from the flame and plunge it in a glass of water. The combination of heat and moisture will instantly "age" the screw head; you can repeat the procedure as many times as you like until the head looks appropriate to your piece of furniture—but do let it cool before you use it.

Check the piece over for other obvious modern additions, such as magnetic latches, plastic castors, or Plexiglas panes. Nearly all of these can be replaced with antique-style hardware or, as in the case of Plexiglas, with genuine glass. If your cupboard, bookcase, or china closet is supposed to look as if it is more than a hundred years old, I would suggest that you do as many antique restorers do and use old glass salvaged from old house windows as replacements. You won't realize how much of a difference there is between old glass with all its imperfections and new glass until you place the two side by side and note how differently they reflect natural light.

While reproductions continue to have a bad reputation in the antiques business, they have been here for centuries and will continue to remain popular as long as antiques are hard to find and cost too much. I have no problem justifying the place and purpose of reproductions, so long as they are truthfully represented. While antiques dealers, myself included, worry not so much about the present owner misrepresenting the piece as we do the second, third, or fourth owners, twenty, thirty, or forty years from now, much of the problem could be avoided if you and I would carve, brand, or somehow permanently inscribe the date on which

◄ Signing Your Work

we completed our reproduction in a spot that could be readily seen, yet would not detract from the beauty of the piece, such as on the underside of a table, inside a drawer, or beneath an arm. Granted, a brand could be sanded off, a label removed, or a carving covered, but the scar, the glue mark, or the difference in the color, regardless how subtle, can alert the cautious buyer.

Shopping List

— linseed oil
— turpentine
— shellac
— denatured alcohol
— paste wax
— paint

— no. 120 sandpaper
— no. 220 sandpaper
— metal file
— distressing "tools"
— no. 00 steel wool
— no. 000 steel wool
— brushes
— clean rags

CHAPTER II
Formulas and Recipes

While each of these formulas has been tested, it is impossible to guarantee how each will react in every situation. For that reason, I strongly recommend that you test each mixture on an inconspicuous spot on your furniture before applying it to the entire piece. If a particular formula does not respond or perform in the expected manner, experiment with various proportions of ingredients, but, as always, test it first.

Many of the ingredients required in the following recipes are highly flammable. Never apply direct heat to any flammable liquid. Instead, use the traditional double boiler method: a smaller container sitting in a larger container of water. Heat the water, and the water will then heat the ingredients in the smaller container. It's not only neater, but safer, too.

One thing to remember: "Boiled linseed oil" is NOT raw linseed oil that you boil at home. At the hardware store you will find both "raw linseed oil" and "boiled linseed oil." Do not confuse the two and do not attempt to turn raw linseed oil into boiled linseed oil by heating it. If you do, you run the risk of starting a fire.

And, as always, assume that every ingredient is toxic and that it shouldn't be inhaled or swallowed. Read and observe all cautions printed on the container and keep all chemicals and ingredients stored safely out of the reach of curious children and innocent pets. I urge you to wear safety glasses at all times, and when working around liquids, wear neoprene gloves, a long-sleeved shirt, and a heavy work apron. If you have a history of allergies, I also recommend that you wear a charcoal respirator whenever mixing and using any of these solutions.

Brass, Antiquing

1 cup distilled water
1 tablespoon trisodium phosphate (TSP)
½ teaspoon liver of sulfur

Wash item with lacquer thinner to remove any coatings. (If tarnished, see following recipes.) Heat water to boiling, stir in TSP.

Pour into glass container and add liver of sulfur. Using wooden tongs, string, or other nonmetallic material, dip item in hot solution for 2–5 seconds, pull out to check color. Repeat for darker color. When desired color is obtained, rinse under cold running water. Dry, then rub with no. 0000 steel wool or coarse cloth to imitate use. Seal with paste wax or light misting of aerosol lacquer.

Brass Cleanser (for dirt and mild tarnish)

> 1 part water
> 1 part household ammonia

Combine ingredients in a glass container. Insert item, let soak, then remove and rub with cloth until clean. Seal with paste wax or lacquer.

Brass Cleanser (for tarnish)

> vinegar
> salt

Soak item in vinegar. Moisten rag with vinegar, dip in salt and rub item. Rinse with vinegar. Dry immediately. Seal with paste wax or lacquer.

Brass Cleanser (for tarnish)

> lemon slice
> salt

Dip a slice of lemon in salt, then rub item. Rinse with vinegar, dry immediately, then seal with paste wax or lacquer.

Brass Cleanser (for tarnish)

> 2 parts vinegar
> 1 part lemon juice

Combine ingredients, then insert item and let soak until tarnish is loosened. Remove and rub dry with cloth. Seal with paste wax or lacquer.

Copper, Antiquing

—see Brass, Antiquing

Copper Cleanser

—see Brass Cleanser

Furniture Finish Cleanser

1 part turpentine
3 parts boiled linseed oil

Combine ingredients and warm in a double boiler (or set container in a pan of hot water, but *do not* apply heat directly to container). Dip rag into mixture, then rub onto surface with a cloth or no. 0000 steel wool; buff dry.

Furniture Finish Cleanser *(for thick varnish finishes only)*

1 quart hot water
1 tablespoon laundry detergent
3 tablespoons boiled linseed oil (tung oil or mineral oil)
3 tablespoons turpentine

Stir detergent into hot water, then add oil and turpentine. Rub onto finish while still warm with cloth or no. 0000 steel wool. Buff dry.

Furniture Polish

1 pint boiled linseed oil or mineral oil
1 ounce beeswax
1 pint turpentine

Heat the oil in a double boiler, then add the beeswax. Stir until melted; remove from heat and immediately stir in the turpentine. Let the solution cool. Apply with a soft cloth, then buff dry.

For a tinted furniture polish that will disguise shallow scratches, dissolve your choice of tinting color in the turpentine before adding it to the wax and oil.

Furniture Polish (with a fine abrasive)

> 1 cup boiled linseed oil or mineral oil
> 1 cup denatured alcohol
> 1 cup vinegar
> 1 ounce rottenstone

Combine the liquid ingredients and stir thoroughly; add rottenstone as you continue stirring. Apply with a soft cloth, rubbing in the direction of the grain. Buff with a clean cloth until dry.

Furniture Finish Reviver (varnish or oil)

> 1 part turpentine
> 1 part boiled linseed oil (or mineral oil)

Combine ingredients and apply with no. 0000 steel wool or a cloth. Buff dry with clean cloth.

Furniture Finish Reviver (shellac)

> 2 parts mineral oil
> 1 part clear liquid shellac

Combine ingredients and apply with no. 0000 steel wool or a cloth. Buff dry with clean cloth.

Furniture Finish Reviver (heavily crazed shellac)

> 2 parts turpentine
> 2 parts boiled linseed oil
> 4 parts denatured alcohol

Combine ingredients and apply with no. 0000 steel wool or a cloth. Buff dry with clean cloth.

Furniture Finish Reviver (heavily crazed lacquer)

> 2 parts turpentine
> 2 parts boiled linseed oil
> 4 parts lacquer thinner

Combine ingredients and apply with no. 0000 steel wool or a cloth. Buff dry with clean cloth.

Hand Cleaner

1 cup turpentine
3 tablespoons water
3 tablespoons liquid soap

Combine and stir thoroughly. Shake before using. Pour small amount into palm of hand, then rub hands together, working mixture into your skin. Wipe off with clean cloth.

Leather Cleanser

1 cup warm water
1 teaspoon liquid soap
1 teaspoon vinegar

Mix ingredients thoroughly. Dip clean cloth into mixture, then rub gently on leather. Wipe dry.

Leather Dressing

10 fluid ounces benzene
1 ounce beeswax
1 fluid ounce neat's-foot oil
6 fluid ounces lanolin

Shave the beeswax into 1 cup of benzene (highly flammable) and slowly heat in a double boiler until wax is melted. Remove from heat, stir in remaining benzene and other ingredients. While still warm, rub on liberally with a cloth, working mixture into the leather. Buff dry with a clean cloth. Repeat if necessary the following day or any time the leather again appears dry and lifeless.

Leather Dressing

2 parts anhydrous lanolin
3 parts pure neat's-foot oil

Slowly melt anhydrous lanolin in a double boiler, then stir in neat's-foot oil. Stir thoroughly. Remove from the heat. While still warm, work into leather using soft cloth. Buff dry.

Leather Reviver

2 parts denatured alcohol
3 parts castor oil

Mix ingredients together; using a soft cloth, rub into clean leather until absorbed. Let sit for one to two days, then apply a light coat of castor oil alone. Rub into leather until absorbed.

Marble Sealer

1 part beeswax
1 part turpentine

Pour turpentine over beeswax shavings and stir until beeswax dissolves. Set in pan of hot water until warm. Brush on clean marble, let cool, then buff off excess.

Milk Paint

instant nonfat dry milk
hot water
acrylic paint or pigment

Slowly add hot water to dry milk until you have a mixture the consistency of syrup. Tint the mixture the desired color by slowly adding powdered pigments or acrylic paint.

Milk Paint

2 cups slaked lime (dehydrated lime)
½ cup water
1 pint cottage cheese
skim milk
powdered pigments

Combine the lime and water thoroughly, then let stand for 24 hours. Stir in cottage cheese, then let stand for an additional 24 hours. Add skim milk and stir until a syrup-like consistency is reached. Tint mixture the desired color by slowly adding powdered pigments.

Neutralizer (for use on wood or marble that has been treated with ammonia or bleach)

1 part cold water
1 part vinegar

Combine and flush liberally. Wipe dry immediately.

Paint and Varnish Remover *(Warning: not recommended for fine woods, veneers, inlay, or valuable antiques.)*

3 pounds trisodium phosphate (TSP)
1 gallon hot water

Stir the TSP into the hot water until dissolved. Apply liberally with a brush; repeat until finish is softened.

Stain, Pigmented Wiping

1 pint turpentine
6 fluid ounces boiled linseed oil
tints or pigments (see following list)
½ fluid ounce japan drier

Combine turpentine and boiled linseed oil; stir thoroughly. Slowly add tints or pigments until desired color is achieved. Stir in japan drier. Store in tightly closed container. Note ingredients and their proportion on label.

dark brown—burnt umber

dark reddish brown—burnt sienna

*yellow—raw sienna, yellow ochre, chrome yellow

*medium brown—Vandyke brown, raw umber

*red—rose pink, red lead, red oxide

blue—ultramarine blue

*black—lampblack

*basic wood colors

Stain, Tobacco

> 1 plug chewing tobacco
> 1 pint household ammonia

Place tobacco and ammonia in a jar, seal, and store one week. Carefully uncap jar and set outside to release ammonia fumes, then strain through cheesecloth. Before using, dampen wood with clear water, then apply heavy coat of tobacco stain. Allow the wood to absorb the stain, but wipe it off before it evaporates. Wipe off excess, let dry. Remove any raised fibers with medium steel wool the next day; repeat staining process for darker color.

Stain, Varnish *(Not recommended for fine furniture or antiques.)*

> 1 pint varnish
> universal tinting color or artist oil paint

Add tint or paint to varnish a few drops at a time, stirring thoroughly. Do not overtint. Each coat of varnish will darken color.

Stain, Walnut

Method A—Cover a bucket of green walnut husks with a gallon of rainwater for 3 days. Add one tablespoon dry sodium carbonate (soda ash), then place over low heat and let simmer for 3 days. Remove from heat, let cool, then strain through cheesecloth. Pour into jars or bottles, seal, and store in a dark cabinet.

Method B—Cover a bucket of green walnut husks with a gallon of rainwater for 3 days. Add one tablespoon dry sodium carbonate (soda ash), then place over low heat and let simmer for 6 to 8 hours. Remove from heat, let cool enough to pour unstrained into glass container(s). Set containers in direct sunlight for 2 weeks, then strain through cheesecloth. Pour into jars or bottles, seal, and store in dark cabinet.

Stain, Water

Place ingredient (see following list) in pan, cover with water, then bring to a boil. Reduce heat and add 1 tablespoon caustic soda per gallon of water. Cover and simmer 6 hours. Pour into glass jars, cap, and set in sunlight for one week. Strain through cheesecloth, pour into jars, seal, and store in dark cabinet.

These stains call for much experimentation, as depth of color and tint depend on the proportion of the ingredient to the water.

> Suggested ingredients:

> Brazilwood—reddish
> Chicory root—yellowish brown
> Tobacco—brown
> Dragon's blood—red
> chestnut—brown
> tea or coffee—brown

Stripper, Solvent

> 1 quart lacquer thinner
> 1 quart denatured alcohol

Combine ingredients, apply with no. 00 steel wool. Mixture evaporates quickly, limiting size of area that can be stripped at one time.

Tack Rag

> cheesecloth
> turpentine
> varnish

Take a section of clean cheesecloth, unfold it, and dip it in turpentine. Wring it out, then start adding varnish a few drops at a time, working it into the cheesecloth until it becomes sticky. Refold the cheesecloth and store it in a self-sealing sandwich bag. If it dries out before it becomes too dirty to discard, simply repeat the process.

Water Rinse (for rinsing stripper sludge)

> two quarts warm water
> one cup trisodium phosphate (TSP)
> four tablespoons laundry detergent
> two quarts cool water

Mix warm water, TSP, and detergent thoroughly, then add two quarts of cold water to cool solution before using it to remove the sludge. (Warning: water may raise the grain of the wood, loosen veneer, and swell thin slats. Wipe dry as soon as possible to avoid water damage to wood.)

Wax Finish (medium strength)

> 1 part turpentine
> 1 part melted beeswax
> 1 part boiled linseed oil

Warm turpentine in a double boiler, adding beeswax and stirring until it dissolves. Add oil, continuing to stir. Remove from heat, brush on the wood while still warm, and allow to dry. Buff with a clean, soft cloth.

Wax Finish (high durability)

> 1 pint turpentine
> 1 pound carnauba wax
> 1 pound paraffin wax

Heat turpentine in a double boiler, adding wax shavings and stirring until melted. Remove from heat, pour into container, and let cool. If wax dries too hard to use, remelt and add more turpentine.

Wax, Tinted

> quality paste wax
> oil-based tint

Place quality paste wax in a double boiler and slowly melt it; when wax is liquid, add oil-based tint of appropriate color (example: lampblack for black wax). Stir to mix thoroughly; pour back into container and allow to cool and harden.

Wood Sealer

> 4 parts denatured alcohol
> 2 parts shellac

Dilute liquid shellac with denatured alcohol. Stir thoroughly. Store in a glass container.

CHAPTER 12
Sources of Restoration Supplies and Information

I can remember being told as a college freshman that the biggest difference between an undergraduate and a graduate student is that a graduate student knows where to go to find out what he doesn't know.

I have since discovered that one of the biggest differences between an amateur and a professional refinisher is that a professional knows where to go to get what he doesn't have.

To help narrow the difference between the weekend refinisher and the weekday professional, I have listed the names and addresses of several of the companies that professional refinishers turn to when they need a special stain, an unusual piece of hardware, or a particular type of veneer. Most of these companies are very small, very fast, and very efficient. The only drawback I have run into is that most have a minimum order amount that is generally more than the cost of what I need at one particular time. If you find that the ten dollars of brass knobs that you need falls fifteen dollars short of the minimum required per order, then let me make two suggestions: first, you can find a friend who might also want to order something from that catalog; or second, you can do as I do and buy something you've always wanted—like a picture frame clamp, a five-blade scraper set, or a do-it-yourself clock kit. Believe me, it isn't difficult to spend thirty dollars with a good woodworking or reproduction hardware catalog.

I have attempted to categorize the companies I have included under headings representing their particular strength, that is, hardware, caning supplies, trunk parts, and so forth, but almost all of these companies offer a variety of parts and supplies. It isn't unusual to find a company that stocks tools, varnishes, hardware, hinges, books, sandpaper, drill bits, and stripper, so just because a company is listed under one category, don't assume that they stock only that type of material.

Just as handling costs have forced companies to institute a minimum charge per order, printing costs have forced several to charge a fee for their catalog. To save time, I would recommend that you call first to see if they have what you need and to find out how much their catalog costs. If you would rather write, include a large self-addressed, stamped envelope for their reply or, if you are lucky, for them to slip a catalog into.

Finally, while this list is extensive, it is by no means conclusive. New companies are emerging every month, and many take several years to become widely known. I would suggest that you read regional antiques and craft magazines and newspapers (see list after Sources), adding the names of individuals and companies who advertise their services and products to this list. I would also appreciate learning about these firms (or any of those I've listed that have gone out of business or changed their address) so that I can update my own list for eventual publication. My address appears later in the book.

CANE AND BASKET SUPPLIES

Peerless Rattan
P.O. Box 636
Yonkers, NY 10702
(914) 968-4046

H. H. Perkins Company
10 South Bradley Road
Woodbridge, CT 06525
(203) 389-9501

Frank's Cane & Rush Supply
7252 Heil Avenue
Huntington Beach, CA 92647
(714) 847-0707

Connecticut Cane & Reed Co.
P.O. Box 7620
Manchester, CT 06040
(203) 646-6586

Cane and Basket Supply Co.
1283 S. Cochran Avenue
Los Angeles, CA 90019
(213) 939-9644

FURNITURE PLANS AND KITS

Mason & Sullivan Clocks
586 Higgins Crowell Road
West Yarmouth, Cape Cod,
MA 02673
(617) 778-0475

Shaker Workshops
P.O. Box 1028
Concord, MA 01742
(617) 646-8985

GLASS, CUSTOM

Century Glass & Mirror Co.
1417 N. Washington Street
Dallas, TX 75204

B & L Antiquarie
P.O. Box 453
Lexington, MI 48450
(313) 359-8623

HARDWARE, PARTS, AND SUPPLIES

Wise Company
P.O. Box 118
Arabi, LA 70032
(504) 277-7551

Williamsburg Blacksmiths
Goshen Road Route 9
Williamsburg, MA 01096
(413) 268-7341

HARDWARE, PARTS, AND SUPPLIES

Van Dyke's
P.O. Box 278
Woonsocket, SD 57385
(605) 796-4425

Tuxedo Carvings
Tuxedo, NY 10987
(914) 351-4544

Thomas H. Kramer, Inc.
805 Depot Street
Columbus, IN 47201
(812) 379-4097

Ritter & Son Hardware
P.O. Box 578
Gualala, CA 95445
(800) 358-9120

Period Hardware
P.O. Box 1357
Pacifica, CA 94044

Paxton Hardware, LTD
7818 Bradshaw Road
Upper Falls, Maryland
(301) 592-8505

19th Century Company
P.O. Box 1455
Upland, CA 91786

Muff's Antiques
135 S. Glassell Street
Orange, CA 92666
(714) 997-0243

Horton Brasses
P.O. Box 95
Cromwell, CT 06416
(203) 635-4400

Heirlooms
709 E. 14th Street
Big Spring, TX 79720
(915) 263-8640

Good Pickin's
P.O. Box 666
Jefferson, TX 75657
(214) 665-3222

Furniture Revival & Co.
P.O. Box 994
Corvallis, OR 97330
(503) 754-6323

18th Century Hardware
131 East Third Street
Derry, PA 15627
(412) 694-2708

Kayne & Son
Custom Forged Hardware
76 Daniel Road
Candler, NC 28715
(704) 667-8868

Colonial Lock Company
172 Main Street
Terryville, CT 06786
(203) 584-0311

Brass Tree
308 N. Main Street
St. Charles, MO 63301
(314) 947-7707

Ball and Ball
463 W. Lincoln Highway
Exton, PA 19341
(215) 363-7330

Antique Hardware Store
43 Bridge Street
Frenchtown, NJ 08825
(201) 996-4040

Antique Hardware Company
P.O. Box 1592
Torrance, CA 90505
(213) 378-5990

HOME RESTORATIONS

San Francisco Victoriana
2245 Palou Avenue
San Francisco, CA 94124
(415) 648-0313

Renovator's Supply
Millers Falls, MA 01349
(413) 659-2211

HOME RESTORATIONS

HouseParts
417 Second Street
Eureka, CA 95501
(800) 634-2600

Bona Decorative Hardware
2227 Beechmont
Cincinnati, OH 45230
(513) 232-4300

LIGHTING

Rejuvenation Lamp
& Fixture Co.
901 N. Skidmore
Portland, OR 97217

Squaw Alley Incorporated
106 W. Water Street
Naperville, IL 60540
(312) 357-0200

MISCELLANEOUS

Turner & Seymour
(decorative nails)
P.O. Box 358
Torrington, CT 06790
(203) 489-9214

Grainger's
(motors, exhaust fans,
compressors)
5959 W. Howard Street
Chicago, IL 60648
(312) 928-1912

Wood and Leather Craft
Star Route
Callicoon, NY 12723
(914) 887-4195

Automatic Music Roll
Company
(player pianos, jukeboxes,
radios)
P.O. Box 3194
Seattle, WA 98114
(206) 633-3664

PAINT

Old-Fashioned Milk Paint
Company
P.O. Box 222
Groton, MA 01450
(617) 448-6336

PIERCED TIN PANELS

Country Accents
RD 2 Box 293
Stockton, NJ 08559
(201) 996-2885

REFINISHING SUPPLIES

Gaston Wood Finishes
P.O. Box 1246
Bloomington, IN 47402
(812) 339-9111

Mohawk Finishing Products
Route 30 North
Amsterdam, NY 12010
(518) 843-1380

Behlen's
Route 30 North
Amsterdam, NY 12010
(518) 843-1380

TOOLS AND SPECIALTIES

Woodworkers' Store
21801 Industrial Boulevard
Rogers, MN 55374
(612) 428-2899

Brookstone
127 Vose Farm Road
Peterborough, NH 03458
(603) 924-7181

Constantine's
2050 Eastchester Road
Bronx, NY 10461
(800) 223-8087

Barap Specialties
835 Bellows Avenue
Frankfort, MI 49635
(616) 352-9863

TRUNK PARTS

Charlotte Ford Trunks, LTD
P.O. Box 536
Spearman, TX 79081
(806) 659-3027

Antique Trunk Company
3706 W. 169th Street
Cleveland, OH 44111
(216) 941-8618

VENEERS AND WOOD

Mountain Lumber
Route 2 Box 43–1
Ruckersville, VA 22968
(804) 985-3646

Bob Morgan Woodworking
Supplies
1123 Bardstown Road
Louisville, KY 40204
(502) 456-2545

Craftsman Lumber Company
P.O. Box 222
Groton, MA 01450
(617) 448-6336

Artistry in Veneers
450 Oak Tree Street
South Plainfield, NJ 07080
(201) 668-1430

The most current source of information on antiques, furniture restoration, and firms that offer reproduction parts, refinishing supplies, and restoration services is your area antiques newspaper or magazine. In addition to including articles and columns on furniture refinishing, most will have several restoration-related advertisements. I would strongly recommend that you write to any of the publications listed below and ask for a recent sample copy. You may wish to subscribe to several, especially if you live in an area that is covered by more than one. A small local paper with emphasis on area auctions, shows, and shops can be complemented with one of the national monthlies, which will keep you current on new discoveries, important conferences, and major auction houses.

◀ **Antiques Publications**

Adrian Antique Market
123 N. Main
Adrian, MI 49221

American Ceramics
15 West 44th Street
New York, NY 10036

American Clay Exchange
800 Murray Drive
El Cajon, CA 92020

American Collectors Journal
P.O. Box 407
Kewanee, IL 61443

American Heritage
P.O. Box 977
Farmingdale, NY 11737

Antiquarian Magazine
P.O. Box 798
Huntington, NY 11743

Antique & Auction News
P.O. Box 500
Mount Joy, PA 17552

Antique & Collectibles
1000 Pioneer Way
El Cajon, CA 92020

Antique Collector
527 Madison Avenue
New York, NY 10022

Antique Gazette
929 Davidson Avenue
Nashville, TN 37205

Antique Market Report
P.O. Box 12830
Wichita, KS 67277

Antique Monthly
Drawer 2
Tuscaloosa, AL 35401

Antique Monthly
P.O. Box 37105
Washington, DC 20013

Antique Press
12403 N. Florida Avenue
Tampa, FL 33612

Antique Review
12 East Stafford Street
Worthington, OH 43085

Antique Showcase Magazine
Canfield Ontario NOA 1CO
Canada

Antique Trader Weekly
P.O. Box 1050
Dubuque, IA 52001

Antique Traveler
P.O. Box 757
Mineola, TX 75773

AntiqueWeek
P.O. Box 90
Knightstown, IN 46148

Antiques & Art Around
Florida
P.O. Box 7584
Hollywood Hills, FL 33081

Antiques & Collectibles
P.O. Box 268
Greenvale, NY 11548

Antiques & Collectibles
Magazine
7723 Billings Way
Sacramento, CA 95832

Antiques & Collectibles News
P.O. Box 171713
Arlington, TX 76003

Antiques & Collecting Hobbies
1006 S. Michigan Avenue
Chicago, IL 60605

Antiques & Arts Weekly
5 Church Hill Road
Newtown, CT 06470–9987

Antiques & Fine Arts
434 S. First Street
San Jose, CA 95113

Antiques Magazine
P.O. Box 1975
Marion, OH 43305

Antiques of the Great NE
P.O. Box 277
Hunter, NY 12442

Antiques Today
P.O. Box 3897
Sonora, CA 95370

Antiques West
P.O. Box 2828
San Anselmo, CA 94960

Architectural Digest
P.O. Box 10040
Des Moines, IA 50340

Arizona Antique News
P.O. Box 26536
Phoenix, AZ 85068

Art & Antique Adventures
P.O. Box 4168
Santa Rosa, CA 95402

Art & Antique Auction
Review
IFM Building
Old Saybrook, CT 06475

Art & Antiques
89 Fifth Avenue
New York, NY 10003

Art & Auction
250 West 57th Street
New York, NY 10019

Arts & Crafts Quarterly
P.O. Box 3592 Station E
Trenton, NJ 08629

Buckeye Marketeer
16 E. Henderson Road
Columbus, OH 43214

Cape Cod Antiques & Arts
P.O. Box 400
Yarmouth Port, MA 02675

Cape Cod Antiques Monthly
P.O. Box 340
East Sandwich, MA 02537

Carolina Antique News
P.O. Box 241114
Charlotte, NC 28224

Collect America
P.O. Box 777
Waynesboro, TN 38485

Collector
P.O. Box 158
Heyworth, IL 61745

Collector
467 N. Main Street
Pomona, CA 91768

Collector
P.O. Box 730
Quechee, VT 05059

Collector Editions Magazine
170 Fifth Avenue
New York, NY 10010

Collectors Journal
P.O. Box 601
Vinton, IA 52349

Collectors Marketplace
P.O. Box 975
Rootstown, OH 44272

Collectors Mart
15100 Kellogg
Wichita, KS 67235

Collectors News
P.O. Box 156
Grundy Center, IA 50638

Collectors Showcase
P.O. Box 6929
San Diego, CA 92106

Country Americana
Magazine
P.O. Box 228
Washington, NJ 07882

Fine Woodworking
63 S. Main Street
P.O. Box 355
Taunton, CT 06470

Flea Marketeer
6569 Dixie Highway
Clarkston, MI 48016

Herald
Friends of Greenfield Village
Dearborn, MI 48121

Historical Gazette
P.O. Box 527
Vashan, WA 98070

International Collectors Alert
10076 Boca Entrada Boulevard
Boca Raton, FL 33433

Journal of Decorative Arts
2399 NE Second Avenue
Miami, FL 33137

Kovels on Antiques
P.O. Box 22200
Beachwood, OH 44122

Long Island Heritage
P.O. Box 471
Glen Cove, NY 11542

Maine Antique Digest
P.O. Box 645
Waldoboro, ME 04572

Magazine Antiques
980 Madison Avenue
New York, NY 10021

MassBay Antiques
P.O. Box 192
Ipswich, MA 01938

Mid-Atlantic Antiques
P.O. Box 908
Henderson, NC 27536

Midwest Antique Review
P.O. Box 90
Ottumwa, IA 52501

New England Antiques
Journal
4 Church Street
Ware, MA 01082

New York Antique
Almanac
P.O. Box 335
Lawrence, NY 11559

Northern Collector
P.O. Box 189
Gonvick, MN 56644

Nostalgiaworld
P.O. Box 231
North Haven, CT 06473

NY-PA Collector
Drawer C
Fishers, NY 14453

Ohio Antique Review
P.O. Box 538
Worthington, OH 43085

Old News Gazette
4928 Government Street
Baton Rouge, LA 70806

Old Stuff
P.O. Box 230220
Tigard, OR 97223

Renningers Antique Guide
P.O. Box 495
Lafayette Hill, PA 19444

Rocky Mountain States
Collector
Drawer 1107
Decatur, GA 30031

Southern Antiques
P.O. Box 1550
Lake City, FL 32056

Spinning Wheel
Fame Avenue
Hanover, PA 17331

Victorian Homes
P.O. Box 61
Millers Falls, MA 01349

West Coast Peddler
P.O. Box 5134
Whittier, CA 90607

Yankee
Dublin, NH 03444

Yesteryear
P.O. Box 2
Princeton, WI 54968

Glossary

acrylic—a synthetic resin used in water-base paints.

alligatoring—numerous small cracks in a finish, often the sign of an aging or thick finish.

aniline dye—a man-made tint that can be dissolved in water or alcohol and used to change the color of wood.

apron—the board between the tops of the legs which supports the top or, in the case of a chair, the seat; also called the "skirt."

benzene—a cleaning fluid and solvent; it evaporates quickly and is highly flammable; also called "naphtha."

bleeding—a situation in which the stain seeps out of the wood and into the finish, generally the result of applying a finish before the stain has dried.

boiled linseed oil—oil processed from the flax seed to which special drying agents have been added; not produced by simply boiling raw linseed oil.

bristle—a natural fiber used in brushes.

burl veneer—thin slices of wood cut from a warty growth on a tree; distinguished by unusual swirling grain pattern; highly valued by furniture craftsmen.

burn-in stick—a repair material used to replace missing wood, it is heated until it melts into the cavity, is allowed to cool, then is sanded smooth; also called "shellac stick" or "lacquer stick."

butt joint—a means of joining two pieces of wood simply by gluing the two flat surfaces together.

caustic soda—sodium hydroxide; also called lye.

China wood oil—another name for **tung oil**.

closed-grain wood—woods such as maple and birch that have small, tight pores.

crazing—a mild form of alligatoring, characterized by thousands of microscopic cracks in the finish.

denatured alcohol—ethyl alcohol to which poisonous chemicals have been added to enable it to be used as a solvent for shellac.

distressing—purposely inflicting signs of age to a wood or finish.

driers—chemicals that hasten the drying time of finishes such as varnish, lacquer, linseed oil, and tung oil.

dovetail—a means of joining two pieces of wood together at right angles to one another using an alternating series of slots and projections that increase the gluing surface and strength of the joint.

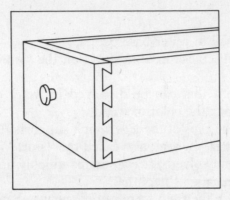

dowel—a round rod, either wood or metal.

escutcheon—a key plate.

epoxy glue—an extremely durable adhesive often used to bond woods that have been previously glued.

filler—see **paste filler**.

fish eyes—small craters in a new finish that are the result of an adverse reaction between the finish and foreign substances, such as wax or oil, on the surface.

flaking—a condition that exists when the finish begins peeling off the wood.

flattening agent—an additive to varnish or lacquer that reduces the amount of gloss in the finish when it dries.

French polish—a nineteenth-century finishing technique in which a specially prepared pad is dipped in shellac and whisked across the wood in a prescribed pattern.

fuming—a means of changing the color of certain woods containing tannin by exposing them to the fumes of ammonia in an airtight container.

graining—the act of duplicating the grain pattern of a type of wood using paints, stains, or glazes.

glides—metal or plastic disks tacked to the bottom of furniture legs to prevent marring of the floor.

hardwood—wood that comes from trees bearing broad leaves, such as oak, walnut, and maple.

heartwood—wood from the center of a tree.

hue—color.

inlay—decorative veneer or thin metals applied flush with the surface of the wood.

japan colors—tinted pigments dissolved in either lacquer or turpentine.

japan drier—a chemical added to stains and varnishes to reduce the drying time.

kiln—heated chamber designed for drying fresh-cut lumber.

linseed oil—oil processed from flax seed, formerly used as a wood finish, but no longer popular because of its inability to dry properly.

methylene chloride—a chemical used as the active ingredient in paint and varnish remover.

mineral oil—a lightweight oil.

mineral spirits—often called "turpentine" or "paint thinner."

miter—joint formed when two boards meet at an angle to one another.

mortise—an opening, usually rectangular, in a board that receives a second board, called the tenon, forming a mortise-and-tenon joint (also see **tenon**).

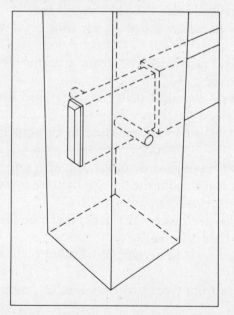

neoprene—a synthetic rubber highly resistant to solvents.

open-grain wood—woods such as oak, mahogany, and walnut that have large, obvious pores; also called "coarse-grain wood."

orange peel—term used to describe a rough finish, generally lacquer that has been sprayed improperly.

overspray—dried particles of a sprayed finish, such as lacquer, that land on a freshly sprayed area, but do not dissolve.

paraffin oil—a lightweight oil, often called **mineral oil**.

particleboard—board made from wood chips compressed and glued together; also called "fiberboard."

paste filler—a material, often powdered silex, that is thinned with mineral spirits and used to fill the pores in woods such as oak, ash, and mahogany.

patina—the overall effect of the aging process on wood, metal, or a finish, generally characterized by a muting of the colors and a satin finish.

penetrating oil stain—a stain that relies more on dyes than pigments to change the color of the wood.

pigmented oil stain—a stain that relies more on tinted pigments than dyes to change the color of the wood.

pegged joint—a mortise-and-tenon joint that is secured by inserting a length of dowel through both boards; also called a "pinned joint."

plain sawn—the standard means of cutting a board, which results in a long, wavy grain pattern; also called "flat-grained."

polyurethane—a resin which, when added to varnish, creates a more durable finish.

pumice—a fine, powdered abrasive ground from volcanic glass and used to rub out finishes.

resin—a man-made or natural chemical that dries to a hard film; a critical ingredient in wood finishes.

rottenstone—a powdered form of limestone used to rub out finishes.

quartersawn—a means of slicing a board, often oak, that reveals the medullary rays that travel from the core of the tree toward the bark; also called "tiger oak" or "flake oak."

sapwood—the portion of the tree nearest the bark; it can be identified in a board by its lighter color.

sealer—any thin finish used as a first coat; also called a "wash coat."

softwood—wood that comes from trees that bear needles, such as pine and fir.

spline—a thin, flat strip of wood glued into slots cut the entire length of two boards to be butt-jointed; it increases the glue surface and the strength of the joint.

spontaneous combustion—a fire caused by the heat generated by oxidizing oils in rags thrown in a pile rather than laid out to dry.

tannin—an acid found in woods such as oak, hickory, and mahogany; it reacts with certain chemicals, such as ammonia, to change the color of the wood.

tenon—the end of a board that is inserted into a mortise or opening in a second board; an exposed tenon passes entirely through the second board (also see **mortise**).

tung oil—an oil processed from the seeds of the tung tree; also called "nut oil" or "china nut oil."

turning—a spindle or knob that has been made or "turned" on a lathe.

universal tinting colors—liquid tints that can be mixed with either water or mineral spirits.

varnish stain—a varnish to which colored pigments have been added.

veneer—a thin layer of wood glued atop what is often an inferior piece of wood; thickness can range from $1/100$ to $1/4$ inch.

wood dough—a soft patching material that comes in a number of colors; unlike wood putty, it hardens and can be sanded smooth afterward, making it suitable for small to medium-sized repairs on raw wood.

wood putty—a soft patching material that comes in a number of colors; unlike wood dough, it does not harden, thus is used for shallow, cosmetic repairs on a finished surface.

Index

About the Author

Bruce Johnson lives in Durham, North Carolina, where he and his wife, Dr. Lydia Jeffries, have restored an Arts and Crafts bungalow for their collection of Gustav Stickley furniture. Johnson divides his time between his refinishing workshop, his search for Arts and Crafts antiques, and his word processor, where he writes his syndicated newspaper column ''Knock on Wood'' and his regular Country Living magazine feature ''Antiques Across America.'' In addition to writing *The Official Identification and Price Guide to the Arts and Crafts Movement* (House of Collectibles, 1988), Johnson is the organizer of the Arts and Crafts conference and antique show held in February at the Grove Park Inn outside Asheville, N.C. He is often accompanied on his travels by his young son Eric.

If you have additional information regarding sources of restoration supplies and materials, formulas, antiques-related publications, or new products, please write to:

Bruce E. Johnson
P.O. Box 6660
Durham, NC 27708

We are sorry, but the volume of mail prohibits personal replies.